Fleeing from History

Fleeing from History

Zionism, Israel, and the United States

YLANA N. MILLER

EU GPSR Authorised Representative:
Logos Europe, 9 rue Nicolas Poussin, 17000, La Rochelle, France
contact@logoseurope.eu

For information, contact State University of New York Press, Albany, NY
www.sunypress.edu

Library of Congress Cataloging-in-Publication Data

Name: Miller, Ylana N., author.
Title: Fleeing from history: Zionism, Israel, and the United States / Ylana N. Miller, author.
Description: Albany : State University of New York Press, [2025] | Includes bibliographical references and index.
Identifiers: ISBN 9798855804027 (hardcover : alk. paper) | ISBN 9798855804041 (ebook)
Further information is available at the Library of Congress.

For my children and grandchildren

Contents

Part III. Making Meaning After Violence

Acknowledgments

This book is the product of many years of research during which the history I sought to understand never stopped evolving. Yet core conflicts have remained resistant to change.

Fifty years ago, when I wrote my dissertation on "Government and Society in Rural Palestine, 1920–1948," I hoped to understand how it was that Palestinian Arabs "lost" their homes in 1948 despite their numerical superiority both in demography and in land ownership. By the time I published my research I had learned that the subject of Palestine and Palestinians triggered responses that interfered with the intellectual freedom I had enjoyed in doing my archival research.

It is therefore with particular appreciation that I must thank both the Department of History and the Master's in Liberal Arts program of Duke University for allowing me to continue teaching while pursuing an additional career path as a psychoanalyst. This position gave me continuing access to students and library resources, both of which have been critical to my research, without constraints. In addition, I want to thank the Josiah Charles Trent Memorial Foundation for providing funding that enabled my work in Israeli archives. Chapter 5 of this book is based on an article, "Creating Unity Through History: The Eichmann Trial as Transition," published in the *Journal of Modern Jewish Studies* 1, no. 2 (2002). I thank the journal for allowing me to include this material.

Over the years I have spent considerable time at the Israel State Archives and the Central Zionist Archives in Jerusalem, in addition to working at the Center for Jewish History in the YIVO Archives and in the American Jewish Historical Society files. I am happy to acknowledge and thank the archivists as well as staff at all these locations who made my research possible.

Once I began to consider publishing this work, I had significant technical help from Neil Berman of The On Button, without whom I could not have pursued this next step. Professor Malachi HaCohen encouraged me at a critical moment, and my editor, Michael Rinella, was remarkably persistent under challenging circumstances in shepherding the manuscript through multiple stages. Among those was obtaining evaluations from anonymous readers. I want also to thank those readers who contributed significantly to improving the book.

I am more than fortunate to have two children, Joshua and Zinaida Miller, whose own experiences as academics allowed them to contribute valuable practical advice and to keep me aware, as always, of the ways in which generational differences enrich our understandings of history. Their partners, Ruby Tapia and Robert Blecher, have also been generous with their wisdom and support. Finally, there is no doubt that this work would not have reached the light of day without the constant, unflagging, and determined encouragement of my husband, Martin Miller, who read every word more than once. Our partnership has been and remains a source of intellectual as well as personal sustenance for more years than I care to record here.

It remains for me to say that of course I am the only one responsible for the substance of everything in this book.

Cast of Characters

Arendt, Hannah. (b. 1906, Germany, d. 1975, New York)
Philosopher, political theorist, and historian. Arendt was forced to leave Germany in 1933, lived in Paris until 1941 when she moved to the United States. She was known for her early work on totalitarianism (*The Origins of Totalitarianism*, 1951), articles on émigré life, Zionism, and the Eichmann trial, but eventually for substantial writings on political theory that have contributed to the ongoing postmortem literature on her work.

Ben-Gurion, David. (b. 1886, Russian Empire, d. 1973, Israel)
Arrived in Palestine in 1906 and was an active member of Poalei Zion, leaving in 1912 to study law in Constantinople. After the outbreak of World War I, he was deported but eventually returned to Palestine while serving in the Jewish Legion. Became secretary-general of the Histadrut (National Trade Union) in 1921 and a founder of the Ahdut Ha-Avodah Party.

In 1930, he was among the founders of the Mapai Party (Labor). Joined the Zionist Executive and became chair in 1933. In 1935, he was elected chair of the World Zionist Organization and the Jewish Agency. As a leader of Labor, he played an instrumental role throughout the period of the British mandate in Palestine. This contributed to his dominating role in discussions of partitioning Palestine as well as the issuance of the Declaration of Independence of Israel on May 14, 1948. He was the first prime minister of the new state, in office from 1948 to 1953, and then again from 1955 to 1963.

Blaustein, Jacob. (b. 1892, Baltimore, d. 1970, Baltimore)
American entrepreneur, philanthropist, and diplomat who founded the American Oil Company with his father. After World War II he led the

American Jewish Committee's delegation to the Paris Peace Conference and later served as senior vice president of the Conference on Jewish Material Claims Against Germany. Served as a regular member of the US delegation to the UN and was active in advocating for human rights. President of the American Jewish Committee, 1949–1954, Blaustein supported the establishment of Israel while simultaneously working to ensure clarity regarding the relationship between American and Israeli Jews.

Camus, Albert. (b. 1913, Algeria, d. 1960, France)
Algerian–French journalist and novelist who was also a member of the French Resistance during World War II. Known both for his ties to existentialism and for his conflicted responses to the movement for Algerian independence waged by the National Liberation Front, or FLN, from 1954 to 1962.

Friedmann, Georges. (b. 1902, Paris, d. 1977, Paris)
French sociologist and philosopher whose primary interest was the study of labor movements. During World War II he lost his academic position and participated in the French Resistance. An early interest in the Communist Party and the USSR (the Union of Soviet Socialist Republics, or the Soviet Union) was followed by a more critical perspective that led to what has been described as a humanist sociology. Friedmann served as president of the International Sociological Association from 1956 to 1959.

Goldmann, Nahum. (b. 1895, Russian Empire, d. 1982, West Germany)
Jewish leader, diplomat, and statesman who was active in the Zionist movement as well as multiple Jewish institutions throughout his life. In 1929 he worked with Jacob Klatzkin on the publication of the Encyclopedia Judaica in German. In 1936 Goldmann and Rabbi Stephen Wise worked to establish the World Jewish Congress. Having lost his German citizenship in 1935, Goldmann eventually settled in New York where he continued his Zionist and Jewish activism. During the war, he and Wise actively opposed efforts by Peter Bergson and others to mobilize public pressure for the rescue of Jews in Europe. Goldmann played a major role in supporting the partition of Palestine and after the war in negotiating German reparations through the Claims Conference. After World War II he was instrumental in efforts to organize the American Jewish world as well as on the international stage. His activities included creation of the Conference of Presidents of Jewish Organizations, acting as president of

the World Jewish Congress, 1951–1978, and chair of the World Zionist Organization, 1956–1968.

Jabotinsky, Vladimir (Ze'ev). (b. 1880 Russian Empire, d. 1940, New York State)
Journalist, writer, translator, and Zionist activist. He was a cofounder of the Jewish Legion within the British Army during World War I. He was the leader of Revisionist Zionism and the Betar youth movement. Barred from returning to Palestine by the mandatory government in 1930, he lived in Europe (Paris until 1936 and then London) until moving to the US in 1940. Jabotinsky was viewed as a formidable opponent by David Ben-Gurion with whom he made an agreement in 1934 hoping to diminish the conflict between Labor and the Revisionists. That agreement failed due to refusal to accept it by Mapai Party members. After his death, his wish to be interred in Israel was delayed until 1964.

Koestler, Arthur. (b. 1905, Budapest, d. 1983, London)
Journalist, writer of fiction and nonfiction, as well as a political activist. Joined the Communist Party in 1931 but left it in 1938. Known for *Darkness at Noon*, published in 1940, signaling his disappointment in the USSR. Koestler worked briefly with Jabotinsky in Palestine and Berlin. He was a European intellectual who lived in Berlin, Paris, and Vienna. He reported from Spain during the Spanish Civil War and traveled to the USSR. He eventually settled in London.

Magnes, Judah. (b. 1877, San Francisco, d. 1948, New York)
A Reform rabbi active both as a pulpit rabbi in New York City and on the executive of the American Jewish Committee. Active as a Zionist and settled in Jerusalem in 1923. There he participated in preparations to establish Hebrew University and became chancellor when it opened in 1925. He remained in that position until 1935 when he became president. Starting in 1929 he articulated a binationalist vision for Palestine. By 1942 he helped establish the Ihud Association, which opposed partition and supported a binational state. In this he was supported by Martin Buber and Hannah Arendt, among others.

Meir, Golda. (b. 1898, Russian Empire, d. 1978, Jerusalem)
Born in the Russian Empire, moved to the US in 1906 with her family, and immigrated to Palestine in 1921. She was an activist in Labor Party

politics during the period of the British mandate, serving on the Executive Committee of the Histadrut. Meir served as ambassador to the USSR, 1948–1949; minister of labor, 1949–1956; foreign minister, 1956–1966; and prime minister, 1969–1974.

Memmi, Albert. (b. 1920, Tunisia, d. 2020, France)
French-Tunisian Jewish writer who moved to Paris in 1956. Known for his writings on colonialism as well as novels drawing on life in North Africa. These include *The Colonizer and the Colonized*, published in 1957, and *Decolonization and the Decolonized*, published in 2006.

Prinz, Joachim. (b. 1902, Germany, d. 1988, New Jersey)
German rabbi who was expelled from Germany in 1937. Took a position as a congregational rabbi in Newark, New Jersey, and was active in the Zionist movement. He became a civil rights activist in the US, most notably speaking with Martin Luther King at the March on Washington in 1963. Prinz was a leader in the World Zionist Organization and president of the American Jewish Congress from 1958 to 1966.

Steiner, George. (b. 1929, France, d. 2020, Cambridge, England)
Franco-American writer, professor, and prominent literary critic. He left France for the United States in 1940, was educated in the US, Britain, and France. Steiner had a long, very distinguished academic career and was a prolific writer, contributing to multiple fields of knowledge.

Stone, I. F. (b. 1907, Philadelphia, d. 1989, Boston)
Independent investigative journalist and writer. Political radical who published *I.F. Stone's Weekly* from 1953 to 1971. Continued to write for the *New York Review of Books* afterwards.

Uris, Leon. (b. 1924, Baltimore, d. 2003, New York State)
Bestselling novelist known for historical fiction. Author of the widely read book *Exodus*, published in 1958.

Introduction

As I write this introduction, a new, devastating war between Israel and Hamas continues to rage in Gaza. At the same time, competing demonstrations and passionate writings reveal the ways in which conflict between Israelis and Palestinians has been incorporated into the American political landscape. For those with little or no personal experience of earlier wars, it is hard to grasp the justification for an American policy of support for Israeli actions in Gaza. For others, who have long identified with Israel—whether as Jews or as Christian Zionists—there is shock in experiencing not only the apparent resurgence of anti-Semitism, but equally the ways in which it appears based on the assumption of merging Jewish with Israeli identity, making Jews responsible for actions over which they have no control. To some, all these developments may seem unexpected. I very much hope that this book will contribute to making it clear that they are the current outcome of a long history in which the trajectory of relations between the US and Israel emerged in the context of an ever changing global political and cultural environment.

Central to this history are the choices that European Jews faced in the nineteenth and twentieth centuries. As earlier definitions of identity and community shifted in response to the development of political, cultural, and economic modernity, Jewish leaders and thinkers grappled with opportunities as well as challenges. While the gradual opening of citizenship to Jews, first in France and then elsewhere, held out a promise of freedom from segregation, it also generated fears of loss as well as uncertainty. As the nineteenth century moved toward its end, new formulations maintained the insistence on Jewish difference from others while modern political parties offered a variety of "solutions" to this difference. Inevitably, Jews themselves chose a variety of paths—acting to assimilate within emerging national collectives, working to transform their surroundings in order to belong as Jews, migrating to find alternative political environments, and holding on to traditional ways of life as forms of collective comfort. Some of these options were more available in Western Europe as opposed to Eastern Europe.[1]

Distinct from these was a line of development that intertwined a long traditional history with specifically modern projects. Historically, religious Jews had maintained a connection with the Land of Israel (Eretz Israel) that was understood as their place of origin as well as their hoped for return in the time of the messiah. In the meantime, however, Jews continued to live in that land as a religious minority now governed by the Ottoman Empire as they had for centuries. It was only in the nineteenth century that this tradition and practice came to be integrated into the Zionist movement, which redefined it to meet conditions in the modern era.

Zionism, whose origins can be found in the works of multiple individuals, was part of a broader set of movements that sought Jewish transformation of various sorts. It was, however, distinguished by two specific elements: (1) renewed focus on the Land of Israel as a place for Jewish growth apart from the diaspora and (2) the importance of separating Jews from the diaspora in order to create a new way of life and allow Jewish culture to flourish.[2]

Before World War I Zionism took shape in the form of new Jewish migration to Palestine and a set of institutions supporting that community within the Ottoman Empire. While these early migrants undertook practical work on the ground, the movement's leadership continued to pursue political and diplomatic goals. A recent anthology, *The Zionist Ideas*, organizes its subject around six schools of thought and covers over one hundred years of documentation.[3] Any study of Zionism thus inevitably requires clarity as to periodization and substantive focus.

Central to the argument I am making here is the distinction between Zionism before 1967 and afterwards. It is my contention that before 1967 those who defined themselves as Zionists represented a broad spectrum of largely secular Jews living primarily in Palestine, Europe, and the United States. Their adherence to Zionist ideas was driven by a variety of conditions, and their understanding of Jewish history ranged from understanding anti-Semitism or exile, or both, as key to a view based on commitment to historical traditions that had adapted over centuries to a variety of environments. In the US particularly, Zionism appealed to a minority of Jews only while anti-Zionism coexisted with it, as with other formulations of Jewish community.[4]

Even after establishment of the state of Israel in 1948, debate and differences about the desired goals of Zionism continued among European Jewish intellectuals and Americans as well as in Israel.[5] This book seeks to examine the ways in which Zionism—not as an ideology, but as a field of cultural and political debate—developed over time, in changing contexts. It looks particularly at the ways in which selected individuals articulated and fought for competing ideas while engaged in an ongoing struggle for communal existence. This process did not end in 1948 when Israel came into existence, but the field in which Zionism was debated was radically altered as it became, over time, an ideology identified with a state and its policies.

Throughout this history, Zionism as a field of debate was characterized by a dynamic in which some came to be seen as legitimate and part of the community while others came to be marginalized. It was a process inherent in the functioning of Zionism as an effort to redefine Jewish community and history in the modern world, as well as to control the relationship of Jews to non-Jews.

In this book, this history will be examined in the context of a central paradox or contradiction inherent in Zionism from its start. While Zionism, like other nationalisms, conceived itself as seeking self-determination, it was inevitably formed from the first by the fact of seeking to create its homeland in a territory already governed by one empire and ultimately with the help of another. This reality—and its extension in the post-1948 world—was a critical factor in determining the outcome of internal competitions for power and self-definition, as well as the ongoing conflicts to define who belonged and who didn't in a process experienced as existential but always subject to division.

This history can be understood in part through the roles played by individuals with significant public roles. Some—such as David Ben-Gurion, Hannah Arendt, Nahum Goldmann, and Golda Meir—participated in different ways over the course of decades. Others—such as Judah Magnes, Ze'ev Jabotinsky, and Jacob Bloustein—intervened at critical moments. Still others—such as Arthur Koestler, I. F. Stone, and Leon Uris—provided insight into broader public views through fiction or journalism.[6] Over time, the relationships of individuals to Jewish identity and community came to mirror as well as to form a changing dynamic. Until 1948, Zionism was a movement that could encompass a variety of visions for the future, adapting or resisting as participants met with changing conditions.

Once Israel existed, it posed a series of questions for those who had been earlier adherents. The new reality of a state that had come into being through war as well as contradictory international circumstances required that Zionists redefine their own positions with regard to the complexity of the relationship between Israel/Israelis and Jews/Judaism. There were those who felt that the success of statehood was a turning point that differentiated those who lived in its territory from those that remained outside. There were others who viewed the state as a project to be supported by the external Jewish community or as an ongoing effort to gather in the diaspora. Whether Zionism would survive its success was subject to discussion.

Israel's birth shortly after the end of World War II and the shock of the Holocaust could not but have a profound effect on all these discussions. If Zionism had emerged as a movement to understand history and use it actively, it was now to be associated with a state that viewed itself as on a permanent defensive. If Zionists initially sought to redefine Jewish identity in ways that allowed them to maintain values of European culture while asserting an age-old claim in Palestine, Israelis now faced the daunting task of translating competing visions into institutions and policies narrowed to the immediate, practical tasks of providing for a specific population and territory.

Yet the lack of fit between Israel as a state and Jews/Judaism as transnational phenomena could not be resolved in 1948/49 and became formative of a new arena. In this arena, the relationships between Israel and worldwide Jewry became more various and the competitions for primacy inevitably helped determine winners and losers. In a relatively short time, the primary interlocutor for Israel and Israelis became not Europe but rather the United States and the American Jewish community. The relationships among them shifted over time from an initial effort to establish borders to a gradual merging, leading to an eventual symbiosis and mutual projections that are now gradually giving way to renewed separateness.

Today, the US-Israel relationship is subject to a variety of conflicts, but almost all of them are occurring in an environment that has come to assume fundamental polarity between Palestinian Arabs and Israeli Jews, a conflict that has come to be aligned in various ways to external actors. This book is intended to complicate current assumptions and to create a longer historical view of the process that narrowed discussions of Zionism and Israel down to zero-sum perspectives.

Multiple recent publications address the relationship of American Jews to Israel while others seek to explain shifts in that relationship. A sample of titles alone conveys recognition of tensions. Dov Waxman's book *Trouble in the Tribe: The American Jewish Conflict over Israel,* published in 2016, offers an analysis of the growing conflict over Israel among American Jews. Eric Alterman's book *We Are Not One: A History of America's Fight over Israel,* published in 2023, offers a narrative that traces the debates about Israel in the US over the decades. Unlike Waxman or Alterman, Daniel Gordis's *We Stand Divided: The Rift Between American Jews and Israel* (2019) seeks to downplay the rift. In contrast, Geoffrey Levin's *Our Palestine Question: Israel and American Jewish Dissent, 1948–1978* seeks to recover a history that had been submerged and points to a counter-history. A different angle that is nevertheless relevant is offered by Salim Yaqub in his book *Imperfect Strangers,* dealing with Americans, Arabs, and US–Middle East relations in the 1970s.[7] All of these and more are emerging while conversations about Zionism and Israel have once again made evident the way in which frameworks of analysis shift over time, opening questions that appeared settled. In addition to the concerns raised by the aforementioned studies, it has become more possible to consider the relationship between Zionism and colonialism as well as the meaning of exile and diaspora in this context.[8]

The history I am offering is a contribution to understanding how and why these questions are arising in recent years. It describes a process occurring over many decades and including the ways in which European Jews played a significant role that was based on complex, plural understandings of what it meant to be Jewish as a minority. Although I cannot include here the more recent literature on Jewish life in the Arab world and the writings about Arab Jewish identity, it is important to recognize that these too have challenged earlier understandings of Zionism and Israel.[9] It is my view that this growing challenge to earlier American and American Jewish assumptions about the fit between the US and Israel is a product of buried histories as well as the construction of narratives with political value.

In the current environment, it is inevitable that this book will be read precisely in the lexicon I hope to challenge. Is it Zionist or anti-Zionist? Pro-Palestinian or anti-Palestinian? Pro-Israeli or anti-Israeli? What about Zionism as a colonialist, settler movement and Israel as the product of original sin? Zionism as the quest for Jewish safety and modernity that built on a long history? Can any of these positions be reconciled with the possibility that Zionism proved to be a remarkably successful enterprise as much because of the historical era in which it developed as because of its adherents? Or with the possibility that it outlived its own era to become something entirely different masquerading under that same name?

I am not at all interested in labels or discussions that serve only to secure ongoing divisions and reinforce stagnant claims of righteousness on various sides. If I were analyzing the Israeli-Palestinian conflict I would be seeking to understand the forces that have clearly benefited from maintaining an ongoing tension and, so far, have resulted in ongoing tragedy particularly for Palestinians but also for Israelis. That is, however, not my subject in this book.

What I hope to recover is an era in which European Jewish intellectuals, leaders, and activists who were leaving their traditional lives and communities understood that politics was and had to be intrinsic to their personal and communal identities but did so while maintaining multiple frameworks of possibility. It is precisely the disappearance of such capacity that has largely accompanied the loss of depth in conversation since 1967. As the reliance on two states (Israel and the US) to protect Jews developed after 1967 when action came to be valued while politics played a secondary role, the different experiences and perspectives (particularly of European Jews) were either forgotten or reinterpreted to support current needs. In the process, an emphasis on Jewish unity replaced the value of Jewish pluralism and, ironically, two populations that had not experienced the wrenching effects of Nazism or Fascism themselves now operated as though their own survival was permanently at risk. For the purposes of this book, the significance of these developments is twofold. First, just when Israel proved its power through military victory, it appeared to lose tolerance for the far more complex tasks of assessing the risks and benefits of formulating options for coexistence with Palestinian or other Arabs. Second, accompanying this development was the dramatic impact of Israeli victory on American Jews who now shifted from a complex negotiation of competitive, plural Jewish identities to an investment in Israel as the self-evident defender of the Jewish people, with the attendant advantage that this seemed to offer a path to continuity without any need to consider differences in their histories. The fact that this development largely coincided with increased US-Israel strategic ties further elided any concerns about potential contradictions.

Tracing this history—and its attendant conversations—has required paying close attention to the context in which it developed. Just as the quest for Jewish self-determination was intrinsically linked to ongoing negotiation of interdependent relations with others, so Jewish and Israeli communities have remained broadly subject to developments in their surroundings. Where Zionism in its origins attracted adherents among activists, Jewish thinkers, secular intellectuals, refugees, and many others in various locations, after 1948 state definitions began to create a new framework of thought and discussion.

In this book, I seek to emphasize the ways in which historically shifting frameworks encompass the field in which Zionists have defined and redefined their project. Rather than utilizing commonly accepted terminology to describe the ways in which Jews navigated their relations with the non-Jewish European world (examples include assimilation versus separatism, universalism versus particularism), I seek to show that a movement clearly dedicated to the transformation of Jewish life can best be understood as a process of formation and reformation, always in the presence of an "other," seeking a variety of responses.

This perspective allows us to grasp that the commonly understood reentry into history that Zionists sought was a complex effort to gain recognition and overcome long-standing stigma. Looked at in this way, it is easier to see that the success achieved in 1948 with statehood and military victory exposed a longer-term deficit or conundrum. European Jews participating in the Zionist movement sought power to create their own selves and communities. That power went with the striving for respect, support, and self-confidence. This craving, already evident in the idea of negating the diaspora, could not but be intensified by the realization of the devastation wrought by the Holocaust. American Jews, in contrast, were largely free of the shame and perceptions of living in exile. They were, however, only beginning to grasp the vast gap between their fate and that of the communities they had left behind. Nor were they prepared to confront their own choices largely to remain quiet during the war.

Israeli and American Jews took pleasure in gaining power after 1948. In the hope that Jews would no longer be subject to historical humiliations and helplessness, it was difficult for most to consider the impact of their success on others—particularly on Palestinians—who were losing lives, homes, and roots. In 1948/49 powerful drives to self-defense and preservation generally heightened perceptions of hostility on all sides with little room to distinguish Palestinians from Arab states. By 1967, however, the failure to acknowledge or recognize Palestinian needs for acknowledgment of their own histories was woven into broader patterns of fear and denial. Facing their own histories not from the perspective of victims, but from that of what Michael Rothberg has called implicated subjects, proved a daunting challenge for both Israeli and American Jews. Having only so recently achieved some measure of security, the reluctance to pay its price could be understandable, but the coalescence of an American state that has evaded facing its own history with a Jewish state fearful of losing its legitimacy lent added strength to a newly forming alliance based not on moral or democratic values but rather on the priority of national security.

My book focuses on the prehistory that prepared the ground for this development. It argues first for two central lines of development that help shift the parameters defining the historical evolution of Zionism from a self-contained, Jewish endeavor to one that is, from its origins, intrinsically linked to and altered by the different contexts in which ideas and individuals of the movement emerge and flourish or are marginalized. This is therefore a study that integrates Zionism as a field of political thought and action into a history that has alternately encouraged its expansion and limited its scope. It offers contexts that help explain the choices and shifts that often appear internal but remain subject to the surrounding world. It searches to place Zionism and the quest for Jewish continuity in juxtaposition with forces that constantly define the lenses that shape understanding of this process.

Second, but related, crucial to this study is the argument that the shift in the diaspora Zionist center of gravity from European dominance to that of the US should be understood as representing a break and change rather than continuity. It is for this reason that the book covers the years from the beginning of the Palestine mandate in 1920 to the aftermath of the 1973 war. This was the period in which European developments played a key role until, subsequent to war in 1967, the US and American Jews moved onto center stage.

This is not a book that addresses the Palestinian Arab–Israeli Jewish conflict directly but one that seeks to recognize that Zionism from its start had impacts on and was affected by a variety of hierarchies structuring the power within which Zionist Jews defined their goals.

In order to do so, the central consideration of Zionism and Israel is intertwined with the consecutive triangular constellations of power that both encouraged and limited actualization of the territorial project. These consisted of Great Britain, Palestinian Arabs, and Zionist leaders under the mandate; European states, Israel, and Arab states after 1948; and US Jews, the US government, and Israel leading up to war in 1967. By 1975, however, this dynamic had shifted when solidification of US-Israel connections in a changing region narrowed the space in which earlier intellectual, political, and cultural debates had existed. This book is an effort to challenge any assumptions of inevitability for this development and to raise questions about the factors that played a role in it.

This study is based on wide-ranging research and reading of relevant archival materials in Israel and the US as well as the secondary literature. It is intended to introduce and open up a variety of historical questions that have not yet been addressed in the existing literature, but which do speak to scholarly work emerging on Zionism, colonialism, and American Jewish history recently.

A few themes, names, and events appear and reappear as I make an argument that the gradual emergence of increasingly intense cooperation between the US and Israeli governments was not only the outcome of a historical process, but that it was directly linked to Israel's assuming a much more powerful regional role. As this took shape, critical voices in the US gradually faded into the background while realities on the ground took shape around existing states; nonstate actors were often identified as terrorists, thus easily viewed as illegitimate.

Two subjects are particularly significant in my consideration of this history. The first is the pivotal role played by the Adolf Eichmann trial as it acted not only to place the Holocaust at the center of Israeli and American Jewish consciousness but to shift the relationship between these two groups. In the aftermath of the trial the Israeli claim to represent those who had perished in Europe contained two critical elements: the assertion of primacy in the international Jewish community and, by implication, the centrality of the Holocaust to modern Jewish history. I argue that these shifts contributed to the changing ways in which American and Israeli Jews viewed one another after the war of 1967.

Second, the role of Nahum Goldmann in this history bears explanation, given that he has largely disappeared from accounts of Israeli history and is therefore much less known to younger historians. This marginalization of Goldmann's efforts as a Zionist and as a Jewish activist is a direct example of the ways in which the views of cosmopolitan European Jews over time became secondary to both Israeli and American leaders. Although a committed Zionist, Goldmann never lost sight of the international realities that contributed to the fate of the Jewish state and people as both took shape after World War II. These realities included the Palestinian Arabs as well as the Arab world more broadly. More than that, Goldmann understood the Cold War and had opinions on the position of a small state in this context. In addition, Goldmann was committed to the ongoing presence of a Jewish diaspora that he believed required educational institutions and whose views he believed should be taken seriously by Israeli leaders. That Goldmann often differed in his views from those of leading Israeli government officials and at the same time served in multiple institutional roles within the Jewish world contributed to his being seen as a "maverick." As a result, he has often been viewed with ambivalence and no full biography of his life has yet been written despite the very plentiful archival materials available in multiple languages. In this book, Goldmann serves to reflect the sensibility of a European Jewish activist who retained connections with a wide network across Europe, Israel, and the US while seeking to institutionalize his understanding of Jewish peoplehood.[10]

My title, *Fleeing from History*, refers to a current reality that is in part the result of the history I am describing. In the United States today, teaching history has become subject to political debates about the legitimacy of including elements that challenge American self-images as well as make manifest the contradiction between professed values and actualities. In Israel, there has long been conflict regarding the inclusion of Palestinian Arab history in the story of Zionism. Here too the desire to be recognized in particular ways has interfered with the need to face history in its completeness. I address these issues by pointing out the ways in which Zionism and the state of Israel have relied on the construction of narratives that, over time, have linked both to the United States. These developments are intimately related to concrete needs on the part of Israel and to American Jewish commitments to merging two aspects of their identities, the Jewish and American.

In order to place this history into a broader global context in which competing narratives, values, and understandings have developed, I include a discussion of the most relevant movement for decolonization—the war in Algeria. I do so because that war and its aftermath contributed significantly to the environment within which the US and Israel were navigating in the post–World War II world. At the same time, the traumatic violence of that conflict was an important reflection of the emerging discourse around colonialism and racism that made it difficult for Palestinian Arabs and Israeli Jews to imagine their own experiences in ways that might generate empathy rather than intensified competition for external support.

That competition unfolded during a Cold War that set one ideology against another to justify struggles for power and control. Inevitably, it devolved into choices for leaderships in emerging states.

My inclusion of the war in Algeria and its impact on Palestinian Arabs is meant to make clear the parallel ways in which violent eras had an ongoing impact on all concerned. One of those impacts on Israeli Jews might be described as a collective solipsism. Claims to exceptionalism rooted in European Jewish history and supported by a variety of narratives thus carved Israel's history as understood by its population out of the region in which it existed. This was true despite the reality that Israel's population increasingly consisted of groups whose own history had been lived in the Middle East for centuries. It is with this reality in mind that I could not address the history of Zionism and Israel without making clear the ways it echoed its surroundings.

The organization of materials in this history entails attention to simultaneous and intersecting developments. Moreover, it requires recognition of the ways in which political and military realities acquire meaning through multiple narratives and vocabularies. Where political and military decision-making is often necessarily short term, interpretation and analysis are often grounded in long-term perspectives. Since I hope to show the interplay between the political and intellectual, the chapters that follow are organized only loosely in chronological order within a broader narrative that requires attention to thematic elements, some of which repeat under various headings.

CHAPTER 1: FOUNDATIONAL CURRENTS, 1917–1948

This chapter introduces the post–World War I translation of Zionism as ideology and movement into a concrete political project with international support. It covers the period during which Great Britain controlled the League of Nations mandate for Palestine, creating a political field in which Arab and Jewish communities struggled to establish political legitimacy in the eyes of a government with its own interests in the area. It is in this context that multiple leading Zionist figures contested competing policies as well as alternative visions for the future with statehood being only one potential outcome. At the same time, concrete material developments external to Palestine had a defining impact on the ultimate shape of the state that emerged in 1948. Among the figures discussed here is one whose work as a Zionist and Jewish activist has largely been sidelined. Nahum Goldmann has been called a statesman without a state and his role in this book is important precisely because he represented the thinking of a cosmopolitan European Jew while working to ensure levels of Jewish unity, space for a Jewish diaspora critique, and a global perspective.

CHAPTER 2: MAKING THE STATE THE SOURCE OF SECURITY, 1948–1962

This chapter looks at the post-1948 challenges to aligning community with statehood by examining the differing views of Zionism articulated by Prime Minister David Ben-Gurion, Nahum Goldmann, and Jacob Blaustein, head of the American Jewish Committee. This is a period in which the new state of Israel was able to draw on two European states for needed support and resources. The reparations agreement with Germany, negotiated by Nahum Goldmann in the early fifties, was significant not only for its material effects but equally for its political implications. Agreements with France in the fifties provided wished-for military resources and support, again with political effects. Critical to this era of continuing European state significance for the new nation was the context of an Algerian-French war that sharpened questions about national identity, nationalist legitimacy, and justifications for political violence. At stake were varying views of desirable relations between diaspora and state. Underlying these differences were conflicts as to whose voice was to count and how to ensure Jewish security. Israel, created as a refuge for Jews, adopted a European model of nation-statehood. Algeria, in its fight for independence against European colonization, also adopted a view of statehood as the source of security. In both cases statehood also came to determine who was to belong. This chapter ends with mention of the kidnapping of Adolf Eichmann in 1960 to introduce one of the events that had pivotal significance in shaping a national history for Israeli and American Jews.

CHAPTER 3: SHIFTING PERSPECTIVES: EUROPEAN AND AMERICAN JEWISH CONSTRUCTIONS, 1948–1962

As American Jews and Israeli leaders were contending with their post-1948 relationships as well as with the decimation of the prewar European Jewish communities, writers of fiction, journalists, and public intellectuals were producing descriptions of the new Jewish state. The meanings of

American and Israeli policymaking were thus constructed in the context of intellectual debates with various narratives offering validity to some actions while marginalizing others.

Dynamic as a process and visible only in retrospect, this emergence of new grounds for interpreting history as well as experience can be viewed through the lenses of particular writers and thinkers. This chapter looks specifically at the shift from European Jewish perspectives to those of American Jews.

Two themes emerge as significant ways of differentiating the ways in which the European Jewish intellectuals discussed here reacted to the new state as opposed to the views of American Jews. Most striking was the way in which those who had lived in Europe, and hence had experienced life as a minority when the Nazis came to power, had retained minority and cosmopolitan sensibilities in the face of experienced persecution. In this way they retained the perspective of outsiders as well as critics. Included here as well is the voice of Albert Camus who, like Hannah Arendt, supported political changes while retaining a commitment to pluralism in the face of growing ethnonationalism.

Chapter 4: Transnational Challenges: Cold War and Decolonization, 1956–1966

It was in the period of 1956 to 1966 that international standing decisively shifted from European imperial states to the rivalry of the US and USSR. With that shift came a tightening of ideological rivalry, a competitive arms race, and efforts to delegitimize opposing political, economic, and cultural systems. Efforts to organize and control client states played a significant part in the global rivalry.

The political narratives in this era grew out of the Cold War and the attendant decolonization that expanded the arena of independent states. This chapter details the ways in which the state of Israel took shape in the context of regional developments and ongoing differences as to the priorities of Jews in the US and Israel. Central to these developments were the competitive claims to legitimacy and support that were voiced by nationalist movements in hopes of gaining international acceptance. It was in this environment that the Arab-Israeli conflict took shape, creating additional pressure on the Israeli leadership to justify its position with regard to Palestinian Arab refugees.

Chapter 5: Re-creating the Jewish People, 1960–1966

As the Israeli state gained military and political strength it continued to face regional isolation and the failure of efforts to redefine the ongoing, unresolved claims of Palestinian Arabs so as to eliminate a competing national narrative. Palestinians were viewed by Israeli policy as refugees to be assimilated or a minority to be contained. At the same time, the majority of American Jews continued to enjoy the postwar diminution of anti-Semitism and the opening of new opportunities to participate in American politics as well as economic growth.

It was in this context that Prime Minister Ben-Gurion announced the capture of Adolf Eichmann in Argentina and the intent to try him in Israel. This chapter details two narrative consequences that began to alter the balance between Israeli and American Jews as well as to marginalize the voices of European Jewish intellectuals. It makes the argument that the Eichmann trial served to create a particular narrative in which the Holocaust was viewed as a crime against the Jews. Since the Holocaust had annihilated most of the European Jewish communities, Israel was the voice of those who had been murdered and therefore attained a moral purpose in representing them. In addition, testimony from survivors was expected to educate the Israeli population and, with it, international Jewry. This chapter thus argues that the trial was pivotal in creating a history that drew together American and Israeli Jews while marginalizing any discussion of the complex, long-standing existence of Jews in Europe. In addition, this chapter makes clear that the attack on Hannah Arendt's critical views served to draw a boundary around those who subscribed to the official position on the trial.

Chapter 6: Ruptures and Meaning, 1962–1967

Despite the existence of an Israeli state now with an institutional framework to support the writing and teaching of Jewish histories, the postwar era was characterized by the existence of multiple narratives and narrators. In the period from 1948 to 1967 Jewish efforts to find meaning in the multiple losses of this era emerged in a world that also saw Palestinians and Algerians writing about the ruptures and losses of their existences. This chapter explores these intersecting efforts, the political contexts in which they developed, and the struggles to formulate national cultures matching nation-states as the primary vehicles for power and identity. Although attention is paid to Palestinian and Algerian cultural production, the focus is on alternative Zionist/Jewish memories and definitions. The divergence between European Jewish intellectual perspectives and those of American Jews makes evident the movement toward a dominant narrative that would marginalize those with counterhistorical views.

Chapter 7: The War to End All Wars, 1965–1967

The Six-Day War of 1967 broke out after a period of increasing tension and uncertainty in the region. In its aftermath it became clear that, contrary to some earlier expectations, decisive military victory led not to peaceful resolution but rather to multiple new conflicts as well as continuing violence. The new material reality of territorial conquest and demographic changes was accompanied by interpretations that were rooted in earlier narratives but were now shaped by competing hopes for the future.

This chapter begins by examining developments in the two years prior to war, including the decreasing power of Zionism as an ideology as well as the diverging paths of Israeli and American Jewish lives. It details the lead-up to war, its development over six days, and ends with the immediate aftermath. This aftermath was characterized by intensified international attention paid to the Arab-Israeli conflict and deeper Cold War penetration.

Chapter 8: Too Many Cooks Spoil the Broth: 1967 and Its Aftermath

This final chapter details the political and cultural responses that divided Jewish communities in Israel and the US after 1967. The newly intensified identification of the organized American Jewish community with Israel was accompanied by the strengthening of US engagement and direct diplomatic intervention in addition to increased military support. At the same time, divisions inside both Jewish communities revived questions about the nature of Zionism and its relationship to Judaism. As religious nationalism and settlement activity took on new meanings, critics expressed fears and warned that the absence of clear plans for diplomatic settlement and negotiation would alter the nature of the Jewish state. At the same time, the post-1967 period signaled the return of Palestinian Arabs both literally in the occupied territories and politically in a movement with gathering strength.

By 1977/78, it had become clear that Zionism as a political arena no longer allowed for the open debate and imagination of earlier years.

Part I

Creating a State

Chapter 1

Foundational Currents, 1917–1948

For many today Zionism is understood to be both the ideology of and the force behind policies pursued by the state of Israel. As a result many view Zionism as a dirty word, equated with racism, imperialism, ethnic cleansing, and occupation. For others Zionism has come to be equated with often unquestioned support for Israeli governments and commitment to the idea of a Jewish state chronically imperiled, with a variety of consequent implications for definitions of Jewish community as well as loyalty.

However, this constellation of definitions is the product of complex histories. Historically, Zionism consisted of multiple threads woven across multiple borders. This book argues that understanding this history is enhanced when we understand Zionism to consist of arenas, intellectual and political, within which participants developed a new language and practice of Jewish politics. This process began before the first World Zionist Congress convened in 1897 and was dramatically curtailed in the aftermath of the war in 1967, which was quickly followed by that of 1973.

The Balfour Declaration of 1917—issued by the British government and supported by the US and France—accorded international recognition to the Zionist claim of a Jewish national right in Palestine.[1] The literature on this subject is voluminous and needs no repetition here. What is significant is the impact that this development had on Zionism and its further evolution. This moment was the first concrete evidence supporting Theodor Herzl's argument that the international community (i.e., European powers) needed this solution to the Jewish Question.[2] While Herzl had sought to convince the Ottoman sultan that Jewish immigration would benefit his regime, World War I ensured that the Zionist project would be linked to as well as dependent on British imperial interests. This was also the moment in which a new dynamic triangle took shape: British administration, the World Zionist Organization, and a Palestinian Arab community newly severed from its historical networks.

The years of the Palestine mandate awarded to Great Britain by the League of Nations, from 1920 to 1948, were tumultuous and marked by unexpected shifts in global power, as well as the emergence of competing seductive ideologies promising dramatic solutions to a variety of perceived inequities. Zionism was one of many such ideologies that reorganized history and promised transformation. Before 1917 it had been carried to Palestine by various self-selected groups and institutions while in European countries it competed with a variety of alternative formulations of the potential relationships between Jews as a minority and non-Jewish majorities in the modern era.[3]

Once the mandate was in place, however, the World Zionist Organization came to be dominated by a leadership working within the Yishuv (the Jewish community in Palestine) in collaboration with Zionist leaders who remained outside Palestine but worked within the paradigm of supporting the enterprise of building a national home. Internal debates now were about the best ways to develop a national community in Palestine; at stake were a variety of perspectives on the desired character of immigration, the nature of institutions, security in the face of numerous challenges, and the ultimate political goals. Central to Zionist ideology was a drive to enable Jewish autonomy and self-determination. Inherent was the contradiction of needing to rely on external supports that could not be controlled, and thus adapting to a changing environment while insisting on national authenticity as well as continuity. Starting with the Balfour Declaration and the establishment of the mandate, the need was for a structure that would allow the Zionist vision to be implemented. Outside Jewish organizations were also a critical source of support—material as well as political. It was in navigating this field that the success of particular leaderships was determined.[4]

Retrospective views often credit Zionist leadership with substantial agency while minimizing the roles of British administration, Palestinian Arab leadership, and perhaps most importantly, the international context within which the Yishuv grew far more rapidly than initially expected. Notably, an emphasis on the loss of European Jews who perished in the Holocaust (and thus deprived the Zionist movement of its expected constituency) has obscured to some extent the degree to which the large-scale immigration of the thirties was transformative. A project undertaken with the expectation of decades to develop gradually turned into one altered permanently by the effects of simultaneous internal warfare and external claims for refuge. Ironically, in an environment of Arab revolt (1936–1939) and growing anticipation of European war, the views of Ze'ev Jabotinsky and the Revisionist Party, which emphasized rapid establishment of a Jewish national entity, were gradually adopted by the leadership of mainstream Zionism. Earlier plans to control immigration in the service of creating a community dominated by Labor Zionism's priorities were abandoned. Expectations of development over time now gave way to growing awareness that time was limited.[5]

Perceived needs for action and political combat determined the course of the Zionist movement and the Yishuv from the mid-1930s to 1948. As a result, the complex discussions that had characterized institution building and intellectual developments in the Zionist arena before this period now existed at a greater remove from daily material realities. And those material realities seemed to marginalize the concerns of some, while endowing others with the authority to represent a movement that was to emerge after World War II as both historically prescient and for many now unquestionably the best hope for Jewish continuity.

Sketching the Debates

Attraction to Zionism in its earliest years grew out of the ways in which it offered a new intertwining of historical Jewish orientations with modern formulations of cultural and political structures that might allow Jewish participation in a world dominated by others. At its core, however, were two very specific elements that differentiated it from alternative solutions to this challenge. The first rested in the belief that Jews or Judaism, or both, could not survive within Europe and therefore required separateness as well as a territorial home. The second element inherent in Zionist analysis can be conceived of as a belief in the need for power—whether conceptualized as self-defense or self-determination, control over Jewish life or in relation to others. This element clearly linked Zionism to its development in a Europe of national movements and nation-states.

Individuals who were attracted to Zionism as a way of thinking about Jewish life and history came from very diverse personal circumstances. Six who represent significant and at times competing voices as well as experiences are representative of the potentialities as well as limitations of activists and intellectuals who linked Jewish life one way or another to Palestine under the mandate. Although there were activists in the movement from a broader territorial base, the ones discussed here and formed by life in Europe or the United States accurately represent the political spectrum that existed during the formative era. Their understandings of Zionism developed between 1920 and 1940 when Britain governed Palestine under a vague commitment to develop the Jewish National Home. What that meant was not only variously interpreted by the British and Palestinian Arabs but also defined in different ways by Zionists.

David Ben-Gurion, the first prime minister of Israel and leader of its Labor Party, came to the territory of Palestine in 1906, well before World War I, from a small town, Plonsk, Poland, then controlled by the Russian Empire.[6] He arrived at the age of twenty, steeped in a Jewish community life and the attacks on it of Eastern Europe. Although he studied law in Istanbul from 1912 to 1914, he was from the first an activist and one focused on the locality in which he sought to mobilize Jews for settlement. It was in this context that his commitment took shape to redemption of a Jewish nation drawing on its biblical origins and devoted to revival of its prediaspora past. While Palestine at this time was a part of the Ottoman Empire, Ben-Gurion's activism before World War I was predicated less on diplomacy and more on changing the immediate environment through settlement, labor organization, and political action. This perspective then gave priority to changing the realities in Palestine and creating the Jewish power to do so despite local resistance.

There was, however, another significance to the timing and circumstances of Ben-Gurion's migration to Palestine. It ensured that his political path moved from one empire to another and then to a third. His early years in the Russian Empire were characterized by the experience of small-town Jewish communal life within a periodically hostile environment linked to autocracy. His years in Palestine before World War I were spent again within a minority community forming its own distinct collective and hoping for benign neglect if not support from an autocratic sovereign. Finally, when Palestine was effectively part of the British Empire, hopes for gaining greater self-determination remained dependent on distant power and the mobilization of collective force. Thus Ben-Gurion's history lent itself to a very particular definition of Zionism and its goals—identifying Zionism with the survival of a Jewish communal existence explicitly set apart from its surroundings, bound by history and defense of its boundaries, and wary of those outside. Within the three empires Jewish communities historically had existed with their own internal structures and collective identities, modified in some ways as they adapted to a changing environment but never identifying themselves with it. It was in this context that Ben-Gurion built his personal route to power through a number of institutions and party structures that were defined under the umbrella of labor as ideology but were powered by their appeal to a particular historical Jewish existence and linked to effectiveness in the material world of Palestine.

Very much in contrast to Ben-Gurion, Ze'ev Jabotinsky—leader of the Revisionist Party that stepped out of the World Zionist Organization in 1935—grew up in the cosmopolitan environment of Odessa in a Jewish family that acculturated to the Russian world in which they lived. His familial and personal history entailed travel, literary pursuits, and journalism, which all contributed to a comfortable worldliness. His personal gifts led to the acquisition of multiple languages and ease in their cultural worlds. More like that of Herzl than that of Ben-Gurion, Jabotinsky's path to Zionism ran through personal struggles to find a place in a world of intensifying nationalisms and ideologies. As a journalist and writer who came to Zionism without substantial Jewish education, Jabotinsky was drawn to Zionism as a national movement offering its adherents power to chart their own course.

Jabotinsky's politics and activism were thus conceived outside Palestine and first manifest in efforts to support Jewish self-defense in Russia, as well as in writing and public speaking. By the time of World War I, his experiences led him to work for a Jewish military presence (the Jewish Legion) that he believed would buttress Zionist claims for political recognition. This was a politics that sought to link mobilization in Eastern Europe with the ultimately liberal goals of Western European polities. The militant nationalism of Jabotinsky's movement contained the idealism of European nationalist uprisings and their drive for power and recognition as well as independence. Much like Herzl, the vision of statehood Jabotinsky sought was one of a liberal state that could belong to the European world he admired. Where Ben-Gurion believed in a Jewish mission and its distinctiveness, a model for others, Jabotinsky was committed to rescuing Jews from their vulnerability and endowing them with equality, normalizing their participation in a larger world.[7]

Both Ben-Gurion and Jabotinsky were schooled within the Russian Empire at a time of significant political and cultural turmoil. While individuals were thus drawn in a variety of directions within a world of competing ideologies, this was nevertheless a world in which being Jewish carried a collective meaning—whether acknowledged or not. Nahum Goldmann and Hannah Arendt, in contrast, were born into a German world that allowed individuals a more fluid relationship to both Judaism and German national construction. Access to a German culture and education could serve a variety of purposes; Arendt and Goldmann chose very differently but both carried with them throughout their lives the impact of this world.

As Goldmann tells his story, his life integrated aspects of the collective Jewish world of his grandparents (marked by the rabbinical education and leadership of his grandfather) with the opportunities for education and personal development available in pre–World War I Germany. Among other things this meant that he did not experience the shame and stigma that accompanied the pogroms nor did he grow up in a Jewish world set apart from its surroundings. Equally significant, he was accorded the opportunity to gain a secular education without sacrificing Jewish knowledge and connection.[8]

Hannah Arendt, in contrast, was very much a product of the German world in which she was raised. Encouraged to acknowledge and take pride in her Jewish identity, she experienced this as a fact unaccompanied by choices other than those that determined how one lived with this reality. Growing up in a world that prized German culture and education, her relationship to Jews and Judaism was from the first inflected by politics and a relationship to the dominant Christian world. Arendt's participation in the Zionist movement was thus shaped by the political world in which she lived by the early thirties. Initially she found in it a combination that remained present in her life—attachment to a powerful older male mentor and immersion in action driven among other things by ideas. Zionism for Arendt was practical and represented a break from her past thinking.[9]

For Golda Meir Zionism offered instead the promise of reconnecting threads and integrating personal history with the creation of community. Although her family emigrated when she was seven years old and thus shared the experiences of immigrants fleeing from the Russian Empire to the promise of the US, Golda was driven by personal dissatisfaction as well as political passion to find resolution through the Socialist Zionist movement. In this choice she threaded an ideology with European roots into an American education. She ultimately found that she could only pursue the search for a secular Jewish identity by emigrating to Palestine in 1921. Once there, however, it was precisely her ability to communicate with American audiences that gave her added value within the mainstream Zionist leadership.[10]

In dramatic contrast, Rabbi Judah Magnes brought to Palestine a distinctly diaspora Jewish and specifically American outlook. Growing up in California in an observant immigrant family, Magnes grew into a cosmopolitan intellectual—schooled in Germany as well as the US, practicing as a rabbi but always reaching beyond any single congregation, ultimately defining his Zionism in Palestine through his role as president of the Hebrew University and as a critic on various fronts. Where Meir sought to be a part of the community she wished to build and lead, Magnes often acted as a deliberate outsider, living with multiple contradictions.[11]

Structuring the Conversations and the Gaps

From 1920 until 1948 the debates and conversations that characterized Zionism as a movement took place in the context of British/international commitment to the development of a Jewish National Home in Palestine. These were accompanied over time by the emergence of new threats to Jewish life in Europe as well as intensifying resistance to Zionism in Palestine/the Middle East. Responses to these developments were far from uniform, and those who sought to influence Zionist policies reacted from personal as well as historical and political considerations.

If Zionism was from the first predicated on identifying threats to the continuities of Jewish life and Judaism, its prescriptions circled around a number of poles. The weight accorded to a variety of goals was distributed from perspectives that ranged along a spectrum of relationships with the world beyond that of particular Jewish communities.

One of the most common differences within Zionism—dating from its origins as an organized movement—was that between cultural Zionism and political Zionism. This division is also historically linked to leading spokespersons Ahad HaAm vs. Herzl and to the differences between those who saw a Jewish state as the answer to anti-Semitism in Europe, along with the negation of the diaspora, as opposed to those who questioned the goal of statehood and believed that the diaspora would be a permanent component of Jewish life. What both these strands had in common, however, was a focus on Palestine as central to Jewish history as well as a recognition of historical crisis requiring active response. Once Great

Britain took control of its mandate, however, the relative balance shifted. The mandate, however one chose to define the Jewish National Home, clearly created a new political arena and with it new constellations of institutions as well as power.[12]

The Palestine mandate coincided in timing with the extinction of European Jewry as a well-organized, diverse, and historically rooted population. For Russian Jews the revolution of 1917 served ultimately as a final undermining of Jewish community life, with its distinctive culture, and disappointment for those who had believed that revolution would solve the Jewish Question by creating an inclusive society. For Western European Jewry the rise of fascism in its multiple forms led ultimately to physical extinction, exile, and mourning for the potentials that died as well. Thus, ideologies that had offered robust competition to the Zionist project were slowly drained of significance while the Jewish community of Palestine, the Yishuv, gradually took on a character molded by its own experience. It was only in the United States that an alternative remained credible, but it too was inevitably altered in these years.

Palestine

It is impossible to understand the world in which Zionists were formulating their views without juxtaposing this process with the simultaneous fragmentation of what had been the Ottoman Empire. Subjected to a gradual penetration of European power and nationalism over time, the Ottoman Empire's final demise after World War I was a tale foretold. As a result, elite populations within the empire, and in particular Arab elites, had already operated in an environment requiring adaptation and defense. The early presence of Zionist settlers—representing to a large degree Jewish responses to European nationalism as well—inevitably triggered concerns understandable only in this context. They ranged from immediate, on the ground responses to broader calls for Ottoman protection.[13]

When the war's end brought the final dissolution of the empire along with British and French control over what had been its Arab provinces, an elite accustomed to a world without internal borders was faced with already feared foreign occupations as well as new, powerful obstacles to defending their own structures, traditions, and ways of life. In the newly constituted Palestine mandate, moreover, this change was accompanied by a radical revision of community lives and relationships. Palestinian Arab elites were faced with a governing authority that had committed itself to the growth and development of a Jewish National Home along with recognition of a Jewish Agency committed to immigration as well as expanded settlement on Palestinian land. These commitments were made not simply as a consequence of British victory and imperial power; they were founded on a Christian acceptance of Jewish rights to return to a land that was the source of their historical development as a people. That this theological/ideological understanding coincided well with British interests is clear; nevertheless it is also significant that a Jewish project undertaken during a period of multiple political loyalties and uncertainties was now directly linked to British power, and written into international law at a moment of British/French/American dominance. Inevitably this shift altered not only the dynamics and identifications of Palestinian Arabs but also the dynamics and identifications of Zionist Jews.[14]

EUROPE

In the post–World War I world of Europe and the US, Zionism gained credibility slowly, but its attraction was enhanced by the twin developments of spreading anti-Semitism combined with intensified nationalisms. While the Russian Revolution of 1917 introduced a period of uncertainty for Jews as for others in the empire, Western Europe experienced its own political experiments and, over time, intensification of ideological conflicts. For individual Jews and Jewish families, responses mirrored the worlds in which they lived and reflected assessments of their possibilities.

Nevertheless, the existence of the Palestine mandate with its promise of a Jewish National Home and a right to participate in the Zionist project clearly provided an ideological framework specific to Jewish history and culture, as well as a national identity that had the potential to free Jews of the complexities many faced in the European nationalist worlds. When material conditions further deteriorated, and as fascism emerged with the specific threat of Nazism gaining ground, Jewish migration to Palestine took on broader dimensions.

The migration of Jews in the 1930s no longer depended on ideological commitments to Zionism or the building of a new society. Increasingly it took on force as a strategy for survival. Moreover, the reluctance of the US and other countries to extend refuge gave added credibility to the Zionist reading of history, which asserted the need for a Jewish home separated from Europe in hopes of negating anti-Semitism by negating the diaspora.[15]

The paradox of this search for security in a Palestine under British control was the reality that by 1939 Arab-Jewish conflict had contributed to a new White Paper that effectively voided the Balfour Declaration.[16] The

British policy announced in the White Paper of 1939 satisfied neither the Palestinian Arab community nor the Jewish community. It was formulated in the aftermath of the Arab revolt, expectations of war in Europe, and failed efforts to arrive at a resolution to local conflict. The White Paper announced a British policy that would limit Jewish immigration to and land purchase in Palestine while working toward a unitary independent Palestinian state over ten years. Thus, the moment that confirmed the need for Zionism also underlined its vulnerability and the ways in which it brought with it the challenges of seeking safety in territorial control. The early Zionist settlers hoped to transform themselves as well as their communities and leave the impact of their presence to the British to manage. Meeting the limits of that premise at a time of deepening threat enhanced a variety of reactions that altered the nature of the movement itself. Palestinian Arabs simultaneously had to face internal fracturing and conflicts; these contributed to the deepening polarization and violence accompanying the efforts to make nationalism fit in a world that was not organized to accommodate its insistence on new forms of identity as well as economy. As the British stepped back to reevaluate their own national interests in the face of war in Europe, Arabs and Jews in Palestine were left to make decisions for survival of their communities with little possibility for viewing this task as one that could be shared. In less than twenty years of British mandate, the inequality of communal power in Palestine had only increased but so had the distortions in perceptions of self and other.[17]

CHALLENGES OF THOUGHT VERSUS ACTION

While the British Empire controlled Palestine and dominated much of the Arab world, Palestinian Arabs and Jews coexisted without ultimate responsibility for the territory they shared. In some cases this meant that local communities—villagers and settlers—found ways both to accommodate and to manage conflict. In other cases it meant that leaders and thinkers formulated frameworks within which to imagine the future—personal as well as communal. In the case of Palestinian Arabs, the background to this process was the centuries-long network of connections with the surrounding former provinces of the Ottoman Empire and their struggle in more recent times with Western penetration. For Zionist Jews, the background was largely the disappointment of wishes to be part of modern European projects and a drive to create an arena for the reestablishment of a Jewish polity as well as safety. Inevitably, these two developments—each focused on internal drives—were largely oblivious if not hostile to one another.

Central to these realities was the fact that modern nationalism and the nation-state had become the dominant paradigm for thinking about political life in the twentieth century. Yet the ways in which nationalism could accommodate historical claims to territory as well as leadership in the Middle East obscured deeper unresolved conflicts for both Muslims and Jews. As an ideology linked to secularism, nationalism provided a distinctive, emotionally powerful alternative to the traditions and authority of religions that had evolved and accommodated changes over centuries. These conflicts were present in a variety of ways both within the Zionist movement and in resistance to it. Under the mandate, the struggles were broad and the space to debate open.

Early discussions among Zionists revolved around several key differences. The founding disagreement of Ahad HaAm with Herzl incorporated in some ways the themes that would be carried forward within the Yishuv. Those like HaAm who emphasized Jewish culture and Judaism would see themselves as building a morally just society as well as the center of Jewish life to serve an ongoing diaspora. Those who were drawn to Herzl's secular vision would focus on creating a Jewish state that would ideally lead to negation of the diaspora and the normalization of Jewish life along with the eradication of anti-Semitism. These were broad, abstract categories that nevertheless took specific shape as individuals made their choices in the Yishuv.

The Palestine mandate for the first time drew boundaries around the territory thus designated. It incorporated the land historically known by Jews as Eretz Israel and thus all the communities located within it: the Jewish settlements that had drawn Jews over the centuries as well as the more recent immigrants who came as part of the Zionist project. By 1922, however, the first conflicts over British designation of this territory had already alienated some Arabs as well as some Zionists. While Palestinian Arabs saw themselves as connected with the lands of Syria and protested the separations imposed, Revisionist Zionists protested the British decision to grant Abdullah, son of their ally the sherif of Mecca, control over Transjordan, which was now removed from the purview of the Balfour Declaration and thus the Jewish National Home.[18]

The Zionist movement now had recognized status and permission to create a Jewish National Home. It also now had a local community within which rivals would contest the nature of that home, and an ongoing external movement expected to provide support but also made up of those with their own views of Zionist priorities and goals. From the first, an internal contradiction was rooted in the reality of needing British support to achieve what was conceptualized as a separatist national presence, eventually to be embodied in a national state, yet one that would require adaptation to the changing international environment. The facility with which different individuals articulated their ideas and made their choices of action in this environment contributed to the emergence of dominant leaderships on the one hand, and marginalized groups on the other, with Zionism as an arena for political discussion changing in the process.

David Ben-Gurion was the central figure that emerged through the Yishuv and by 1948 came to be identified with its success. Known for the forcefulness of his positions, the effectiveness of his political ascent through Labor Zionist institutions, and eventually for his mobilization of Jews as well as Judaism in the service of the state, Ben-Gurion betrayed little conflict in his central commitment to Zionism as a Jewish nationalist movement. Despite his ideological link to the Labor Zionist movement, with its emphasis on the valuing of work, settlement, and theoretical socialism, Ben-Gurion operated in a world of practical politics and pragmatism. This was particularly evident in his rivalry with Ze'ev Jabotinsky, whom he came to denounce for his militarism despite effectively moving closer over time to the need for the use of force.[19]

But this relationship, which changed over time, was characterized by other ways in which Ben-Gurion could define himself precisely through difference. For a number of reasons, voluntary and involuntary, Jabotinsky's activism was largely outside of Palestine, in a Europe experiencing the intensification of anti-Semitism and hostility to cosmopolitan Jews. Ben-Gurion, in contrast, focused always on the Yishuv where his consistency, apparent "moderation," ability to rise through communal institutions, and flexibility when articulating political goals all served him well. The moral framework of Labor Zionist ideology was well suited to establishing the Yishuv as a progressive, modern, and competent enterprise, working within a British imperial framework while steadily developing skills that would eventually be needed to support autonomy. It was precisely the ambiguity of political goals as well as the care to legitimize Zionism via an integration of historical claims with rights based on labor that further enhanced Ben-Gurion's strengths as a leader.[20]

Despite the external validation contained in the Palestine mandate, however, there were those who struggled with the translation of Zionism as an idea into reality on the ground. Judah Magnes, who moved to Palestine in 1923 in search of a personal integration of his intellectual, political, and spiritual commitments, brought with him the realities of American experiences. His conflicts could not easily be externalized nor did they allow him to accept the inevitability of confrontation between the two national communities. As president of the Hebrew University, as a rabbi, and as an American, Magnes ultimately became part of a group that sought agreement with Arab spokespersons rather than with the British authorities. Their pursuit of a binational Palestine did not interfere with their perception of themselves as part of the Zionist movement, nor were they viewed as outsiders despite the fact that they were a small minority, clearly offering thoughtful assessments rather than actively engaged in party politics or military preparations. They saw themselves rather as representing a Jewish national presence that depended not on being a majority nor on homogeneity but rather on an ethical and humanistic community rethinking the relationship of Jews to the modern, changing world they lived in.[21]

Ben-Gurion, and with him, Golda Meir, and Jabotinsky carried the distinct experiences of Eastern European Jews. Their early lives incorporated a world of significant transformation not only for Jews as a collective but equally for the world in which they lived. In contrast, Judah Magnes, Hannah Arendt, and Nahum Goldmann each brought to their views of Zionism pride in their own complex heritages and personal choices unavailable to the large number of Jews being displaced and afraid, whether in the Russian Empire, then the USSR, or in Western Europe after World War I. Their personal quests could not be answered by a Jewish statehood that offered survival and "normalization," nor were they prepared to give up the cosmopolitanism that they valued even in the face of its link to potential vulnerability. Yet each of these individuals remained connected to the Zionist project in the era of its becoming a reality under the mandate.

During this period general subjects of debate and conflict circled around differing visions of the society Zionists hoped to construct, leading among other things to conflicts over who should be allowed to immigrate to Palestine in the Zionist quotas. Where Labor Zionists invested in the purchase and development of land settlements, the majority of immigrants continued to be urban dwellers. By the thirties, when European conditions forced emigration on many, they often came as individuals with commercial backgrounds or professional skills rather than pioneers eager to redeem themselves with physical labor. The growing institutional power and structure dominated by Labor Zionism thus played a formative role in determining not only the priorities of the Yishuv but also its responses to a changing environment. Within that environment of increased threat resulting from Arab opposition, changes in British policy, and heightened urgency within, the Zionist leadership made choices that set in motion a narrowing of theoretical debate and the emergence of an identity that could claim moderation as well as moral justification at a time when both were at risk in the international arena. This was, moreover, an identity now predicated on rooted localism with appeal to components of the external world but limited by focus on the particularity of the Yishuv.

By 1939, Ben-Gurion's commitment to fight the new British policy, while supporting Britain in the war, summarized the narrowed space within which Zionist leaders could maneuver. The Revisionist insistence that the whole of Palestine (including Trans-Jordan) was rightfully to be part of a Jewish state was marginalized in a world within which partition of the land west of the Jordan became a best possible outcome. Appeals to a negotiated settlement with Arab leaders receded as the role of force became more prominent. The debates about the creation of a transformed Jewish society reflecting "new" men and women were less relevant while rescue and refuge emerged as more immediate tasks. Immigration, earlier controlled and linked to "building" the land, came to be displaced by immigration as the vehicle for demographic expansion. Finally, dependence on Great Britain and European Jewry ceded place to the US and its Jewish community. By the end of World War II the Zionist arena had been significantly altered, and so had the world in which it existed.

The immediate surroundings of the Yishuv now consisted of a growing number of independent Arab states, along with a Palestinian Arab community that had been deeply fractured in the course of the mandate but whose cause was already significantly identified with broader regional nationalist aspirations. In Europe, the original wellspring of Zionism and its demographic source, the war did far more than annihilate millions while producing the refugees who could now be viewed as logically to be absorbed by the Yishuv. The war also obscured the realities of richly functioning European Jewish communities with a variety of ideological movements that had challenged Zionist ideas. Moreover, the destruction of those communities ironically contributed to the vindication of Zionist narratives of history and appeared to make Zionism the most prescient of Jewish political arguments. In the US, anti-Zionist activists now found their voices losing an audience in the face of American Jewish mobilization.[22]

Toward Statehood

For three years, from 1945 to 1948, the future of Palestine remained undetermined and subject to a multitude of perspectives as well as interests.[23] Given British physical control and legal standing, it was anticipated that the British government would have primary claims to determining further developments as could be expected by Arab state leaders as well as the Palestinian Arab community. The White Paper of 1939 had outlined a future unitary Palestinian state within which the Jewish National Home would remain but whose growth would be subject to majority approval, that is, Arab consent. The plan was predicated on British support for a transitional period of unified structural change entailing a continuing British presence and the support to make it work. It was also linked to British aspirations in the broader Arab world that had been created at the height of imperial expansion in the region. Ironically, this meant that Palestinian Arab aspirations were thus dependent on the continuation of an imperial presence that had otherwise come to be reviled because of its support of the Balfour Declaration and all that followed.[24]

For the Zionist leadership the White Paper signaled the potential loss of what they viewed as rightfully the object of the Balfour Declaration—that is, Jewish statehood. Although they had acquiesced in the earlier partition of territory and worked to maintain their claim that Jewish settlement was not at odds with Arab rights, the White Paper was viewed by Ben-Gurion and his supporters as a sign of the need to rethink their own strategy. Reacting in the context of a changed international balance of power, Ben-Gurion, Rabbi Abba Hillel Silver, Nahum Goldmann, and others shifted their attention to the US and a focus on attaining Jewish statehood. While the path to success was complex and by no means predetermined, it was an effort supported by the outcomes of the war. Recognition of the devastation and the mass killings of the war, coupled with the continued presence of displaced persons in Europe, required American support as well as financial investment. Despite British and US State Department concerns, American policy with regard to Palestine was formulated through a lens that saw Zionist claims and Jewish refugees as clearly linked. It was a framework calculated to appeal both to moral right and to identification with a project based on self-reliance.[25]

Ben-Gurion's strategy was consistent with the analysis first offered by Herzl in *The Jewish State*. Herzl argued that the Zionist movement could gain international support because it offered the dominant powers something that they would welcome—a solution to the Jewish Question. Although the accuracy of this insight was not evident in Herzl's lifetime and thus his diplomatic efforts failed, it appeared that after World War I there was enough international interest among the winning powers to support the project. After World War II, however, the victorious states were by no means in agreement with each other as they sought to deal with the effects of the war; they faced the realities of an alliance now fractured and a shift from the dominance of European global empires to the lead of a US adjusting to its newly acquired position. In this atmosphere, Palestinian Arab appeals to British justice and fairness could not compete with Zionist militancy coupled with claims now buttressed by the literal homelessness of Jews in Europe.

At the same time, the positions of the Zionist leadership were challenged not only by Arab spokespersons and British authorities. They were also questioned by those who had supported the political project of creating a Jewish National Home but vigorously opposed the plan for partition and Jewish statehood. In its place they argued for a binational state in which Jews and Arabs would have equality. This position was maintained by those like Judah Magnes and Martin Buber who had long held the view that the Zionist project as they conceived it could only thrive with negotiated agreement between Arabs and Jews. In the aftermath of World War II, Judah Magnes formed Ihud, which opposed partition and supported a binational state. Hannah Arendt and Martin Buber both participated in Ihud. They articulated strong apprehension about the long-term implications of the partition plan, which would inevitably lead to military confrontation and a Jewish state surrounded by a hostile region. This, in turn, would require ongoing dependence on external supports.[26]

The binationalists have long been viewed as idealists, unrealistic in their hopes that Palestinian Arabs would agree to the ongoing presence of a Jewish National Home, whatever its nature. Most were intellectuals, not politicians, operating out of a number of belief systems—moral/ethical, religious, and some Marxist. There is little doubt that their objectives required a long-term commitment on the part of authorities willing to support the project of coexistence. That commitment had never been an active part of British policy nor was it a Zionist priority any more than it was supported by Arab leaders.

Nevertheless, in the history of Zionist debates, the binationalists were not only prescient but represented a critical set of voices that questioned the intensifying focus on statehood and indiscriminate immigration as central to Jewish survival or redemption. The urgency of action impelled by immediate needs, in their view, was endangering the ultimate outcome Zionists sought. In standing back, they opened themselves to be seen as naïve and unrealistic. In retrospect it is also important to see that underlying their views was a resistance to the form of nationalism now adopted as the mainstream definition of Zionism, as well as to the emerging Arab nationalism(s) that were supported, directly or indirectly, by European powers to legitimate their own construction of the Arab Middle East.

Central to postwar developments was the priority given by Western powers to European and American interests in the face of Soviet policies. While the Allies had fought together against the Axis, each of these wartime alliances contained ongoing differences within them. With regard to the US and Great Britain, it is critical to recognize that the temporary alliance with the USSR did not obviate the longer-term perception of threat, while the temporary mobilization against Germany did not eliminate the longer-term view of German potential to serve Western needs. It was in this context of shifting relationships and transitions that the future of Palestine, as of other colonial holdings, came to be determined. Britain and France, weakened by the war, continued to operate with a view to maintaining international positions. The US was formulating positions in which there was hope of aligning with anticolonialism, while continuing to shore up Western European allies.

Palestinian Arabs and Jews had to make their case in a world in which their needs were largely irrelevant to those making decisions about their destinies. Under these conditions, ability to act independently became critical while any plan dependent on outside investment—economic or military—was unlikely to succeed. While the Zionist movement was internally divided, it had substantial advantages in navigating the international terrain. In Palestine itself, David Ben-Gurion led with unambivalent intent and institutional strength. In the US, the American Jewish leadership was mobilized and increasingly united in the aftermath of a war whose destructiveness became clear as did the failure of rescue actions. Tying these two primary communities together was a web of communal organizations including the already well functioning machinery of the World Zionist Organization. In the years from 1945 to 1948, the many differences among Jews in Palestine and in the US became less visible, while the importance of a unified stance grew.

There was, however, another factor that entered into the choices made by those who hoped to shape the Zionist project. Under the mandate, the security of the Yishuv relied ultimately on British responsibility for Jewish welfare. For those who saw Zionism as necessitating the creation of a new Jewish society, the presence of this imperial authority was not a source of legitimation, but it did nevertheless function to provide time for the upbuilding they hoped would lead only ultimately to a form of statehood. For those who came fleeing persecution, Palestine initially provided a haven within the British Empire, linked to British interests.

After the war, however, safety had taken on a whole new meaning. Deep disappointment with the international responses to Nazism combined with the very real sense of British betrayal that the White Paper signaled. In addition, there was now the reality of surviving, displaced Jews in Europe, as well as of the League of Arab States that adopted the Palestine Question as central to regional interests. To the degree that a primary Palestinian Arab leader, Hajj Amin al-Husseini, had been actively complicit with Nazi leadership, and a variety of other events in the region during wartime had signaled Arab sympathy with the Axis, these factors combined to generate intensified feelings of vulnerability and an emphasis on security as having priority.[27]

In this context, Ben-Gurion's insistence on statehood and unlimited immigration offered a powerful promise of recovery. A state in which Jews were the majority, which could grow quickly through immigration, and where they could take care of themselves offered an important corrective to the experiences of failed promises and disappointments that had piled up in the immediate prologue to the fight for statehood. Any plan that required coexistence with those viewed as hostile to Jewish needs was easily discounted by many, and the wish for a place governed as the extension of family was powerful. Although the forties yielded a series of efforts to conceptualize Arab-Jewish coexistence in Palestine, none could gain the needed support as the mainstream Zionist leadership moved to insist on control of its own territory and polity, even if it was geographically more limited than had been hoped.[28]

Ultimately, the coinciding of American and Soviet support for the partition of Palestine helped set the stage for a military confrontation that left each population in Palestine—Jewish and Arab—to seek support from their own extended communities in a conflict that gave further evidence of the inequalities that had developed under the mandate. When Israel, as a Jewish state, was declared independent in May 1948, many of the fundamental questions that had been part of the Zionist project had not been settled. Nevertheless, the dominant Mapai Party controlled the new government and its leader, David Ben-Gurion, was in a position to organize as well as to articulate the defining era of the new state.

At this point, two of the individuals who had played important roles during the mandate were no longer able to do so. Ze'ev Jabotinsky had died in New York in 1940. His wish to have his body buried in the new Jewish state could not be fulfilled until 1964, when Levi Eshkol was prime minister. This was a result of the bitterness and rivalry that had come to characterize Ben-Gurion's attitude toward his Revisionist rivals, as well as the personal antagonism he felt toward Jabotinsky himself.

At another point on the spectrum, Judah Magnes could no longer continue advocacy of coexistence and a federalized state in Palestine. His stroke in New York in October 1948 prevented him from returning to the new state. While recognized as a significant voice both in the US and in Israel, Magnes too had lived to see his visions of Zionism marginalized.

Hannah Arendt, who had actively supported Magnes and his struggle against partition, remained in the US, continuing her academic work and maintaining a decreased engagement with Zionism, which had now yielded an outcome that she saw as dangerous. She did, however, continue to participate in events such as a discussion of Palestinian refugees in 1958, and she would reemerge as a focus of attention with her publication of *Eichmann in Jerusalem* in 1962.

Nahum Goldmann, sometimes labeled a statesman without a state, continued to be actively engaged but never within the Israeli political system. Having been instrumental in the achievement of partition, he maintained his role as a link between Israel and the diaspora while also feeling free to express views and take positions that were not always in accord with those of the Israeli leadership. Goldmann, like Arendt, continued to have deep ties with the Europe and particularly Germany in which their own understanding of politics, as well as specifically Jewish life, had been formed. Unlike Arendt, however, Goldmann also sought to play a role in the American Jewish organizational world, thus working to maintain diaspora links to which he was committed.[29]

Finally, Golda Meir now served the Israeli government as a long-standing member of Mapai and a loyal supporter of its first prime minister. She had come to the US during 1948 to raise funds for and strengthen the investment of American Jewish communities in the new state. Her first government position was as ambassador to the USSR, inaugurating an ongoing presence in the Israeli leadership that would later lead to her becoming prime minister.

By 1948, many of the competing voices defining Zionist goals or critical of Zionism as a whole were quieted. At the same time, new challenges emerged—beginning with the question of whether Zionism could be viewed as having achieved its goals and therefore would best be dissolved, as Israel sought to define itself in the world and with regard to a diaspora that showed little sign of disappearing.

Chapter 2

Making the State the Source of Security, 1948–1967

Establishing the Terrain

It is common knowledge that the War of 1967, often referred to as the Six-Day War, was transformative in a series of ways. It was the point of origin for the Israeli occupation of East Jerusalem, the West Bank, the Golan Heights, Sinai, and Gaza. It was also a turning point in the US-Israel relationship; it helped cement an identification of American Jews with Israel, including an emphasis on the Holocaust as a significant component of what came to be seen as a shared history. While all these developments have been detailed in a variety of studies, there are questions that have not been asked, as though the answers were self-evident. Why and how did the war take on the emotional significance that it did? What were the antecedents that prepared Americans and American Jews in particular to respond as they did? That this response was linked to sharper polarization of views on Arab-Israeli conflict as well as less tolerance for alternative views is an important aspect of the shift, which inaugurated an era of Israeli regional dominance linked directly to US global aspirations.

It is with a view to understanding how the period before this war prepared the ground for it to take on powerful meaning that this study examines antecedent dynamics. Central to those dynamics was the replacement of Europe and European Jewry, in all their complexity of relationship to the Zionist project, with an alliance of Israel and the US based in part on a reimagining of both history and statehood. Tracing this process entails a careful examination of several threads: the ways in which Israeli statehood affected the process of defining a national identity; the transformation of Jewish institutional leadership, organization, and practice after 1948; and the challenge of formulating the legitimacy of US assumption of global power not only against the USSR but equally in contrast to European historically colonial models.

Throughout the period under consideration, 1948–1967, we can see the underlying conflict between a quest for power (often experienced as defensive) to have control and ideologies that relied on moral advantage as well as equity for support.

The establishment of the state of Israel in 1948 did not end ongoing debate about the implications of seeking statehood for the Jewish community in Palestine (the Yishuv), but it did significantly transform the terms of discussion. While earlier disagreements revolved around the likely consequences with regard to Arab-Jewish relations as well as concerns about the ways in which war might affect the nature of the state, these issues became largely moot once the state came into being. Nevertheless, questions about the nature of this new state, its definition as a Jewish state, and its relationship to diaspora communities became all the more pressing. One way of examining this conversation as it evolved in the period from 1948 to 1967 is to examine the relationships of individuals rooted in three quite different Jewish political cultures: Jacob Blaustein of the American Jewish Committee; Nahum Goldmann, whose activities articulated a particular representation of cosmopolitan European Jewish culture; and David Ben-Gurion, the first Israeli prime minister. At one level the tensions in these relationships made evident the unresolved questions that continued to obscure the boundaries of an Israeli polity in formation. Thus, the uncertain physical boundaries of the state (due to the fact that the war of 1948 ended without treaties) were accompanied by continuing debate on questions related to the boundaries of legitimate participation in policy debates (on citizenship, on foreign policy, and so on). At a second level, however, these relationships can also stand in for consideration of the search for a usable national history to serve the state's efforts to continue defining its constituency while maintaining the resources viewed as essential to its survival.

With the Declaration of Independence in May 1948, and specifically as a consequence of war, Israel came into being as a Jewish state with an overwhelmingly Jewish majority. Despite this success of the Zionist project, however, it remained very much a work in progress, with considerable internal differences only further exacerbated by the encouragement of immigration that doubled its population over the next six years.[1] Led by David Ben-Gurion and the Mapai Party, Israeli attention was focused on consolidating the gains of war as well as maintaining and expanding Jewish population, while developing institutions such as the Israel Defense Forces, all with a view to creating a powerful national identification with the state, which was bolstered by the perception of being surrounded by hostile forces.[2]

For Jewish and Zionist leaders who resided outside the state, however, the new political situation aroused very different considerations. While support for Zionism (with its insistence on the need for a Jewish homeland as refuge as well as national center) was significantly bolstered by the realities of World War II and its aftermath, this shift only enhanced the need to redefine the meanings of Zionism as a state-building project, and of Jewish communal life in its relationship to that project.

In the early years of statehood, Ben-Gurion's emphasis on *mamlachtiut* (statism) necessitated the use of various tactics to manage competing centers of power. Choosing to absorb some and to negotiate with others, the focus was on dealing with immediate demands and interests while delaying confrontations unlikely to serve these purposes. In crucial areas this resulted in a policy of deciding not to decide in hopes that time would enable resolution. In the case of the relationship between the World Zionist Organization and the government of Israel, Ben-Gurion and Nahum Goldmann were key players in negotiating a Status Law that ensured an ongoing role for the World Zionist Organization in areas with significant impact on development of the state. Equally critical, however, was the fact that this legislation appeared to underwrite the ongoing significance of a Zionist movement after statehood, creating a formal claim by representatives of the Zionist movement to priority in connecting the state to the diaspora.[3]

David Ben-Gurion questioned the meaning of poststate Zionism in the diaspora and challenged the World Zionist Organization's claim for priority over other groups such as the American Jewish Committee (AJC). Nevertheless, he conceded on the Knesset legislation, which recognized the World Zionist Organization as "the authorized agency which will continue to operate in the State of Israel for the development and settlement of the country, the absorption of immigrants from the Diaspora and the coordination of the activities in Israel of Jewish institutions and organizations active in those fields."[4]

The law further encouraged the World Zionist Organization to work for the unity of all sections of Jewry as necessary for Israel's mission (of ingathering) and "to broaden its basis" for that purpose. The AJC watched carefully as the Status Law was considered, its representatives expressing their concern in response to any effort to appoint a sole representative of American Jewish relations with the Israeli government. At the same time, Nahum Goldmann worked in support of the law, as well as on efforts to bring the AJC under a broad umbrella that allowed better control over the interaction between American Jewish leaderships and the Israeli government. Despite the efforts to regularize relations, the fifties were marked by continuing differences of perspective and active efforts to manage them. The nature of these differences sheds light not only on the politics involved but equally on the historical experiences contributing to various conceptualizations of Jewish communal fear and needs.[5]

For American Jews who continued to live as a minority with no intention of moving, statehood could be welcomed and even arouse pride. However, security as well as identity remained largely bounded by the relationship to the US, which required ongoing efforts to integrate and to decrease exclusionary barriers.[6] For Zionists in the US, however, the challenge posed by statehood was different. In the decades prior to 1948, American Zionism had had its differences internally and with European Zionist leaders. After 1948 questions were raised about the purpose and viability of an ongoing Zionist movement as well as the definitions of Zionism outside the state. Beyond theoretical conceptualization, this was an arena in which power and control over state policies remained subject to significant conflict, triggered in part by the fact that this was also the domain within which European Jews (often now living in the US), American, and Israeli Jews all had a stake.

The conversation on these subjects took place at a variety of levels and within various groups. To understand its impact at the institutional level, the focus in this analysis remains on the leadership and on the ways in which discussions developed over the period from 1948 to 1967. In the interests of analyzing shifts over time, it is important to recognize what can be seen in retrospect as periods of significant change in the process of creating an Israeli-American Jewish alliance, which was based eventually on much broader identification with the state.

In the early fifties, Prime Minister David Ben-Gurion had to contend with challenges posed both by Jacob Blaustein, director of the American Jewish Committee, and by Nahum Goldmann, a prominent Zionist activist. Goldmann, though born in Lithuania and educated in Germany, was now pursuing his Zionist commitments largely in the US. As an individual who had already played an important role in the years leading to statehood, he was eager to continue using his diplomatic skills and expressing his critical views within the Zionist movement, but his participation was not limited by participation in the newly created Israeli political system. Thus, while Blaustein confronted Ben-Gurion with the expectation of articulating clear distinctions between Israel and the American Jewish community, Goldmann was eager to link American Jews to Israel but to do so in a way that allowed for the creation of intermediary institutions and representatives in partnership with the state.[7] The triangle was sustained by two central contradictions characterizing Israeli self-determination as a nation-state. The model of nation-statehood is based on the premise of a national community finding recognition in political form, while Israel came into existence in the process of defining its national constituency and with clearly competing claims by those living in its territory as opposed to those outside. The Yishuv leadership, having led the fight for independence, asserted its right to define the nation, but chose to do so not on the basis of citizenship and territorial definition, but rather on the basis of a particular reading of Zionism that emphasized active ingathering of Jews as a vehicle for building the state. The result was an internal contradiction between claims to political separateness and the reality of failure to separate.

This phenomenon was intimately related to the second, inevitable contradiction that Israeli leaders faced. The state they had founded and defended resided within a region just emerging from long-term integration within various imperial systems. Israel came into being as a state with a population and legal structure also formed in that world, but with a leadership determined to distinguish it from its surroundings, as well as to deal with regional challenges by mobilizing external supports in the service of its own very powerful imagined community. Circumstances seemed to favor this project, but in the years before 1967 ongoing debate and critique from those who were being asked to provide those supports made visible the efforts required to make it work and the existence of alternative views.[8]

Status and Responsibility

It was no coincidence that in 1951 and 1952 Jacob Blaustein and Nahum Goldmann articulated two very different alternatives in discussions with

Ben-Gurion. While each one ultimately gained recognition, the results maintained a measure of tension and resulted in a resurfacing of discussion ten years later. In the meantime, conditions in Israel and its position in the world had changed, with the state having firmly established itself.

While the American Jewish Committee was a non-Zionist organization, it had been actively engaged in supporting practical aspects of the Jewish settlement in Palestine under the mandate. It did so in the context of the broader commitment to representing the interests of American Jews within the US and to the US government. Given its clear stance, the AJC could not support any implication that Jews in the US resided in exile or had any obligation to immigrate to the new Jewish state. Its leadership thus recognized that with the establishment of the state there would be a need to ensure clear Israeli recognition of this position. In August 1950, Prime Minister David Ben-Gurion responded with a statement to Jacob Blaustein, affirming "the state of Israel represents and speaks only on behalf of its own citizens and in no way presumes to represent or speak in the name of the Jews who are citizens of any other country." Recognizing the particular concerns of the AJC, Ben-Gurion further added that "any weakening of American Jewry, any disruption of its communal life, any lowering of its sense of security and diminution of its status, is a definite loss to Jews everywhere and to Israel in particular."[9]

Ben-Gurion's statement was intended to avoid conflict with a community whose support he felt was crucial for the new state. At the same time, this public clarity did not and could not resolve the internal contradiction of a position that depended on maintaining a Zionist ideology based not only on ingathering but on the superiority of Jewish life within the state, while simultaneously seeking to mobilize widespread support in the strongest diaspora community—the United States. This tension was to a degree exposed by the more complex negotiations accompanying the ultimate passage of what came to be known as the Israeli Nationality Law in 1952.

Discussions of the Israeli Nationality Law convey these differences quite clearly. They also tell us that in the fifties what were viewed as troubling aspects of the Israeli state were noted and addressed by AJC leaders as well as some of their constituency. One of the most notable contrasts was that between an Israeli policy based on strengthening majority dominance in the state, and an American Jewish perspective particularly sensitive to the dangers of discrimination against minorities. In considering the new Israeli Nationality Law in 1952, the administrative committee of the AJC was described as "greatly disturbed that the recent Israeli Nationality Law seems to discriminate between the Jewish majority and the minorities now living in Israel. . . . we believe that humanity and justice require that all legal residents of Israel and legal immigrants into Israel should be granted equal rights including the right of citizenship."[10]

Additional concerns were raised with regard to the way in which the Israeli Law of Return automatically granted citizenship to Jewish immigrants seeking residency. This was viewed as raising issues of double loyalty and discrimination. Throughout the discussions, there was also confusion as well as concern about the Israeli decision to include nationality and religion on identity cards, particularly in light of the fact that nationality was Jewish or Arab rather than Israeli. In contrast to American ideas of citizenship, it was clear that Israel was establishing categories based on its self-defined status as a Jewish state. However, the exact meaning of that definition and what were to be the categories of inclusion or exclusion remained subject to vigorous debate.

While the AJC retained its focus on evaluating Israeli actions in the context of its historical emphasis on Jewish integration in the US, American Zionists found themselves in the odd position of feeling undervalued by the prime minister of the new Jewish state.[11] Viewing themselves as very instrumental in mobilizing and maintaining support for statehood, they discovered that their success bred a new set of challenges. Zionism had been an international movement that created an arena for vibrant debate within various communities and among them. Its party structure had also ensured significant ideological confrontations. Once the success of its primary goal (now defined as statehood) was ensured, however, there were those who believed there was no longer any point to this organizational structure. According to Ben-Gurion on the one hand, and a number of critics on the other, it was important to distinguish Israelis from Jews who might or might not support the state but had no intention of migrating to it. In Ben-Gurion's view, Zionism now required a willingness to be an active participant in the project of building within the new state.[12]

A loyal opposition to this point of view was eloquently articulated by Nahum Goldmann. As a Zionist whose base of operations was in extrastate organizations, Goldmann was on close personal terms with the Israeli political establishment and worked on projects that had significant impact on the state, such as mobilizing support for partition in the forties and negotiating German reparations in the fifties. At the same time, he was unwilling to limit his political perspective within the boundaries of any state; after 1948 he positioned himself in such a way as to maintain organizational supports while simultaneously articulating alternative views of Israeli policies. In these ways, Goldmann worked from two European Jewish experiences. On the one hand, his education and life circumstances made him very much an individual with cosmopolitan skills, such as familiarity with multiple languages; on the other, he worked out of a history in which Jewish communities had collective identities that influenced their relationships to states. Where Ben-Gurion spoke from what was emerging as the Israeli effort to equate community with state, Goldmann spoke within a belief that the community would remain larger than the state, could not be subsumed by it, but that both required effective communication and understanding of common interests.[13]

Goldmann and Ben-Gurion both worked within powerful beliefs in the importance of what they were doing for the future of Jewish communal life, and their orientation toward that future was based on analysis of historical experience. Where Ben-Gurion cast doubt on the long-term existence of a vital American Jewish community, Goldmann worked actively to strengthen its coherence and to support Jewish education outside of Israel. Neither, however, viewed the American Jewish experience as a distinctive model that might offer a valuable alternative for the collective future. It was Europe (East and West), from which the preponderance of both Israeli Jews and American Jews had largely fled, that remained the political/cultural framework for their thinking. It was the history of Jews in Europe, caught between polarities of communalism and assimilation, engaged with the ideologies of nationalism and socialism, identified with the power of expanding states allied with dominant cultures that Goldmann and Ben-Gurion, each in his own way, carried with them. Paradoxically, the Holocaust, which made manifest a powerful underside to this history, served primarily to prove right the Zionist analysis; only later and still incompletely did it become possible to integrate the reality of these polarities.

The drive to contain these contradictory relationships to Europe became evident in a project shared by Ben-Gurion and Goldmann, namely, the negotiation of reparations to be paid by Germany to Israel as well as to individual survivors and refugees. In the face of objections from those who opposed such arrangements, Ben-Gurion and Goldmann each supported these negotiations from their own perspectives. For Ben-Gurion, reparations filled immediate needs for the state but also signified a claim that remained disputed, that is, Israel's right to act as heir to

Jewish communities no longer in existence and as a collective voice of a Jewish nation. For Goldmann, in addition to acting as representative of international Zionist and Jewish bodies, the role of mediator provided a route to recognition of his personal relationship to Germany, a dramatic change from the time not long before when he, like many others, had had to flee.[14]

This particular project, which Goldmann considered his most important historical contribution, contained key elements marking the particular moment. Goldmann was instrumental in developing a relationship with West German chancellor Konrad Adenauer that was based on common language but also on a significant capacity for emotional detachment. Where others reacted with anger to the idea of negotiations with Germany, seeing it as the acceptance of "blood money," Goldmann saw it as the logical, rational outcome of having achieved statehood. In this he joined Moshe Sharett (Israeli foreign minister), Ben-Gurion, and others who defined the ultimate agreement as a moral victory as well as a practical right. Following the logic of Zionism and of statehood, the Reparations Agreement between Israel and Germany, signed in 1952, underlined the change in power relationships. Goldmann himself thus distinguished between the new situation and the mentality of those who opposed it. The simultaneous negotiations for compensation to Jewish victims of the Nazis who lived outside Israel via the Conference on Jewish Material Claims Against Germany (in which J. Blaustein participated) only further contributed to the movement toward institutional unification of Jews favored by Goldmann.[15]

The context for Israeli-German negotiations was one of continuing fluidity as the Cold War began to take shape, generating US policies in Europe and the Middle East focused on consolidating alliances and military defense. Linked to this process was the creation of an ideological structure intended to maintain alliances in Europe while seeking to distinguish the American position from the colonialism now inexorably losing ground. In this environment, Israeli leaders sought to ensure their own maximum advantage without endangering the US support critical to their success. The process of negotiating reparations clearly had British and American backing throughout, fitting well with the plan to encourage West Germany's rapid recovery from the war. At the same time it was only one of the European states with which Israel hoped to strengthen relations. What role Israel should seek to play in this international arena was still a subject for serious disagreement within Israel as well as between its leaders and others.[16] The reparations treaty was linked by some to the potential for resolving Israeli-Arab conflict as well as resolution of the plight of Palestinian Arab refugees. In these areas, US policymaking played a critical, if not always entirely visible, part.[17]

Remaking Europe and Decolonization

From 1948 to 1967 there were still many mirrors in which Jewish politicians and intellectuals could see themselves, whether located in Israel or in the United States. One that relatively few could allow themselves to see, let alone see themselves in, was that of the Palestinian Arabs. In the course of the Palestine mandate Palestinian Arabs, clearly a numerical majority, had taken on the characteristics of a minority community that did not have control over any semblance of recognized state institutions. Thus already stateless even before the creation of Israel, their position clearly marked the potential emergence of a new regional system in which their integration could, according to various plans, be accomplished through other Arab states or as a minority within the Jewish state. Advocates for a binational solution, questioning the logic of ethnic statehood, were viewed on the whole as unrealistic although their predictions have proved to have significant merit. Equally important, however, is the reality that the goal of organizing the region according to nation-states, which would be experienced as the source of individual as well as external security, was intimately related to the way in which the postwar world was emerging in Europe with strong US intervention.

Both France and Great Britain faced challenges to the empires that had expanded their borders and allowed them to incorporate vast populations. The US, in contrast, developed policies seeking to maintain global power but to establish its claim on the basis of supporting self-determination, independence, and anticolonialism as a counter to communism. While the older imperial states continued with a painful, accelerated process of recognizing the limits of their capacities to impose governance as well as culture, the US was accelerating its own expansion in precisely these areas, offering itself as protector by encouraging state systems that could be relied on to manage the messiness of popular movements articulating a range of desires for recognition as well as reorganization of socioeconomic relationships. It is in this context that the initial support of Israeli independence by both the US and the USSR needs to be understood.

As the Israeli state took shape in this environment, Ben-Gurion's policies contained central contradictions that became formative. While insisting on Zionism as an ideology of Jewish independence and favoring military activism, Ben-Gurion very clearly understood the need for material support and political position to be gained from relationships with European states, at the same time retaining a focus on the long-term goal of moving US policy toward a greater commitment to Israel. Ben-Gurion's version of Zionism thus defined state building as key, and there is little evidence of conflict between his understandings of Jewish history and Zionism. Both were built on a European Jewish experience that left deep traces of conflicted identity and ambiguity long before the Holocaust. Thus, policies that mobilized German and French support for Israeli development had dual advantages—the practical gains attached and the emotional satisfaction of gaining recognition from those who had viewed Jews with contempt. What seems to have been much less clear was the contradiction involved in now looking to these same states, which had been so hostile to Jewish community life, as sources of protection and as models.

It is the war in Algeria, and its implications for Israel, Palestinians, France, and the US, that most clearly illustrates how decisions taken to meet short-range, immediate goals left lasting impressions and short-circuited significant discussions. Located most immediately in the context of decolonization taking place as Cold War polarities hardened, Algeria became the object of various imaginaries and remains a painful reminder of unresolved conflicts that belie the expectations associated with independence and apparent nationalist victory in 1962. From 1954 to 1962, Algeria was a focus of political debate, a test of using military force to solve long-standing inequities of power (economic and social as well as political), and a mirror for the changing international constellations of power. Its language of nationalism and revolution incorporated themes that were to be emblematic of a period in which the search for statehood, independence, and authenticity appeared to pervade widely disparate phenomena, all now seen through the lens of a European colonialism tarnished further by the upheavals of World War II and its aftermath. But the war in Algeria also had very specific characteristics that made it directly relevant to the Israeli-Palestinian conflict, both at the historical moment of its occurrence and as an analytical lens in its aftermath. It contained elements that placed it squarely in the histories of the Middle East and of Europe; it broke out after decades of failures to resolve growing tensions through political change; there were those who predicted the likely outcome of these failures; and in the end the state that emerged was deeply marked by the conditions of its birth. Among those conditions was the necessary appeal to an international audience that appeared to ratify its legitimacy. The US role in this process exemplifies the complexity of policies designed to consolidate power in a way that protected European allies while seeking to distance itself from their colonial past.[18]

For Israeli leaders, the Algerian War coincided with the change of regime in Egypt and thus generated a framework within which French and Israeli interests could come to be seen as easily aligned.[19] On the surface, Israeli policies appeared driven by the search for security as well as by the need to consolidate the state as representative of national interests. Lacking a clearly defined national community, Israel in effect straddled a growing international divide. On the one hand, the government followed policies that looked to European states as well as the US for support; on the other, it sought ties with states emerging from colonialism, particularly in Africa. Zionism as the ideology of the state now underlined the legitimate claims of Jews as a nation to self-determination, while simultaneously serving to support a very specific state project. It was a project based deliberately on the failure to define itself in ways that significantly interfered with the goal of consolidation, as well as of creating a sturdy framework for the legitimacy of its authority. At the time, the decisions not to define either borders or constitution were predicated on avoiding internal conflicts and expecting external ones. Independence thus was understood in large measure as success in creating a political arena within which competing understandings of the nature of the state would continue to operate. In this respect, Israel was only one of many states emerging in this period whose accomplishment of technical independence obscured the actual ongoing process of defining key elements such as inclusion and exclusion, the role of religious institutions and leaderships, models of state-society relationships, and so on. That this process was influenced as much by Ottoman/British precedents and Jewish Middle Eastern immigrants as by the pre-1948 population of the Yishuv was also obscured in the myth of creating a European-dominated and preferred nation-state.

The war in Algeria became an interesting foil in which Jews were inevitably viewed as part of the colonialist enterprise, and, in time, the Algerian Revolution was cited by Palestinians as a model for their own national movement. As a result, it became that much harder to see that there were also underlying conflicts regarding the nature of state- and nation-building that affected developments in both Israel and Algeria.[20]

The final war for Algerian independence, beginning in 1954 and ending in 1962, took on meaning well beyond the conflict that pitted French settlers against the Algerian National Liberation Front (Front de Libération Nationale, or FLN). The context for this war, which incorporated French aspirations for recovery from the effects of World War II as well as renewed international status, and which ultimately helped heighten the role of the international community in defining the emerging postcolonial system of nation-states, also implicated the US and its drive for global position. While politicians, diplomats, and fighters struggled to determine who would control the resources and territory long viewed as an extension of France, or how the vast majority of Algerians would gain recognition and the freedom to define their own cultural identities, this violent struggle also took on symbolic meaning for many far away from its reality. Algeria thus also became a dividing line and a defining moment, contributing to the heightening of ideological polarizations. It was in this context that Franz Fanon became a prominent voice articulating the Algerian experience for non-Algerians, particularly for the New Left.[21]

In recent years a number of works have sought to recover aspects of this period that had been largely suppressed or forgotten. In some cases, the connections being newly made are particularly fruitful and suggestive of the ways in which two very distinct phenomena, historically seen as at odds with one another, can be more fully understood both in dialogue with and as formative of each other. Thus, Michael Rothberg, in *Multidirectional Memory,* uses the memorialization of the Holocaust and the Algerian War to argue against views of collective memory that pit one group of victims against another.[22] Jeffrey Isaac argues for the usefulness of analyzing the works of Hannah Arendt and Albert Camus (intellectuals significantly challenged by these events) in relationship to one another.[23] Aamir Mufti writes about the "Jewish Question and the Crisis of Postcolonial Culture."[24] In a volume *on Memory and Violence in the Middle East and North Africa,* edited by Ussama Makdisi and Paul A. Silverstein, James McDougall reexamines the history of the Algerian War by looking at "the presence of the past as a system of meaning and its effective force in shaping political understanding, programs and action."[25]

For purposes of this study, two aspects of this analysis are significant: the ways in which violence comes to be naturalized in Algerian history while alternative routes have been foreclosed; and the way in which "the constitution of history as self-knowledge, in turn is simultaneously both a factor in shaping the form of social struggles, and a crucial object of struggle, in which the goal of each antagonist is to gain the cultural authority to exercise 'the force attached to the legitimate enunciation of history's meaning.' " Thus, according to McDougall, "From the mid-1960s, the reappropriation and 'decolonization' . . . of Algerian history was a major preoccupation not only for Algeria's intellectuals but, more crucially, for a state system whose legitimacy, ratified neither by universal suffrage nor by tradition, remained inseparable from its mythologized . . . origin in resistance and revolution." These statements have resonance for the unsettled histories of Israel/Palestine and for the centrality of its narratives. To understand them, it is important first to clarify the role Algeria played in the shift from a world dominated by Europe to one in which the US vied with the USSR as the source of support for competing forces emerging in the decolonizing world.

Unlike many other colonized areas, Algeria was marked by the relatively long duration of French control, the significant size and impact of French settlement with its profound effects on the native population, and the governing perception that it was a permanent extension of French territory. All these factors contributed to the fact that efforts to remedy the inequities it encompassed were for a long time focused on reforms; those who supported reform believed in the possibility of coexistence between the French and the emerging Algerian movements, which sought cultural as well as political recognition.

It was in the environment of a postwar France struggling to reestablish itself as a significant European force that the war for Algeria became a conflict to define both state and communal boundaries. Shifting from earlier projects based on the continuation of Algeria as an extension of France, the war was fought between an FLN intent on independence/separation and those who were determined to defeat it—as representatives of the French state and a particular conceptualization of French cultural community. As polarization increased, the voices of any who sought to offer alternative views came to be disparaged as colonialist, a term now used less as descriptor or analytical tool and more as a label with which to delegitimize primarily European powers. Thus, the histories of both American and Soviet expansionism remained ideologically separated from this struggle, which both sought to exploit for their own purposes.

Central to the process of decolonization was a conceptualization of states as the vehicles for political authority recognized as legitimate by the international community. Intrinsic to this conception was the assumption that states would act in the name of their citizens, often now redefined as nations, and would provide a measure of security bolstered by an identification of citizens with the state. While it was understood that economic factors were key to creating the stability sought in the aftermath of decolonization, less attention was paid to the radical destabilization created by forces seeking to replace complex social and cultural structures with drives toward national communities. Although decolonization appeared in most instances to be the product of populations rebelling against oppressive imperial authorities, the emergence of these movements cannot be separated from the Cold War context in which they took place. The negotiation, first of European state relationships and then regional state systems, was undertaken by global powers whose positions depended on the reliability of political authorities with control over populations as well as resources.

Thus, it is impossible to separate the outcome of the Algerian struggle from the simultaneous US effort to regulate its relationship with France and to define its own position as one of moral opposition to colonialism. As the war in Algeria intensified, American assessments came to be based on the view that independence was inevitable, generating policies designed to protect US interests, economic as well as political. By the time of the Evian Accords in 1962 (which brought the war in Algeria to an end and granted Algeria independence) the FLN campaign had achieved international support and, with it, an aura of freedom won. Less clear, inevitably, was the nature of the state that would emerge and the uneven impact on Algerians.

Fanon, among others, was instrumental in creating a narrative of Algeria that saw this outcome as inevitable, based on justice and necessity. In this story, violence could play a creative role when exercised in the name of a nationalist movement. In concert with the times, Algeria could be viewed as the story of liberation from an exploitative and oppressive regime that had encouraged foreign settlement, as well as economic inequity coupled with cultural destructiveness. The polarities that had become part of a dominant narrative—fascism against democracy, communism vs. capitalism; colonialism vs. anticolonialism—now emerged as a new framework. In this context, those who suggested alternative stories or understandings, those whose views sought to evade these stark divisions, were largely marginalized; history as it developed was given the authority of inevitability. It is only now, over sixty years later, that there can be some efforts to understand how this view was constituted, along with some understanding of those who foresaw the price to be paid.

At the time, the French-FLN struggle took on meaning not only internationally but also regionally. Although Algerian history was distinctive, the challenge to French control could readily be assimilated to the emerging assertiveness of a more broadly conceived Arabism. This link, whatever its concrete reality (which is questionable), served a variety of purposes and interests. Among those who felt directly affected were, on the one hand, Israeli leaders and, on the other, the Jewish communities of North Africa.[26] That this impact was hardly seamless or uniform offers insight into the fact that Jewish community life continued to be in flux, as Israeli statehood took shape with multiple frameworks for interpreting the risks and opportunities presented. Central to this time period was a process that would eventually give rise to a particular narrative about Israel's position, regional as well as international, while the choices that created that trajectory became less visible. Among the most significant was the choice to define Israel's conflict as one with Arabs rather than with Palestinians. Although it is arguable that this was simply a recognition of existing forces and structures, this is an assumption that should be reexamined.

Ideology and Boundaries—
Debating Nationhood in Full View

In many cases, decolonization entailed, among other things, agreement on the existence of nations claiming rights to self-determination and independence in the form of nation-states. In cases such as that of Algeria and Israel, the nationalist movements required to gain this outcome against strong opposition enhanced the legitimacy of their leaderships as victorious. These two new states were very different in substance and historically set against each other on the axis of colonizer and the colonized. Thus, it has been difficult to note that these developments were both deeply affected by the fact that they took place in the seemingly supportive environment of an emerging postwar international constellation that created its own particular pressures. This fact, in itself, contributed to a phenomenon that accompanied the process of decolonization—that is, the creation of states that did not in reality correspond to developed national bodies with clear boundaries or cultural definitions. Algeria and Israel, moreover, were definitively implicated in the process underlying their emergence—the redefinitions of European states and their relationships to the US. It was in this context that the redefinition of communities and struggles to align community with statehood took place. It was also in this context that alliances across state boundaries emerged to enhance leadership positions and limit domestic debates.

For Algeria, the struggle itself, along with its role as emblematic of postcolonialism, required a definition sharply separating itself from the French authority/culture that had deeply penetrated its modern history. In the case of Israel, that aspect of Zionism that resulted in separateness not only physically from Europe but ideologically from Jewish diaspora existence within the continent now coexisted with the reality that its leadership was deeply identified with European cultures as well as with the quest for recognition precisely from these powers. In both cases, the environment of newly achieved statehood contained an irony of abiding impact—that is, the suppression of knowledge based on painful, conflicted local experience in the service of ideologies that could gain support in the international arena. While generating immediate gains, this process had deeply distorting long-term effects.

For Israeli leadership in the aftermath of 1948/49, consolidation of the gains made through war required an insistence on continuing vulnerability in a region that consisted of territories emerging from European control, with a continuing fluidity of boundaries and internal struggles to create meaningful/effective, political/economic structures. Following the trajectory of British policies under the mandate, Israeli policy focused not on the displaced Palestinian Arab population, but on the governments of Arab states as their proxy. This choice, undertaken in hopes of eliminating any Palestinian claim to political representation, reinforced the emerging assertion of Arabism as a tool for regional organization and the focus of power as well as ideological legitimacy. Israeli policy in this respect was very much in line with British and French perspectives despite the differences between them. The British were hoping to maximize their influence via support of the Arab League while initial French views sought to minimize this challenge to their cultural supremacy.

Thus, Israel participated in the emergence of a regional battlefield within which various states competed, and defined its interests as constructing a Jewish national community that could stand up to this perceived threat to its existence. Lost in the process (which included the ingathering of Jews in Israel) were significant elements of the reality that had characterized historical Arab/Jewish coexistence within the region, but particularly in Palestine.

From the perspective of Israeli governments largely led by David Ben-Gurion, a central organizing concern was that of security. For reasons concrete and inherent in the creation of an effective state, as well as emotionally resonant in the aftermath of World War II, the search for safety was a powerful component of the priority accorded to the creation and strengthening of the Israeli military. This perspective governed decision-making with regard to regional relationships (including the effort to place Arab-Jewish relations beyond the border) and reinforced the search for ties to ensure the maintenance of military superiority. Given limits imposed by US policy, the partners that could fulfill these needs were few.[27] Under these circumstances, it took only a few years for elements in the French and Israeli governments to find their interests well suited to one another.

The coincidence of Egyptian regime change with FLN mobilization in the mid-1950s appeared to underline the values of cooperation to resist the forces of Arab nationalism. This alliance had obvious concrete advantages for the Israeli military and accorded with the broad definition of statism associated with David Ben-Gurion.[28] Less evident was the way in which these developments contributed to creating a particular version of Israeli nationalism, masked by the overt emphasis on Zionism and Jewish nationhood; also largely unnoticed was the shared struggle for who would define legitimate state boundaries and the reality of their fluidity during this time period.

Several realities served to create the stage on which these conflicts were played out. In the Arab Middle East (as in many formerly colonized areas that became independent in the postwar period), the states that emerged were by no means experienced as having fixed borders, nor were governments necessarily accorded community support. Although overt French and British control gradually decreased, political independence was fraught with uncertainties as to models of governance; centuries of Ottoman structures, which had retained a measure of continuity under mandatory rule, now coexisted with models of national states. Efforts to mobilize popular support for state-building were challenged by long-standing patterns of identification with nonstate communities.

Europe remained a site of contested borders as well, with the newer division into East and West having the effect of creating new regional realities, as well as contributing to substantial political and economic reorganizations that extended the roles that both the US and the USSR now actively played as part of this new construction. In this process decolonization was to function as a vehicle establishing new limits for

Europe and new states as battlegrounds for domestic as well as Cold War competition.

The United Nations took shape as a forum within which newly emergent states were represented and heard, but effective control remained limited by the major powers. Nevertheless, it was within this body that states were now recognized and international legitimacy conferred. In very different ways, Israel and Algeria both emerged with the active sanction of this body, which was to become a new institutional framework for the articulation, as well as contestation, of conflicting ideological projects to organize global relationships.

For Israelis, these dynamics intersected in a variety of ways. Central to our concern is the way in which the Israeli state was from the first affected by the perception that survival depended on maintaining external support and thus on creating a narrative that would succeed in that effort. At the same time, the state-building project was one that remained subject to significant debate internally, yet it was often limited by the pressure to perform its nationalism on the international stage and to suppress the unfinished project of nation formation.

The war in Algeria became a part of Israeli nation-building in a number of ways. The most visible was the impact of the alliance with France. Invisible at the time but equally significant historically was the way in which this struggle became a model for the Palestinian national movement. Entwined with both was the reality that Jewish community life was being reshaped by the underlying dilemmas of a historically dramatic sovereignty coexisting with a transformation of minority existence. The relationship between the new Jewish state and its external audiences was fraught at multiple levels in these years when Zionism as classically defined to mean an ingathering came to be intertwined with state interests. Enlarging the Jewish population to ensure continuity simultaneously required adjustment to the reality of needing support from an American Jewish population with no interest in moving. Israel after 1948 absorbed immigration that doubled its population but in the process also imported those who brought experiences of Jewish life and history distinctly different from those of the Yishuv.

The themes that emerged in Israeli appeals for support and in the FLN's fight for independence were constructed to engage the attention as well as actions of the primary global powers in the postwar world. That it was essential to create effective narratives of justification became increasingly evident as the structures that had supported colonial enterprises could no longer be sustained. In these years, 1952 to 1962, the decisive shift from European primacy to bipolar ideological competition was the backdrop on which decolonization emerged as a framework to conceptualize specific alterations in power relationships, as well as to view national liberation movements as either "on the right side of history" or, eventually, as revolutionary upheavals threatening political stability. In any case, these were political developments strongly linked to moral evaluations and to notions of cultural authenticity. They were also, and Algeria was one of the best examples, movements in which violence and action could be seen as part of the necessary transformation and recovery from oppressive systems of exploitation.

For Israelis and those who supported them, this was an era of conflicting identifications and challenges. Admired by some for the heritage of egalitarian ideals and the language of socialism, as well as a Declaration of Independence that promised equal citizenship to all, the first government of the state was faced with immediate decisions that put these commitments in context with challenges to security and survival. Although the dominant narrative that took shape was one that reinforced perceptions of encirclement by enemies and regional isolation, of chronic threat and the military as a central institution, there remained alternative constructions linked to earlier Zionist histories, anchored largely in the prewar European Jewish world or to earlier communal experiences particularly in the Middle East and North Africa.

As nationalist ideologies mobilized in the name of gaining control over the future, being free of external control and correcting injustices, there was little room for recognition of losses attached to historical ruptures. In Algeria, as in Israel, attainment of independence after the experience of traumatic violence was linked to an ongoing rupture with the past, and therefore to urgent needs to formulate histories that conformed to the creation of new communities. In both cases religion continued to provide the materials to claim continuity and authenticity, while new generations were educated into the hybridity of a religious identity bolstered by revolutionary claims and the creation of new states that required refashioned communal identifications.

Re-creating History and Community

In the early years of statehood, formulations of communal belonging and historical development have to occur almost simultaneously. For our purposes, in looking at Israel as it took shape from 1950 to 1962, it is relatively easy to distinguish these levels. On the one hand, the government was enacting laws and policies that clearly defined those to be included and those excluded from the core of Jewish statehood. Thus, regulation of Palestinian Arab citizenship and rights (or lack thereof) along with the Law of Return clearly signaled state priorities and differential citizenships. Coupled with military rule over the Arab population, which was not lifted until 1966, these laws and policies underlined the state's different relationship to Jewish and Arab citizens. Similarly, the incorporation of religious schools in the state system, as well as privileges for religious students, gave symbolic form to the definition of Jewish statehood. At the same time, continuing encouragement of immigration could be seen as linked to the definition of a state of the Jews. Jewish statehood describes the nature of the state as Jewish; a state of the Jews defines it as a state belonging to Jews. The potential contradictions between these two definitions, in addition to the clear conflict between promises of the Declaration of Independence and these policies, were largely ignored in the service of what was taken to be national security. In this context, the use of the Israeli Defense Forces as a vehicle for socializing immigrants, educating them into the ideology of the state and its language, fit the goals of assimilation as well as mobilization.

While there was an obvious ideological fit to now equating state needs with expansion of its Jewish constituency, there was an initial gap of substance between the rhetoric of Jewishness as identity and the real, historical practice of that identity in the many places Jews had lived. While Zionism had predicted the need for Jews to leave Europe, it was changing circumstances in the Middle East and North Africa that forced others to migrate. In different ways, all the immigrants arrived to the expectation that they would cast their past aside and adopt a common future. Paradoxically, however, they were also not encouraged to adopt the history of the Yishuv, which had remained in place, nor was the Yishuv permitted to maintain its own continuity despite the fact that it had remained in place. The year 1948, the Declaration of Independence, and the war, which was viewed as giving birth to the state, all served as a critical dividing line. Before, there was a British mandate, two communities in Palestine, and a Zionist movement working to create a new Hebrew nation. Afterward, there were no British, limited Palestinians, and a Jewish population that brought together those with memories of the mandate, those who had survived the war in Europe, and those whose communities had lived for decades or centuries in the Arab/Muslim world. Zionism motivated only some of these immigrants, and where it did their definitions of it were variable.

Ben-Gurion, first prime minister of Israel, understood the importance of creating links between this population and the state. He also had clear ideas about the ways in which Zionism, now the dominant ideology of the state, was to be understood and taught. His version of a Jewish history to match the needs of the new state relied on linking biblical presence in the land, to which Jews now returned, with the renewal of a national existence that would nurture creative labor—physical as well as intellectual—in the service of an idealized secular mission.[29] Many of those who had chosen to come to Palestine before 1948 shared the sense of participating in a new community, often with a dedication to building for the future. This was, however, not available to many of those who came afterwards. Further complicating the task of creating a national history was the fact that only those who had lived in Palestine before 1948 could understand and experience the transformative nature of the war of that year. Only a much smaller number were in a position to deal with the ways in which the wartime losses as well as gains became formative for the state.

The year 1948 coincided with the postwar realities of Europe and the aftermath of the Holocaust. While immediate attention was focused on recovery and reconstruction, these were also years in which large numbers were again displaced. For the Zionist movement, the immediate focus was on claiming that the solutions for Jewish survivors and for Palestine were inseparable. Significantly less attention was paid to the ways in which World War II, in all its manifestations, had affected individual survivors. It was, of course, assumed that integration into a Jewish community seeking its own state would provide the opportunity for their recovery.

During the first ten years of statehood, neither the traumas of 1948 nor the traumas of World War II and the Holocaust could compete with what was viewed as an ongoing threat to Israel's existence. Mourning was ritualized in various ways, institutions were created, and one trial dealt with conflicts regarding Jewish communal leadership in Hungary and the Zionist movement.[30] At the same time, there were writers who dealt with the war of 1948 in a variety of ways. These were fragmentary responses contributing to the development of a history that could serve as the story of Jews and Israel in a new era. This was a time of multiple histories and moral judgments. They coexisted with the emerging international bipolarity and decision-making regarding Israel's place in that world. While initially some had hopes for neutrality, these were quickly eradicated both by developments in the USSR and the need for sources of concrete support only realistically available from Western Europe and the US. While US policy remained focused on gaining and maintaining ties throughout the Middle East, Israeli leadership sought to strengthen its case for American support at both governmental and popular levels.

By 1960, several developments contributed to an unrecognized but very important shift in the ways that Zionism as an ideology and Israel as a state were to articulate claims for that support. Gradually, a multiplicity of histories would be reorganized and some suppressed. Where Herzl's Zionism had been rooted in the famous slogan—If you will it, it will not be a legend.—and socialist Zionism had clearly built on an optimism not only of the will but of action—the fifties complicated this perspective in a variety of ways.

Where Israeli actions had clearly and with intent led to Palestinian Arab displacement, along with the construction of a particular form of the Jewish state, it was now more politic to emphasize not the power of will or action, but rather the need to react in the face of threat. Where pre-1948 Zionism included, in a variety of ways, the need to live with the Palestinian Arab realities, these could now be viewed as a danger from which Israelis had to be protected. The search for separateness that had characterized Zionist analysis of European Jewish history now was easily transposed but with one critical difference. In Europe it had been seen as an initiative in the face of threat as well as a commitment to the reconstruction of Jewish life; in the Middle East it was redefined as rooted in having no choice, as an existential conflict that would in effect delay the project of facing differences about the nature of Jewish identity and community, while emphasizing the needs of mobilization and unity.

These shifts were threaded through the everyday choices that became constitutive of the ways in which Israeli Jews responded to the challenges of these years, and of the relationship being created between them and American Jews. There were elements in the histories of these two Jewish communities that created a foundation for their coming to see themselves as part of a whole. At the same time, there were significant ways in which the choices of Israeli and American Jews set them apart from one another. By the 1950s, these were communities that were faced with European Jewish survivors who had stayed in a world that both Israelis and Americans had not only left behind but in many cases had seen as worlds to be fled, a Jewish existence of little pride. As they learned of the Holocaust, it was also a world in whose destruction they could feel themselves complicit or responsible in some ways for failure to have rescued European Jews.

Whatever the reality of such regrets, American and Israeli Jews now lived in a world that had seen the devastation of virulent anti-Semitism in the service of state power. They also now had the good fortune to live in a world that was open to recognition of anti-Semitism as a dangerous phenomenon affecting not only Jews but the polities in which they lived.

As a minority, American Jews were finding a variety of paths to integration throughout the US, and the organizations that represented them continued to be of various natures. Zionism, now linked to the existence of Israel, remained central to only a limited sector of the community while anti-Zionism had decreasing appeal. At the same time, Jews were responding to national American politics in a variety of ways, and while some clearly identified themselves with other marginalized groups, others gave greater priority to joining the ascendance of American economic and political power.

In Israel as well there were competing assessments of foreign policy goals and defense needs that gave shape to the ways in which the Jewish state defined its place in the world. One subject that generated divisions within the leadership by the late fifties and early sixties concerned the desirability of developing a nuclear weapons capacity. Ben-Gurion and those who supported him believed that this was an essential step to effective deterrence as well as national survival. Others, including Golda Meir, had significant concerns about the implications of this commitment. It was initially undertaken despite US concerns and pressure for Israel to sign the Nuclear Non-Proliferation Treaty. While Ben-Gurion was eager to gain US support, he had no hesitation about misleading American inspectors when it came to a program that he saw as essential to the protection of the state.[31]

The world in which these developments took place was one in which the language of politics was changing both in response to the Cold War and to the decolonization giving rise to new states. The emergence of nationalist movements that adopted revolutionary, often socialist rhetoric contributed to the redefinitions of political structures as progressive or reactionary, depending on their relationships to the past as well as the nature of the authority they wielded and the alliances they made.

The war in Algeria played a significant role in debates about the relationship between Europeans and Muslims of the Middle East. As the US and the USSR developed an interest in its outcome and in the implications for the regional balance of power, the Israeli leadership came to be located in a set of contradictions that few articulated. This was a leadership that saw itself as on the secular left and as seeking national liberation as well as social justice through the recovery of its own past, as well as construction of a new and hopeful—some would say messianic—future. Nevertheless, they were now making decisions in a world characterized by a shift to Soviet support for nationalist movements in the decolonizing world and increasing divisiveness over responsibility for the ills of colonization.

In a world of East vs. West and a Third World including Egypt as representative of Arab nationalism, Ben-Gurion continued to focus on building a state that gathered in Jews, strengthened its military capacity, and sought US support in the international arena. Confronted with those who linked Zionism to colonialism, however, there was a growing need to ensure a base for the legitimacy of the state that would gain popular adherence as well as justify US support. During a time when there continued to be American concern for the unresolved Palestinian refugee crisis, when more than one American president was critical of Israeli actions, and when American Jews were generally focused on domestic arenas, Israel actively sought to justify its own policies and actions in a way that would gain adherents beyond its borders. In this effort, coupled with the parallel appeals by other states and movements for international approval of the FLN as well as other nationalist movements, Israel competed with a range of states seeking the patronage necessary in a bipolar world with its own constructions of legitimacy.

Into this arena Israel introduced a powerful claim and historical narrative that integrated a particular Jewish history and experience that linked the story of Israeli success to an unrivaled victimization. It was, in addition, a narrative that could seamlessly unite the American and Israeli Jewish communities. The story of Israel's capture of Adolf Eichmann in 1960 and his trial thereafter served both to assert Israel's voice as that of the Jewish people and to insert the Holocaust into public understanding of the state as necessary to prevent the historical vulnerability that had allowed Jews to be annihilated. At a widely publicized trial Eichmann became the visible face in a search for justice that had resonance throughout a world still attuned to World War II. As witnesses testified against him, the trial presented a particular historical view of European Jewish life and experience; this view spoke precisely to the desired audience of Jews who had escaped or survived, who saw Europe as at best the site of failed emancipation and assimilation, or at worst, as the eternal home of anti-Semitic views that prevented the liberation experienced differently in either the US or Israel.

Chapter 3

Shifting Perspectives

European and American Jewish Constructions, 1948–1962

The Eichmann trial and Hannah Arendt's report on it have remained a topic of debate and scholarly interest to this day.[1] The ways in which the Holocaust came to be entwined with both American Jewish identity and debates about Israel have also been subject to continuing discussion.[2] Both developments signaled historical shifts in the relationships between Israel, Europe, and the US. Europe was the historical birthplace of Zionism and remained a source of significant support for the state during the fifties, while the American Jewish community was diverse and Zionism was a primary concern for only a minority once the state had been created. By the time of the Eichmann trial, however, several developments were leading toward a new identification of American Jews with Israel.

Along with the Israeli government focus on the US as the source of critical financial, military, and political resources, the American Jewish community was gaining greater institutional unification and a politically more active leadership. Memories of prewar European Jewish life had vanished with much of its population and many of those who survived felt reluctant to speak of it. In this situation—an Israeli Jewish population made up of multiple communities and an American Jewish world seeking its place—the Eichmann trial played a role that could not be fully anticipated, and the Arendt report signaled a new moment of separation from the complexities of prewar European Jewish life.

These shifts occurred in the course of both American and Israeli policymaking, but their meaning was constructed in the context of intellectual debates as well as narratives that offered particular validity to some actions while marginalizing others. Dynamic as a process and visible only in retrospect, this emergence of new grounds for interpreting history as well as experience can be viewed through the lenses of particular writers and thinkers.

The contrast between European understandings and American constructions of Israel might be represented by the novels of Arthur Koestler and Leon Uris. The political and personal efforts to find meanings in a world shifting from the Europe of the forties to the new polarities of the fifties and sixties can be seen in the writings of Hannah Arendt, continuing her own quests for understanding, and Albert Camus, attempting in a related time to grapple with the emerging violence of an Algerian revolution that also tore his world apart. Algerian Jews, like other North Africans, were caught in a world whose divisions demanded sudden shifts of identity and loss—as articulated by Albert Memmi among others.

While Nahum Goldmann worked to unite American Jews and to support the ongoing diaspora, Rabbi Joachim Prinz[3] brought his German experience into a new world that he saw through a lens different than that of American Jews striving for integration. Goldmann and Prinz, in very different ways, sought to bridge the European–American Jewish divide, each in his own way.

In 1948 I. F. Stone published a book titled *This Is Israel*.[4] The text consisted of Stone's descriptive narrative of the war in Palestine and the birth of Israel. Photos taken by Robert Capa, Jerry Cooke, and Tim Gidal accompanied the text. The book jacket helps us place this book in its context as it offers descriptions of the framework within which it was produced. Stone, a leftist American journalist, had experience in Palestine and was present during the war in 1948. Robert Capa, born in Budapest, was a noted war photographer with direct experience of European dictatorships as well as the Spanish Civil War. Jerry Cooke was schooled in Italy and Germany. Tim Gidal, born in Germany, had photographed throughout Europe, the Middle East, and Asia during World War II. Both Cooke and Gidal were from families that originated in Russia and were deeply affected by the rise of Nazism and fascism in Europe. All four experienced 1948 in the context of a Zionist movement allowing the emergence of an independent Jewish state after the horrors of Europe that they had witnessed. Their eyes were thus on the Jewish community as it fought for survival and what they saw was the promise of a homeland for the homeless. The preface by Bartley Crum expressed a view of the Jewish community as unified and notes the miracles it has performed. And he also asserts that "we Americans, secure in our own position, can, through this book, warm ourselves in the glory of a free people who made a two thousand year dream come true in their own free land."[5]

Crum's romantic view is that of a supportive American outsider. Stone, however, is writing out of intimate understanding of the politics and the military uncertainties that surrounded the ultimate emergence of Israel. He understands that the military victory was accompanied by the creation of a large Palestinian Arab refugee population. He notes the resonance of European Jewish history—the pogroms, the destroyed Jewish villages, the displaced people who survived. He also recognizes the ways in which the Yishuv developed the institutions that ultimately allowed it to win.

The Israel that Stone experienced and wrote about consisted of what he and others saw as pioneers willing to take on the difficulties of creating a new society in which Jews could live free of the limitations and the fear that Europeans had imposed on them. It was also to be a refuge for the survivors of World War II, who needed to feel safe. A war clearly seen as self-defense against multiple armies and a population that had no place else to go won the sympathy not only of I. F. Stone but of many on the left and of Americans who, like Crum, could easily identify with it. But central to this early support was a particular understanding of Zionism and of those who had created the Yishuv—seen now as the evidence that, had there been a Jewish National Home in 1933, there would have been a place for the Jews who perished.[6]

There is, however, an important epilogue to the book, which makes clear the moment of its creation. Here Stone recognizes that, having won the war, Israel had yet to win the peace. Its future, as he saw it, "depended on friendship and commerce with its Arab neighbors, and its wisest looked toward a Middle Eastern Federation."[7] As a radical and as a Jew, Stone viewed Israel in its origins as a progressive society with great promise, as a small state that would need to make peace in its surroundings in order to live up to its promise. He, like many other sympathizers, saw Israel through the lens of Western European and American eyes, failing to grasp the challenges Israel would pose to its surroundings nor the impact of imperial withdrawals from a region deeply affected by such penetration.

By 1967, a mere nineteen years later, Stone used a wider lens when he reviewed a collection of articles published by Jean-Paul Sartre in *Les Temps Modernes*. Here Stone makes reference to the impact on Sartre of both World War II and the Algerian struggle:

> The bulk of the Jews and the Israelis draw from the Hitler period the conviction that, in this world, when threatened one must be prepared to kill or be killed. The Arabs draw from the Algerian conflict the conviction that, even in dealing with so rational and civilized a people as the French, liberation was made possible only by resorting to the gun and the knife. Both Israelis and Arabs in other words feel that only force can assure justice. In this they agree, and this sets them on a collision course. For the Jews believe justice requires the recognition of Israel as a fact; for the Arabs to recognize the fact is to acquiesce in the wrong done them by the conquest of Palestine.[8]

Thus, the symposium that Stone reviewed reflects the status quo—separate articles in separate sections testifying to the Arab fear that such communication would signal a dangerous recognition of Israel.

The delineation of two sections mimics the contemporary perception of conflict as between two nationalist movements—Arab and Jewish. Yet Stone also points to the repression of alternative views on the Arab side and regrets that *Les Temps Modernes*[9] did not "include a Jewish as distinct from Israeli point of view." He points out that in Israel Jewry finds itself defending a society in which a variety of practices (such as the lesser status of non-Jews than Jews) are precisely those which Jews elsewhere fight in their position as a minority. As a Jew bound emotionally to Israel, Stone feels obligated to report the Arab side, "especially since the US press is so overwhelmingly pro-Zionist."[10] He formulates the conflict as a tragedy, as one of right vs. right but also, particularly, as a challenge to the victors—one that will determine who they become. In the nineteen years between 1948 and 1967, Israel had gone from self-determination and a necessary war of survival to a state that Stone felt had accomplished Zionism's dream; the "ingathering of the exiles" in an ironic form—gathering in Arab exiles along with its conquest of land in 1967. Stone saw the choices as ones for Israel to make. And, of equal importance, he was concerned above all with the effects on Israeli Jews of becoming an occupying power, very much in line with his commitment to universal values and questions of meaning.

The two decades between Stone's book and his review were critical in shaping the changing relationship of Israeli and American Jews at a number of levels. George Steiner, literary critic and author, made an effort to describe this relationship in *Life* magazine in 1957.[11] Writing shortly after the Suez/Sinai War and the resulting tension between the US and Israeli governments, Steiner sought an explanation for the support American Jews gave to Israel, despite the disinterest of many in Zionism as an ideology and despite the substantial differences within the community.

Steiner points out the complexity of the American Jewish community, and that despite this diversity of opinions and organizations, this is a community affected by the creation of Israel—"they disagree violently about what Israel means, or should mean, to an American Jew. They discuss the problem of Zionism in radically different ways." He goes on to describe the continuing presence of polarities within the community. The American Zionist Council and the anti-Zionist American Council for Judaism represented very different assessments and the latter was a much smaller organization. Yet the debates made clear that responses to Israel's existence were anything but uniform. More mainstream was the American Jewish Committee, which continued its focus on equality for Jewish minorities. While in contact with Israel, its leadership did not see itself as bound to support Israeli policies.

Steiner then asks the following question: "Why is it that millions of American Jews support the general cause of Israel even though they may not feel themselves committed to the historical traditions and politics of Zionism? Upon what emotional urges are they acting?" Seeking to avoid generalizations, Steiner nevertheless looks for an answer that accounts for this emotional response. As a European by birth and early childhood, Steiner comes to this question in some ways as an outsider. Nevertheless, he pinpoints the ways in which historical events combine with more recent social mobility to create a view of Israel that meets particular needs for many American Jews. That need, rooted in the impact of the Holocaust as well as the still incomplete integration of American Jews in American life, gave significant force to the success of Israel and its military. "Pride and a reawakened sense of historical tradition combine in complex ways to explain the pro-Israel sentiments of the overwhelming majority of American Jews." These sentiments did not, however, translate necessarily into unquestioning acceptance of Israeli policies or opposition to those of the American government that opposed them.

If Stone and Steiner exemplified the shifting public terrain on which American and Israeli Jews were meeting, Koestler and Uris narrated Israel for broader audiences in fictional as well as journalistic forms. As such, they offered various models for the potential identifications of individuals in these two communities. The striking differences between them, however, also marked the ways in which Jewish life was being altered by the gradual fading of the European Jewish context.

Arthur Koestler, journalist and European intellectual, gained significant public recognition as the author of *Darkness at Noon*, published in 1940.[12] By then Koestler had weathered a series of experiences that joined the power of ideologies seeking to transform social and political life with active participation in the major European conflicts of the century. Living in Vienna, Berlin, and Paris, traveling to Palestine, the USSR, and Spain, Koestler lived both the intellectual and the activist engagements that characterized a Europe at war with itself. As a profoundly secular Jew, Koestler came to Zionism as did many others of his class and educational background—with the conflicted aspirations of an outsider seeking to have an impact on his world. Growing up with anti-Semitism as an environmental norm, with a clear Jewish identity that was largely devoid of meaningful religious observance, and educated in modern German culture, Koestler was drawn to Zionism and, in particular, Revisionist Zionism, as promising solutions to his personal dilemmas while also linking him to a world in which he could hope to belong.[13]

Like Jabotinsky, whom he admired and whose version of Zionism he adhered to, Koestler was drawn to the movement in response to European realities but also with a belief in aspects of European political ideologies and values. His quest was neither messianic nor traditional but rather driven by the hope for Jewish "normalization," belonging, and acceptance. In this context, it is also important to point out that "normalization" for Western European Jews or for Jewish intellectuals could as easily incorporate a devaluing of the "shtetl" or Eastern European Jews as it could the wish for a respected Jewish secular identity placed on an even plane with non-Jews. This position is evident in the fact that Koestler's initial contact with Zionism was connected to his belonging to a Jewish fraternity in Vienna—an evident example of seeking equality on European terms.

Koestler himself spent some years in Palestine during the twenties. Here, he had a short experience in a kibbutz, followed by a period of writing as well as editing in a variety of capacities. During these years his engagement with Zionism was intertwined with a number of significant relationships and his own development as a writer. Unlike those who were committed to building their lives in Palestine, however, Koestler remained an outsider despite his belief in the need for a Jewish National Home.

By 1930 Koestler had moved once again to Europe where he remained connected in a variety of ways to the Revisionist Zionists, but he built his own life as a journalist and explorer of a European world increasingly divided as well as dangerous. It was only in 1946 that Koestler published a novel largely based on his earlier experiences in Palestine, *Thieves in the Night*.[14] While clearly showing the context in which it was written and narrating the Jewish development in Palestine, the novel's primary character makes manifest the complexities of that development. Speaking in the self-reflective, critical, and ironic voice of an outsider as well as from a position of support for the project of a Jewish state, this character also displays the European culture from which he perceives Palestine. And, from that perspective, he gives voice to the fears as well as the hopes attached to the Zionist project. Thus, the generational differences between Jewish immigrants from Europe and their children:

> Their parents were the most cosmopolitan race of the earth—they are provincial and chauvinistic. Their parents were sensitive bundles of nerves with awkward bodies—*their* nerves are whipcords and their bodies those of a horde of Hebrew Tarzans roaming in the hills of Galilee. Their parents were intense, intent, over-strung, over-spiced—they are tasteless, spiceless, unleavened and tough. Their parents were notoriously polyglot—they have been brought up in one language which had been hibernating for twenty centuries before being brought artificially back to life.[15]

Koestler understood Zionism as a necessary political project, responding to the urgent needs of European Jews. Unlike I. F. Stone, he did not see its value as tied to its social transformation of the land or of its progressive institutions. Nor did he see it as based on a religious claim and justification. It was in many ways a reparative project—one that allowed Jews to seek control over their own lives and to free themselves for the successes and also the failures of what could be seen as a "normal" national life. Despite the support Koestler expressed, however, his home remained in England and his culture remained that of a multilingual European environment.

In 1949, Koestler published a sequel to his novel, this time a non-fictional account titled *Promise and Fulfilment: Palestine, 1917–1949*.[16] This was Koestler's effort to understand and describe Israel's rebirth as a nation as "a freak phenomenon of history." True to his own intellectual culture, he characterized the narrative as "not about the Jewish race and the country of Israel as such," but rather as a use of that country and its people as "a specimen of humanity to be examined under the social microscope."[17] In this way, Koestler sought to bridge the particular with the universal—to acknowledge the subjective nature of his history while linking it to the search for broader meaning.

Koestler's analysis was decidedly not of a miracle nor did it exclude the role of the British and the claims of Palestinian Arabs. His summary of the Balfour Declaration in which "one nation solemnly promised to a second nation the country of a third" was a succinct recognition of the interests inherent in that document. As he wrote the book, Koestler also anticipated a future in which "few will take an interest in the struggles and shocks to which it [Israel] was exposed in the prenatal stage. Yet nations, like individuals, retain characteristic traces of these experiences. Whatever shape the culture of the new State of Israel may take, its pattern and values will reflect the formative influences both of the early pioneer days . . . and of the tragic suspense and birth labor of the decade starting in 1939."[18]

Reporting on his conversation with Prime Minister David Ben-Gurion, Koestler remarks on the "cultural claustrophilia" that he believes is the common denominator of the Israeli population.[19] In context, Koestler was objecting to an emphasis on Hebrew and Jewish tradition that seemed to distance itself from modern Western culture and democracy. Already in 1949 he felt that the state of Israel could be defined as "an anachronistic ideal realized by ultra-modern means,"[20] a view much later echoed by Tony Judt, another thinker steeped in European history.

In the last section of the book, Koestler examines some of the paradoxes he sees in the emergence of the new state. Among them is the power of clericalism and the Orthodox, who represent only a small minority. For Koestler this clericalism was one of the most serious problems needing resolution. Viewing Israel as a project intended to break away from Orthodoxy, he nevertheless understands that political structures would be likely to put matters of personal status in the hands of religious authorities. Like others of this era, however, he expected that this would be changed over time and could hardly anticipate actual developments that strengthened religious control. Similarly, Koestler's critical analysis of Sabra culture (the culture of Jews born in Israel or the Yishuv) is rooted in what he saw as provincialism, but he expected it to change with time.

In the epilogue, Koestler openly recognizes that the existence of Israel presents a new challenge for diaspora Jews. In his view, they now have the choice of staying outside or migrating and becoming citizens of the Hebrew nation. As far as he was concerned, the Orthodox would be a vanishing minority, and Israel had now fulfilled the mission of Zionism; for those like himself, Koestler did not see any outcome other than to "wish it [Israel] good luck and go their own way, . . . with the nation whose life and culture they share, without reservations or split loyalties."[21]

Koestler's works on Palestine and Israel have largely been forgotten. One could argue that their significance lies precisely in their reflection of a particular time through the eyes of a European Jew who embodied the peculiar mix of cosmopolitan European culture and Jewish identity shaped within the historical moment of imperial domination.

Leon Uris, in contrast, was clearly the product of an American rise to global power, and his novel about the founding of Israel, *Exodus*, has continued to gain attention. *Exodus*, the book (published in 1958) and then the film (in 1960) captured the transformation of Zionism from the lens of a Koestler to the ambition of an American Jew.[22] A recent biography by Ira Nadel documents the consciousness with which Uris sought to alter postwar American views of Jews.[23] Quoting Uris, the author makes clear his distress with "introspective Jewish writing" and the explicit motive for writing *Exodus*: "I was just sick of apologizing—or feeling that it was necessary to apologize. . . . We Jews are not what we have been portrayed to be. In truth, we have been fighters."[24] Thus, he explains, Uris's goal was to remake the image of the Jew and Judaism.

The reviews of *Exodus* were mixed, and critics, including Israelis, were distressed by its rendering of their history (Uri Avnery of *HaOlam HaZeh* in particular), but the book was a longtime bestseller that reflected an ongoing transition in American Jewish life and community.[25] Nadel describes this as follows: "Uris pairs the Jewish catastrophe of the Holocaust with the Jewish triumph of Israel. They became the two pillars of Jewish American identity: 'out of the ashes of Auschwitz, the birth of Israel.' This became part of the mythic American consciousness *Exodus* promotes. New Israel replaced old Europe, which the American Jew welcomed."[26]

Whereas Koestler, like others involved with Zionism and Palestine before 1948, understood the politics as well as long-standing commitments that led to the emergence of Israel, Uris offered Israel as a miracle that could reverse the horrors of the Holocaust and show the world Jewish heroes. The Zionism of Herzl—based on a reading of history and efforts to take advantage of it—now became not an active movement of creation but rather a movement of self-defense, inherently moral and offering a form of redemption. Uris, himself not a historian, was writing a narrative whose storyline was particularly effective in appealing to Americans whose own military victories were viewed as the victory of good over evil.

In the fifties, when American Jews were still absorbing the implications of World War II, Uris offered them a Jewish history that helped assuage any feelings of responsibility for the fate of Jews in Europe. Had those Jews followed the Zionist path, in Uris's story, they might have been saved. In addition, his support for the terror and violence that accompanied the Zionist struggle served to legitimize it as a movement for national liberation as well as revenge.[27] Both themes fit well into the specific challenges of the postwar world for American Jews.

For some in Israel, too, *Exodus* met a contemporary need. David Ben-Gurion, for example, recognized its value as a "piece of propaganda, the greatest thing written about Israel."[28] Teddy Kollek, chief of staff for Ben-Gurion, had met Uris in 1956 and was later to suggest that Uris would be best equipped to write a book on the Eichmann trial.[29]

Intentionally and unwittingly, leaders in Israel and in the American Jewish community were constructing a narrative to connect their histories while marginalizing the daily lives and struggles of the European Jews who had created and populated the Zionist movement before their large-scale disappearance. Israeli and American Jews had survived largely by leaving Europe over decades, for a multitude of reasons. Now they found themselves having to understand their own survival as well as cope with the losses not only of people but of the future that those people represented.

In postwar Palestine, then Israel, the Holocaust had eliminated most of the population Zionism expected to create its future. Instead, the displaced people in postwar Europe became an altogether different political factor, helping to justify the need for a Jewish state as refuge, but also compensation. The burden for the preexisting community was a heavy one, but timing precluded opportunities for public mourning or understanding. The rapidity with which the Jewish population in Palestine shifted to a war in which they had reason to fear further annihilation made it easy to obscure the profound transformation in their fate. Yet gaining statehood and recognition under these circumstances only complicated the process of redefining relationships both within and without. Responding in ways that gave their own choices moral meaning and solace, while delaying the mourning that threatened just below the surface, Israeli Jews shifted attention to immediate demands, with few able to recognize that their own gains in security were accompanied by the radical losses of Palestinian Arabs. Nevertheless, those who had lived in Palestine knew a history that the new immigrants, who doubled Israel's population in four years, did not. In this context, Israeli leaders had to construct, on the one hand, a national history to be taught and, on the other, a narrative that would serve to establish the legitimacy of a state still very much in question throughout the region in which it existed.

Parallel to Israel but building on a very different set of experiences, American Jews had reason to reconsider their relationships to Jewish community as well as to postwar American realities. Greater opportunities for integration as well as acceptance in an expanding US coincided with renewed awareness of difference from the European world (where most had their roots) in which ethnic/minority self-definition had largely been assumed. The devastation of the war and the Holocaust only confirmed a process that saw that world as necessarily coming to an end, but without having anticipated the traumatic manner in which this occurred.

The emergence of Israel thus was part of a world in which American Jews were developing their communal identity in a variety of ways, via multiple institutional paths. The path that Uris offered—for himself and his readers—was one story to bridge differences and link Israeli Jews, American Jews and, of equal importance, the US. *Exodus* offered American Jews an identification with the power of Israeli Jews as a vehicle for transforming their own position.[30]

Exodus, the novel and then the film even more, had paradoxical effects. Creating a dramatic as well as romantic historical narrative, Uris sought to solve his own conflicts—the wish to be a strong, proud Jew who was also an American patriot with no intention of migrating to the new state. Presenting an idealized Zionism and Israel, Uris's work was welcomed by those who believed such an image was in Israel's best interest. For others, it was a dangerous distortion of Israel's reality. Uris's picture was that of an Americanized Israel—replete with the simplified images of a morally pure hero and his non-Jewish American lover rescuing victims of the war, battling for survival as well as justice, creating a state that mirrored American ideals. At the time, it was welcomed by those seeking the comfort of a Jewish identity without conflict. In the longer term, it was a significant piece in the development of a pseudo understanding.

While journalists familiarized Americans with images and descriptions of the Jewish state as seen from the US, and novelists offered stories with different emotional valences, others struggled with the implications of this history and its meanings. Intellectuals of various perspectives took an interest in interpreting a postwar world rapidly evolving into the bipolarities of the Cold War. Understanding developments such as those in Palestine and Algeria, where the bipolar view necessarily excluded more complex realities, could easily be viewed as betrayal from one point of view or another. For those who identified deeply with particular European experiences or thought and considered how the violence and cruelties of twentieth-century European history were intertwined with culture and self-perception, or both, these efforts required a capacity to risk the implications of answers for themselves as well as their altered surroundings.

Among the most well-known thinkers who wrestled with such questions, and were unwilling to answer them either with ideological stances or tribal loyalties, were Albert Camus and Hannah Arendt. Both paid prices, although different ones. And both have received more appreciative attention in recent times as their stances can be disentangled from the conflicts that they lived through, while those conflicts have also received more nuanced recognition that moves beyond the bipolarity that had marginalized those who did not fit its stringent demands.

Entangled with Cold War ideologies were beliefs in the possibilities of new beginnings, political transformations, and ruptures with the past. Israel and then Algeria each represented experiments in the excitement of new creations linked to centuries-old traditions that were to be harnessed in the service of modern political projects born in violent conflicts. In each case there was a past contaminated by shame, humiliation, and powerlessness that required compensation and erasure. It was precisely this need that Uris responded to for American Jews and that Fanon saw in the Algerian struggle.

This formulation and its attendant ideals did not, however, meet the needs of others, whose drive was not toward rupture but rather toward recovery and meaning. For both Arendt and Camus, historical conflicts were experienced on the most intimate personal levels as fragmentation as well as loss. Both experienced displacements not of their own making; the displacements were accompanied by the eruption of violence and brutality, which demanded recognition of their own attachments precisely to the homes that were so rapidly transformed. While the conflicts that Camus and Arendt lived through were widely analyzed by a variety of intellectuals as well as political activists, Camus and Arendt were distinctive because they could never speak from outside or through ideological commitments. Both struggled in very different ways with finding some personal resolutions.

Both also wrote prophetically but inevitably were ignored or denounced for their failure to understand the presumed inevitability of history.

Camus

Albert Camus, born in Algeria in 1913, to a poor and struggling family, came to be recognized as a writer articulating existentialist views, a journalist linked to the French resistance of World War II, and as a winner of the Nobel Prize for literature in 1957.[31] And yet his efforts to speak from a position of personal hybridity and pain also led to his marginalization, as well as rejection by intellectuals, most notably by Jean-Paul Sartre, who had welcomed him in an earlier era. Camus represented within himself the conflicting identifications and loyalties that precluded neat resolution or choices structured on bipolar lines as good or evil. It is only in recent years, as Algeria developed out of the excitement of independence into a long-term process of dealing with internal conflicts (as well as the ongoing relationship with France) that there has been some renewed recognition of Camus as an Algerian who wrote out of attachment and knowledge unavailable to French leftists who supported the FLN without personally experiencing the price that its victory would entail. Arguably, there was an inevitable price to be paid for a long, deeply destructive period of colonialist settlement and exploitation; Camus understood who would pay the price and that the victims would not be defined by comfortable labels of race, national origin, or culture. He was, thus, unable to take pleasure in the violent, brutal struggle nor to see it with the optimism of a Fanon who expected that violence could lead to the release of new social forms.[32] Although Camus did not live to see the outcome of the war in Algeria, his silence and silencing during his last years expressed the recognition of an atmosphere in which there was no room for the coexistence he had sought, nor space to mourn the Algeria he remembered as home. While his lens was trained on France and Algeria, other developments were remaking the context in which this wrenching fight to separate two components of his and others' attachments acquired meaning. In that process, bipolarity diminished complexity and action took precedence over thought.

The war in Algeria signified, among other things, the elimination of a French imperial project and the growing impact of US engagement in projects of global security. With hindsight it is clear that US policies designed to protect postwar alliances often had paradoxical effects. Thus, actions in the name of anticolonialism were nevertheless accompanied by taking on formerly British and French imperial interests in the name of freedom while simultaneously securing US primacy in these alliances. In the Middle East, the Suez/Sinai War of 1956 stood out for its seemingly overt challenge to British and French imperialisms, as well as to Israeli collaboration with them. Nevertheless, by 1958 US policy brought the Cold War, with its attendant division, more fully into the Middle East. The effort to balance an anticolonialist stance with such intervention highlighted inherent contradictions.[33]

Among those contradictions were the effects of US policy on both the Israeli-Arab conflict and on the war in Algeria. As the US framed its policies as anticolonialist, supportive of self-determination and freedom, the FLN recognized the value of gaining international support in its struggle to oust the French, thus using new external actors to counter the one that they wanted to expel. In the process, the language of the struggle and its appeal inevitably played to a political forum being constituted along the lines of Cold War competition for client states.

The war in Algeria has been seen as a laboratory for multiple efforts to make and remake the postwar world as a system of nation-states ultimately represented in a United Nations offering a theoretical forum for international relations and law. Algeria could be seen along the lines of North-South differentiation with attendant racial and cultural distinctions in a conflict labeled revolutionary; it could be seen as asserting the rights of indigenous populations to draw their own borders and systems of governance; from some perspectives, Algeria participated in efforts to create a Third World, Arab nationalist unity, or both.

The war in Algeria also functioned as an important crucible of ideological developments that reflected new dynamics of power in which emerging states, and decolonizing territories, acquired moral as well as political roles. The FLN, among others, knew that its fate was linked to acquiring legitimacy on the global stage. That this need might have impeded resolution of internal conflicts was secondary to achieving independence and separation, creating an arena in which further political and cultural conflicts were to emerge.

The Arab-Israeli conflict of these years, 1948–1962, took shape in this context. While Zionists and their supporters viewed Israel as a new state with its roots in both Jewish history and progressive social movements, the Arab world viewed it as an extension of the imperial/colonial projects now actively being fought. Most of the Arab states gained independence without the struggles engulfing Algeria, but the conflict over Palestine remained an open wound and the unresolved fate of Palestinian refugees continued to serve as a focus for political mobilization. Entwined in the conflict from its beginnings were competing claims of legitimacy and historical narratives.[34]

Israeli policies of this era were inevitably shaped by the framework within which various choices were made. As a new state that was still constructing its own relationship to the nation with which it identified, Israel was the product of ideological and practical choices made in the years immediately prior to independence as well as in the decade thereafter. Zionism, as a contested movement, assumed its role as a state ideology linked to policies of ingathering and the Law of Return.

The Israeli governing elite still contained alternative views on foreign and defense policies, as well as differing assessments of practical possibilities. While Moshe Sharett (Israel's prime minister, 1954–1955) believed that diplomacy held long-term promise for improving regional relationships and Golda Meir took initiatives to create ties with newly independent African states, Ben-Gurion gave primacy to military strength, demographic growth, and reliable support from European and American sources. In the 1950s Ben-Gurion's dominance led to strong ties with France precisely when it was embroiled in the Algerian War, which could only further solidify the view, for Palestinians and many others in the Arab world, of Israel as an arm of imperialism in the Middle East. Moreover, the decision to develop nuclear weapons capabilities as well as the shift to reliance on the US by the 1960s further narrowed Israeli policy options. Now clearly identified with one side of the Cold War and alienated from the Third World, Israel tied its security to military strength and increasing connection to the US as well as to American Jews.

Arendt

Hannah Arendt's trajectory in her relationship to Zionism and the state of Israel can be understood precisely against the backdrop of this shift from a European context to an American one. Arendt, as a refugee displaced and deprived of her homeland by the Nazi takeovers in Europe, experienced her Jewish identity as a given. Her responses as a young woman were shaped by attraction to Zionists who offered political paths to action as well as refuge. As someone who shared the fate of the larger refugee community, first in Paris and then in New York, Arendt found a voice both in German and eventually in English. Her writings in the early years reflected efforts to understand and articulate the nature of the European Jewish Question and Jewish history as well as anti-Semitism. Emerging clearly from the imposed struggle with what it meant to be Jewish in a rapidly changing political world, Arendt defined herself clearly with a critical stance that could not identify with Jewish nationalism, but valued nevertheless the activism of Zionists and others who sought to find meaningful responses to the exclusions of Jews who shared European cultures.[35]

While still in Europe, Arendt's work and writing was colored by the immediacy of her own uncertain status. Once she arrived in the US in 1941, however, Arendt's contributions reflect the impact of some distance as well as longer-term reflections. Her analysis of the war and the role of Jews was intertwined with the effort to understand the deformations of political life as well as possibilities for ethical action. Inevitably, these concerns led Arendt to commentary on, and reconsideration, of the Zionist project. In Europe before the war, she had participated in the efforts of Youth Aliyah and maintained relationships with leaders such as Kurt Blumenfeld as well as scholarly friends, including Gershom Scholem. Now, however, in the postwar period, Arendt became more critical of a movement that was being led to fight for Jewish statehood despite the considerable resistance of Palestinian Arabs among others. It was now Judah Magnes, president of the Hebrew University, and others who articulated positions that Arendt ultimately found compelling and supported.[36]

Both Camus and Arendt resisted ideologies that relied on national separation or were based on the need for force to overcome political conflicts and inequities. While recognizing the validity of movements to correct for historical powerlessness, humiliation, and oppression, both paid close attention to the potential price to be paid when power was gained at the expense of political interaction.

Until 1948 Arendt wrote of Zionism and Jewish history using the pronoun "we." Writing for a broad public, particularly in the *Aufbau* (a New York City newspaper for German-speaking Jewish immigrants) but later also in English language journals, her articles reflected an immediate engagement with developments and a very personal concern that infused the political commentary. Throughout, her arguments in favor of a federated solution for Palestine were also in line with her hopes for European integration. Although firmly committed to the need for Jewish political participation as Jews, she was equally intent on the need to recognize Arab perspectives as well as power.[37]

Despite Israel's military victory in 1948, Arendt remained concerned that the failure to achieve resolution of the continuing conflicts that accompanied statehood would lead only to further militarization as well as isolation. In 1958, she participated in a panel that issued a report on the *Palestine Refugee Problem*, urging active steps toward repatriation and resettlement.[38] This, like other such efforts, gained little attention in an era of political movements that saw nationalism and nation-states as vehicles to correct historic injustices. It is, however, an indicator of Arendt's continuing concerns for a Jewish future and awareness that such a future would most likely be affected by living in an often hostile world that required negotiating relationships as well as recognizing interdependencies.

Goldmann

While Arendt's relationship to Jewish history and existence was shaped by intellectual as well as political concerns, she was never an active participant in Jewish community life or education. Particularly after 1948 and even more after 1967, Arendt integrated her understandings of the history she had lived into broader frameworks and interpretations. This was also the era in which her life in the US provided a changing perspective on current developments.

In contrast, Nahum Goldmann devoted his life to Jewish community with a view to bringing that larger world into its functioning. Like Arendt, Goldmann's connections to Germany and German cultural life were formative, but his version of cosmopolitanism was based in efforts to organize as well as educate among both Zionists and diaspora Jews. A recent book about Goldmann titled *Statesman Without a State* and his own book, *The Jewish Paradox*, both suggest the complexity of Goldmann's path, which was possible only at a specific historical moment in which he sought to ensure Jewish security that was ultimately linked to statehood, but also to maintain a vibrant diaspora with its own Jewish voice.[39] Goldmann's work, moreover, was significant in that he bridged Jewish experience in Europe, Palestine, and the US throughout the critical era in which the politics of Zionism and Jewish communal life shifted from the Europe/Middle East axis to Israel/Palestine/US.

Goldmann came to Zionism with a strong interest in Jewish culture as well as politics. Despite his experiences in Palestine, then Israel, and his intimate knowledge of the Zionist movement, his personal makeup as well as choices resulted in his remaining the consummate insider/outsider always on the edge. Fulfilling a number of official positions in the World Zionist Organization and in the World Jewish Congress, Goldmann never fully committed to a territorial base or constituency. His life throughout was in the company of Zionist and Jewish leaders but always with an eye to the bigger European or American context.

In contrast to Ben-Gurion or Golda Meir, among others, Goldmann never focused on party politics but was deeply engaged with the institutionalization of Jewish life internationally. While initially very much an insider in Zionist and American Jewish organizational life, he eventually found himself marginalized between the two, returning in some ways to his original European position.

In the postwar period Goldmann played a significant role in support of partition as the way to achieve Jewish statehood and end British control of Palestine. In this endeavor, he and Ben-Gurion worked together. However, once Israeli independence had been assured, Goldmann and Ben-Gurion were on different sides of a complex new set of relationships. While Ben-Gurion, as prime minister of the new state, drew clear boundaries between its population and those outside, Goldmann saw Israeli need for external Jewish support as linked to a role for world Jewry in expressing views on Israeli policies. In this position, he was clearly speaking for himself as someone who remained outside the state yet was deeply involved with its fate.

His critique of Israeli policy was rooted in long-standing concerns about the Yishuv's relationship to its Arab surroundings and its international position, particularly with American Jews.[40] Because he did play significant roles in support of Israel, including most prominently his management of the negotiations with Germany over reparations, Goldmann's critique of some Israeli policies remained coupled with commitments to continuing activism in the world of Jewish organizational life and close ties to the Israeli leadership.

In addition to his work in the World Zionist Organization and the World Jewish Congress, Goldmann saw himself as playing an important role in the world of American Jewish organizational life. He describes himself as "resolved to put an end to the chaos in American Jewish life, at least as far as Israeli matters were concerned, because it was continually causing harmful complications. Despite my own dissenting position, I naturally thought it my duty to secure the support of American Jewry for Israeli policy."[41] In order to reconcile the apparent contradiction, Goldmann took the position that standing by Israel in its precarious situation was necessary but that this should be accompanied by the possibility of influencing its external politics. In the aftermath of the Suez/Sinai War of 1956, Goldmann once again acted to "keep the American organizations in line"[42] while simultaneously, in private, expressing his critique of Israeli actions.

Longer term, Goldmann was instrumental in the efforts to reorganize American Jewish life so that it could speak with a unified voice with regard to Israel and foreign policy. Goldmann described his goal as follows: "Since it was impossible to organize the vast majority of Jewry inside the WZO [World Zionist Organization], I had to try another way. The major difficulty was the chaotic nature of American Jewry. . . . There was no institution that could speak in the name of American Jewry as a whole, either to Israel or to the American government."[43]

Taking it upon himself to remedy the situation, Goldmann worked to convene "a conference of the presidents of all major Jewish organizations with the object of creating at least a loosely structured forum for the discussion of all American-Israeli questions."[44] In time, this organization (Conference of Presidents) became an important institutional presence in the effort to signify American Jewish unity. Although the American Jewish Committee refused to join from the first, it eventually participated in this expanding framework for American Jewish organizational leaders.

Despite his multiple positions in Zionist and Jewish organizations, Goldmann retained an individualized, critical perspective that worked against his ever achieving consistent influence or power. In many ways his ability to work within multiple Jewish communities and political arenas reflected the historical moment in which European Jewish intellectuals and leaders found themselves. Educated in worlds and cultures they could no longer live in, they nevertheless carried with them particular historical awareness as well as expectations. Goldmann, who was dubious about the capacity of American Jews to replace what he considered the richness of European Jewish culture, nevertheless sought to mold American Jewish culture along lines that borrowed from European Jewish representation. Although he lived in the US for years, his framework was one of seeking unity rather than accepting the plurality of American Jews. Unlike those like Rabbi Joachim Prinz, whose experiences in Nazi Germany translated into sensitivity to specifically American racial divides and immersion in the daily lives of an American Jewish congregation, Goldmann remained active largely on the planes of diplomacy and leadership. Not entirely at home either in Israel or in the US, he finally returned to living in Europe.

Rabbi Joachim Prinz had played a prominent and courageous role in Berlin during the early years of the Nazi regime. A Zionist from an early age, he did not choose to emigrate despite his pessimism about ongoing Jewish life in Germany but rather to remain in an increasingly dangerous position rooted in German Jewish historical presence. It was only in 1937, when he was warned to leave or face arrest, that Prinz made the decision to leave for the US. Fortunate in his connection with Rabbi Stephen Wise among others, Prinz was able to escape with his family.

Arrival in the US did not provide easy answers to the daily needs of his family nor did Prinz find adjustment to the American Jewish community without its problems. On the contrary, he found American Jews a great disappointment, largely lacking in the Jewish knowledge and worldliness of the European Jewish life he had left behind. Not only did he find the rabbinical world disappointing, but he also found that American Zionism differed in significant ways from his understanding of the ideology as well as the movement to which he adhered.[45]

By 1948 Prinz had become far more familiar with the American Jewish environment from which he assessed the implications of Israel's coming into existence. His reaction, much closer to that of Ben-Gurion than to that of Goldmann, was to say "Zionism is dead. Long live Israel and the Jewish people."[46] His description of the responses he got was "I was attacked by almost everyone, and my friend Nahum Goldmann, who was at that time the president of the World Zionist Organization, did not speak to me for a whole year." Unlike Goldmann, Prinz drew a clear line between the sovereignty of Israel and the ongoing presence of a varied transnational Jewish people. Zionism, in his opinion, had succeeded and no longer had a role to play. Prinz saw that not only had Israel fulfilled Zionist dreams, but also that "the whole Zionist ideology, which presupposes a deterioration of Jewish position all over the Diaspora, is no longer valid."[47] While supporting Israel, Prinz believed that its existence raised new questions demanding new answers for Jews. In this context, he was aware of the need to see Israel as an ongoing project, one in which there was "much provincial chauvinism" creating wrong perspectives and false hopes.[48] In his analysis of the relationship between Israel and the American Jewish community, Prinz believed that American Jewish active interest in Israel needed to be based on a clear separation of Israeli politics from those of the US. In the event of conflict between Israeli interests and those of the US, he was clear on the need to support the country in which American Jews lived in a condition he recognized as historically distinctive. Thus, while Prinz saw the need for American Jews to educate their youth with understanding of Israel, he also felt that "many of the statements on American Jewry which emanate from Jerusalem reveal utter ignorance of the American Jewish community."[49] By 1962, both the interdependence and the gaps affecting the relationship between Israel and the American Jewish community were evident to him.

Frames of Reference and Shifting Identifications

In some ways, Israeli and American Jews were on parallel paths during the period from 1948 to 1961. This was a period in which the losses of historical European Jewish existence were accompanied by promises of normalization, integration, and compensation. Israeli leadership focused on state-building and creating a new nation, ambiguously defined. American Jews were moving into positions of greater material as well as emotional comfort as the barriers of anti-Semitism were diminishing and Jews identified with multiple ways of being American. In both communities, there was a reaching for influence, for recognition, for participation, for self-determination.

The relationships between these two communities were being forged at a variety of levels. The need for a Zionist movement now that it had attained its goal of Jewish statehood was subject to various challenges. While earlier anti-Zionism largely faded, it was not at all clear that there was a consensus as to how Zionism was to be defined. Should it be seen—as Ben-Gurion argued—as supplanted by the existence of the state with Zionists being those Jews who chose to live in its borders? Or, as Goldmann argued, should the Zionist movement continue not only as a source of support for the state but also as a contributor to its policies and decision-making? Was there a new relationship to be created between Israel and the diaspora, based on the reality of coexistence, or was one to be subordinated to the other in defining Jewish political identity and values?

Only limited aspects of these questions were addressed and those largely by figures with organizational positions. Most American Jews were preoccupied with US developments and their own communities. While generally supportive of Israel's existence, few knew much about it.

Responding to American political challenges, there were those in the Jewish community who became activists in various civil rights and progressive movements while others were more wary of jeopardizing their newfound acceptance. It was the era of Jews "becoming white" and having to choose the degree to which they identified with a new status of belonging, with its broader implications.

Largely invisible to most of both Israeli and American Jewish publics were the contradictions inherent in their relationship. Israeli Jews represented the outcome of broad social, political, and cultural developments in European Jewish history. Despite the fact that the Israeli population doubled in the early years of statehood and that much of the immigration was a consequence of transformations in the Middle East, the institutional structure of Israel was clearly built by European Jews. The dominant group, moreover, had arisen out of Zionist migration to Palestine where Labor Zionist movements were primary. Their vision of the Jewish state was infused with a secular, Hebrew culture as well as a strong ethic of independent defense in a hostile world. While accommodations were made with religious leaderships, these were seen as temporary requirements while the state worked to create a national system of education and defense. This was a Zionism based on pride in national success and intentional separation from the diaspora Jewish world. American Jews, whose support was sought, were viewed as incomplete both in their Jewish identity and in their failure to immigrate.

As Israeli Jews focused on their own priorities and the integration of their Jewish refugees, the Palestinian Arabs who remained within Israeli borders were largely invisible and contained by military control. Viewed as a fifth column and often displaced from their homes, the Israeli Arab population was reeling from its own trauma. Immediate conditions prevented almost all from comprehending the long-term consequences of the unresolved war of 1947–1948.

Viewed from the US, however, the situation could be more readily understood. The American Jewish Committee, for example, had historically defined its role as one of protecting minorities. American Jews had understood themselves and European Jews as minorities and thus saw their own interest in legal protection as well as adherence to provisions for equality of status. The American Jews who identified as liberals and supported civil rights in the fifties assumed that Jewish history and belief were part of their commitments.

There were, however, significant missing pieces in the ways that Israeli and American Jews understood one another. Among them was the substantial difference in the impact of 1948 and its consequences. Israeli Jews experienced that war as one for survival and they were not unaware of the effects in transforming the demography of Palestine and giving rise to an overwhelmingly Jewish state that barred entry to Palestinian Arab refugees. American Jews, like other Americans, were still experiencing the aftermath to World War II and had little knowledge of the Arab, let alone Palestinian, worlds. As a result, only a select few might have grasped the ways in which identification with Israel had the effect of eliding the profound tension between a commitment to domestic values of equal rights, on the one hand, and support for Zionism now as a full-fledged nationalist movement with its own state, on the other. For many more, Uris's narrative of a muscular Jewish success story took on the force of historical truth without inconvenient details, all the more so in the context of the emerging American Jewish willingness to assert themselves as part of a global power.

Part II

Europe, America, and Israel

Chapter 4

Transnational Challenges, 1948–1966

In the immediate postwar world, two potentially contradictory developments characterized the restructuring of Europe and, with it, the alterations in control over territories formerly governed from European capitals. In roughly the first fifteen postwar years, movements for independence and decolonization mobilized many populations fighting for national self-determination. Simultaneously, the postwar restructuring of international institutions, and particularly the creation of the UN, was founded on the promise of a vehicle for managing conflicts. As the UN took shape, it embodied both the reality of global power relationships and a growing arena for emerging new states. The UN was the body that gave international assent to the creation of new Jewish and Palestinian states in 1947. It also became a forum in which the FLN was among the first movements to mobilize international support for its struggle. In both cases, the rhetoric of moral legitimacy and national rights ultimately had to gain the support of the US as well as the USSR.

It was in the period of 1956 to 1966 that international standing decisively shifted from European imperial states to the rivalry between the US and USSR. With that shift came a tightening of ideological rivalry, a competitive arms race, and efforts to delegitimize opposing political, economic, and cultural systems. Measures to organize and control client states played a significant part in the global rivalry. The Cold War remained cold between the superpowers, but conflicts in a variety of arenas claimed significant victims in wars that were anything but cold.

As European forces withdrew from various regions, they were replaced by new state formations that often based their legitimacy on nationalist struggles, frequently with claims to revolutionary intentions. In the core territories of the Arab world, states emerged without major violence largely as a result of negotiated withdrawals by the French and the British.[1] In contrast, the Palestine War of 1948 and the Algerian struggle of 1954–1962 gave rise to immediate violence followed by enduring trauma.

Common to all, however, was the tension embodied in the reality that state formations remained incomplete, conflicted representatives of national/religious communities. Political boundaries were subject to challenge, and citizenship was not the equivalent of clear belonging. The promises of independence often gave way to the realities of dealing with the need for external supports that necessitated the suppression of ongoing, conflicting visions of the nation.

Israel/Palestine in Formation

Nationalist powers, in order to mobilize support, necessarily draw on beliefs in collective identity buttressed by claims to shared history, tradition, and authenticity. To Palestine before 1948 Zionism brought a very specific movement that integrated historical claims with current transformation. Based for many of its adherents on the failure of assimilation in Europe and the wish for normalization, it incorporated diverse Jewish experiences on a new foundation. Inevitably, the movement was seen by Palestinian Arabs from the first as a threat, one that took shape under British governance.

When Great Britain finally gave up its mandate and the UN voted for partition of Palestine in 1947, there was no outside power prepared to enable the transition to two states. The Zionist movement, led by David Ben-Gurion and well organized ahead of time, had significant advantages. Palestinian Arabs, in contrast, were already fragmented and weakened by earlier developments; the League of Arab States, which claimed to support them, was itself divided into multiple Arab states just emerging from rule by mandatory powers or, as in the case of Egypt, long-term occupation.[2]

The military victory that ensured Israel's emergence was welcomed by those who saw it in the framework of Jewish suffering during World War II and of Zionist labor to create a new Jewish presence in a historical homeland. The fact that both the US and the USSR provided rapid recognition only further legitimized the new state. Those most immediately involved, in the period after armistices were signed in 1949, expected that negotiations would lead to peace treaties establishing international boundaries, providing for the Palestinian Arab refugees who had fled their homes, and stabilizing regional relationships. That this did not occur was symptomatic of a Zionist project that remained in many ways open ended, with a leadership reluctant to compromise on either territory or refugees, and willing to live with their immediate gains. It was also symptomatic of the gap between Arab state ambitions and Palestinian Arab weaknesses.[3]

Until May 14, 1948, when David Ben-Gurion read aloud the Proclamation of Independence, it was not clear what, other than ongoing conflict, would follow British withdrawal from Palestine. Until shortly before this occasion, representatives of the US State Department worked on a truce that was linked to delay of statehood for both Palestinian Arabs and Jews. Within the Jewish leadership this led to discussion about delay as well. Nevertheless, Ben-Gurion's firm refusal to delay ultimately gained the needed support to move ahead. The Proclamation of Independence itself, also the outcome of earlier discussion, brought together the historical claim to a Jewish homeland in Palestine, the Holocaust of World War II that created survivors needing refuge, the need of Jews more broadly for a homeland, and the UN Partition Resolution that called for two states in Palestine. The Declaration of Independence did not, however, define the borders of the new state at a time of anticipated ongoing conflict.[4]

Central to the proclamation was a commitment to Jewish immigration and a call to the Jewish people all over the world for support in building the state. At the same time, the proclamation also included the commitment to a constituent assembly that would draw up a constitution for the new state by October 1, 1948. It articulated as well the commitment to "uphold the full social and political equality of all its citizens, without distinction of religion, race or sex." Although the proclamation referred to "liberty, justice and peace as conceived by the Prophets of Israel" and expressed "trust in the Rock of Israel," earlier discussions had led to this compromise between secular and religious parties. The proclamation combined historical justifications for Jewish statehood with commitments to democratic government and equal citizenship. While articulating the priority of Jewish immigration and development, it specifically called on Arabs living within the territory of the state to participate as equals and promised representation in state institutions.

While the proclamation was consonant with Zionism as it had evolved in Palestine and spoke to a universality of rights, it can best be understood as aspirational in its commitments. It was not long before it became clear that there would be no resolution to the underlying contradiction between establishing a Jewish state and implementing the promised social and political equality. In theory, it was up to a constituent assembly to formulate a constitution that could give governing form to these commitments, make choices among the many ways in which a Jewish state could be defined, and seek to resolve the tension between serving a territorial citizenry and acting in the name of a worldwide Jewish community. Instead, the first Knesset debated the question of a constitution from February to June 1950 and ultimately gave up the task. Writing a constitution required choices governing the relationship between Jewish religion and Jewish statehood that, for many reasons, proved to be too problematic. Writing a constitution also required determinations as to the rights of citizens without regard to race, religion, or gender in a state that was clearly premised on Jewish needs. There were members of the Knesset who understood that the failure to write a constitution was likely to have negative consequences for the development of the state, but material circumstances, political realities, and the preferences of the prime minister, Ben-Gurion, ultimately led to the "decision not to decide" the fundamental questions that a constitution would have required. As a result, Israel came to be governed by a series of fundamental laws.[5]

Two interrelated realities helped shape the ways in which Israeli leaders made the choices that became formative for the state and the narratives that came to be accepted as its history. Both were now identified with the meaning of Zionism as constitutive of the state. On one hand, the reality of the Holocaust now underlined the Zionist claim that Jews could not be safe as a minority in Europe. At the same time, the demographic transformation of Israel through large-scale migration of Jews from the Arab world after 1948 had the potential to raise questions about the impact of Zionism beyond Europe as well as the coherence of a diverse Jewish population. To the Israeli Jewish leadership, led by the Mapai Party, that valued collectivity as strength and identified with modern European definitions of progress, the goals of statehood were understood to require integration of new immigrants and control over the Palestinian Arabs who had remained in Israel. Neither group was viewed as having valuable contributions to make. The inability to decide on a constitution so as to retain maximum political flexibility was thus also accompanied by policies that linked Zionism as a project to the visions of what was now the elite stratum of a developing state.[6]

As soon as fighting ceased in 1949 it was clear that there was to be a Jewish state with only a relatively small, vulnerable Arab minority and a Transjordanian state that absorbed what was left of Palestine. Gaza remained under Egyptian control. Without peace treaties or mutual recognition between Israel and the Arab states, without resolution of the Palestinian Arab refugee community's position, the war left significant questions open to interpretation. As a result, all the populations affected by the war relied largely on those with authority to explain its meaning and consequences.

At the same time, these elites operated in a world governed by outside powers with their own agendas and controls. The need for financial as well as military supports was accompanied by pressure to appear identified with particular political values and ideological commitments. For Arab leaders a framework of disengagement from imperial powers fit the experiences of their populations. For Israeli leaders Zionism seemed to offer both a narrative of independence and a language of nationalism that was largely shared with Europeans. The result was that as Israeli leaders began to organize the state their connections to Europe played a significant and formative role. While the Jewish refugees helped consolidate the legitimacy of their project, German responsibility and French policies provided important opportunities. In the course of the 1950s, German reparations and French supports (military aid, collaboration in 1956, and enabling the development of nuclear power) contributed to the success of Ben-Gurion's project of building popular identification with the state. Central to that vision was the creation of a military that would mobilize the population, help it to integrate immigrants, and represent the material claim of Israel as both transformative for Jews and ensuring their security. Linked to those developments was the adoption of a historical perspective that saw Israel as a vulnerable island surrounded by enemies necessitating ongoing vigilance and an independent force for security along with external patrons for support.

This was a view not necessarily shared by all Israeli leaders, let alone by American Jewish activists or American politicians. While Israel's Declaration of Independence, with its commitment to a democratic and tolerant state, was quickly recognized by the US, the failure to achieve peace in 1949 reflected important differences between US officials and the Israeli government. Organized American Jewish groups varied in their views, with the AJC in particular supporting the Jewish state while simultaneously maintaining a critical perspective on some of its policies.[7]

The discussions between Jacob Blaustein of the AJC and David Ben-Gurion in these early years were part of a much larger question that accompanied the intense pressures of state-building. That question, as unresolved as those concerning borders and security, had to do with defining the Jewish nation for whom the state had been created, along with defining the relationship between Israeliness and Jewishness. Over the years there have been those who identified the two as closely overlapping as well as those committed to the distinction between them. Some have understood that Israel encompassed a changing population, Arab and Jewish, located within a defined state though one with undefined borders. Others have seen Israel as a Zionist project that existed to rescue, protect, and represent Jews wherever they lived, explicitly or implicitly based on the view that Jews remained vulnerable wherever they were a minority and that only in Israel could they live fully Jewish lives. Decisions made in state-building inevitably affected the process of defining the nation.[8]

Until 1956/57, diplomatic efforts to move beyond armistice agreements to peace treaties were largely stymied by the absence of participants who gave them priority. Palestinian Arabs were reeling from the outcome of the war, and the efforts of some to return to their home villages met with strong measures, which only reinforced Israeli perceptions of their danger. At the same time, Arab states still very much in their own transitions could not function as a unit beyond the commitment to undo the damages in the future while seeing the UN as responsible for the immediate refugee needs.[9] In Israel, Ben-Gurion was quite clear in his preference for the territorial gains of war as well as the ethnic makeup of postwar Israel. As a result, he did not see compromise on these issues as in the interest of the state.[10]

Just as the war itself had largely reflected the disinterest of outside powers in implementing partition, so in the aftermath efforts at resolution were soon to become secondary to a variety of other priorities. The US, France, and Great Britain agreed in 1950 that they would guarantee the territorial status quo, as well as limit the flow of arms to the region. By 1956, these commitments were irrelevant, and Ben-Gurion's return to office a year earlier had largely ensured that Israeli policy would be based on equating military superiority with security. Linked to this policy were relationships both with West Germany and with France, which were given priority over alternative readings of regional realities and possibilities. Ben-Gurion's dominance easily outweighed those in his party, such as Moshe Sharett, who opposed aggressive military initiatives, or Golda Meir, whose focus on domestic development and diplomacy reflected a somewhat different definition of Israeli strengths.[11]

The Suez/Sinai War of 1956 marked a decisive and in some ways ironic moment in which the Arab-Israeli conflict was redefined, Israel's relationships with Europe and the US were altered, and the path to creating new historical narratives emerged. Although the administration of President Dwight Eisenhower sought to gain anticolonial credibility by acting to end the British and French invasion of Egypt while insisting on Israeli withdrawal from Sinai and Gaza, it did not take long before the US announced policies that brought the Cold War more directly into the Middle East. Israeli military action made clear that the victory in 1948 was not a fluke, but rather than ensuring security it contributed to intensification of the arms race in the region, which was also an effect of Cold War rivalries.[12]

As the global rivalry intensified in the context of nationalist movements of decolonization, the leaderships of new states worked to consolidate their own positions, whether through the alliances of the Third World or through finding patronage to support their military and intelligence strengths. In the Middle East, the late fifties and early sixties saw the emergence of blocs labeled as revolutionary vs. conservative with Pan Arabism emerging to challenge state boundaries. Since the Israeli leadership had clearly allied itself with European states, the questions that now arose did so in a narrower context than the one that had existed before 1956. It was in this era of 1958–1967 that Israel and the Arab states, beyond their ongoing conflict, also were shaped by their disputes. The Palestinian Arabs who had paid the price of war were significantly less visible during this period. Reconciliation of separate Arab national identities within a dominant ideology of Pan Arab unity remained elusive.[13]

Competing definitions of collective identities among Arabs and Jews only heightened an ongoing paradox: Arab-Israeli conflict served to delimit differences that served state leaderships while simultaneously suppressing the clarification of state/nation relationships. Thus, Israelis held to a perspective of Arab nationalism that could subsume Palestinians and Arab nationalists into one entity that viewed Israel as the representation of an international Jewish people.[14]

For Israeli and American Jews the period from 1958 to 1966 remained one of fluidity as well as variable interpretations of community, identity, and commitments. Critical to these developments, however, were two threads: searches for security and institutional reorganization. While Israeli Jews lived in an atmosphere of permanent mobilization and collective development, American Jews were responding to more opportunities for integration with differing ways of engaging in the American political arena. At the same time, the Israeli government was challenged by internal conflict and transition in leadership, while in the US Jewish leaders were seeking greater centralization and unity as well as ongoing clarification of the Israel-US relationship.

Navigating US-Israel Relationships

In three key domains, developments during this time helped set the stage for the framework through which Israeli and American Jews would react to the crisis of 1967 and its aftermath. Over this period, as US administrations grew frustrated with their efforts to work with President Nasser and to limit the delivery of military aid to Israel, Prime Minister Ben-Gurion and Deputy Minister of Defense Shimon Peres in particular were invested in developing Israeli nuclear capacity with French support. By the time President John F. Kennedy was inaugurated, the construction of a nuclear reactor in Dimona gave rise to US questioning about whether Israel intended to build nuclear weapons. This did not, however, stop the sale of Hawk missiles to Israel in 1962. As the arms race in the Middle East was heightened by both regional and international competition, Ben-Gurion's emphasis on the priority of military independence could, however, easily coexist with his equally strong pursuit of US support. In the aftermath of the Cuban Missile Crisis followed by the US decision for military action in Vietnam, the potential for Israeli ties to the US based on military effectiveness began to emerge. At the same time, Israeli concerns about German scientists working in Egypt to develop missile technology heightened Israeli claims to vulnerability and American aid.[15]

American Jews like I. F. Stone, whose support for Israel was based on its socialist ideology, pioneering settlements, secular Jewish culture, and postwar rescue of Jewish refugees, remained aware of Israel's incomplete democracy. The AJC, for example maintained its efforts to protect minority rights, whether in the US or in Israel. Most, however, were not focused on Israel in an era when they were coming into their own in the US. In that context, the most salient political divisions arose first from more general fears of communism that threatened many of the intellectual left, whatever their views of the USSR; and, second, from the emergence of a civil rights movement, which some understood in the context of historical anti-Semitism and the moral need to fight discrimination, while others came to see the movement as a challenge to Jewish identity.[16]

The redefinition of Zionism continued, with consequences for Jewish leadership and communal identity, as Jews in Israel and the US slowly adapted to their dramatically different conditions away from Europe. Because the Israeli leadership looked to the US for needed support, and because American Jews now saw new possibilities for maintaining their ethnic distinction along with integration, their connections to one another developed to meet a changing world environment. Prestate Zionism as a political forum was now supplanted by statehood; its European context had been annihilated. Two Jewish populations that had, in very different ways, chosen to leave that world behind now had to deal both with the unanticipated losses and the search for bridges between them.

Two developments during the period from 1960 to 1963 that were ironically at odds with one another helped clarify these tasks: a revival of the discussion between the AJC leadership and Ben-Gurion about the limits to Israeli representation of Jews beyond their borders, and the Eichmann Trial, which placed Israel squarely in the position of speaking for Jews as a whole. Accompanying these developments were underlying processes that shifted the perspectives of American Jews, altering the balance between them and Israel. Jewish institutional life was consolidated and centralized along with the emergence of a Jewish historical narrative that gave the Holocaust meaning in a broader emphasis on dangers to Jewish survival, and there was a temporary obscuring of the complex realities of modern European Jewish life.

Who Speaks for Jews?

Despite temporary resolutions early in the 1950s, two conflicts in which Ben-Gurion's views were challenged arose again in 1960. While differences between Nahum Goldman and Ben-Gurion concerned their theoretical as well as political conflicts as to the need for a Zionist movement, the differences between the AJC leadership and Ben-Gurion arose out of ongoing fears that the Israeli leader spoke as if he represented Jews everywhere. Both of these issues reflected the ongoing lack of clear boundaries and political competition, but they went beyond their apparent subjects to signal substantial differences with regard to Israel-diaspora relations.

Jewish communities in Israel and the US had emerged out of distinct patterns of migration from Europe. While American Jews had largely been driven to the US over time by economic pulls as well as late nineteenth and early twentieth-century anti-Semitism in Eastern Europe, the European

Jews who migrated to Palestine before 1933 were part of a movement that was selective. Arrival in the US signified for many a liberation from the constraints of shtetl existence and eagerness to leave it behind as well as to become American. In contrast, Jews who went to Palestine did so with an ideological bent against diaspora life and commitment to the creation of a new Jewish homeland. Despite their differences, however, what these two shared was a conscious distancing from the historical experience of European Jews as minority communities.

This was not true of one stratum that initially relocated geographically but retained its distinctive relationship to European culture—intellectual Jewish refugees, whether Zionist or not. For them European educations remained formative, shaping their continuing development and choices. Each of these populations had, over time, developed its own institutions and leaders. In the US before 1948 Jewish communities were organized both locally and nationally. In Palestine the Jewish community created the basis for a national government. Intellectuals in Palestine helped create the Hebrew University and a variety of publications while in the US refugees formed substantial presences in universities, publications, and other cultural worlds.[17]

It was only after the war and particularly in the wake of Israel's establishment that a number of Jewish leaders faced the need to clarify the institutional effects of Zionist success. Jacob Blaustein, president of the AJC, remained committed both to the distinctive American identity of the organization and to its independence. Nahum Goldmann, president of the World Zionist Organization, held strongly to his belief in the need for a continuing framework within which Israel was both supported by diaspora Jews and benefited from their active engagement with its development. In 1953, these differences led to the creation of the Conference of Presidents of Major Jewish Organizations, led first by Nahum Goldmann, and to the continued separateness of the AJC, which did not join until 1991.[18] Blaustein and Goldmann reacted in ways that were continuous with their personal histories but also with the cultural/national context(s) that shaped their perceptions. For Blaustein the boundary between American Jews and Israel was clear. Goldmann, who saw himself as a diplomat and participant in the Zionist project, undertook the task of creating an institutional foundation for maintaining a broad base of Israel-diaspora interactions that would fit comfortably with his own transnational/European Jewish identity. Rather than drawing boundaries, Goldmann sought to transcend them and to centralize authority in the diaspora so as to provide an effective, authoritative voice that both supported the Israeli government and was a source that could contribute a different perspective to it. In a later memoir, Goldmann described his view as follows: "During a pretty lively discussion I once told Ben-Gurion that he considered problems from the viewpoint of Sde Boker, his little kibbutz, whereas I saw them from a plane flying twelve thousand metres high. It is a different approach."[19]

The tensions inherent in the process of redefining Jewish boundaries while maintaining communal cohesion surfaced once again in 1960–1962. An AJC report, which was dated July 8, 1957, summarizes the ongoing controversy within the American Zionist community and links it to Ben-Gurion's recent statement to a delegation of the AJC.[20] The memo begins by describing recent conflict (resulting in the founding of the American Jewish League for Israel, which was not a split from the AJC) as "nothing more than the result of a decade of dissatisfaction with the Zionist Movement following the founding of the State of Israel." The memo describes general Zionist loss of prestige and membership, linking the decline to disagreements between General Zionists, a centrist party, and the Israeli Mapai Party that dominated the Israeli government.

The memo, citing a *New York Times* report of May 19, 1957, defines the "core of the matter" as "the danger involved in interference by non-Israeli Jews in the internal affairs of Israel, or vice versa, . . . a danger that goes far beyond confines of the Zionist groups." Detailing specifics of the conflict, the memo recounts charges and countercharges within the Zionist movement that included attacks on Nahum Goldmann's speaking to the American Jewish League for Israel and on the AJC for requesting that Ben-Gurion reaffirm his earlier statement on the relationship of Israelis to world Jewry. Included in the discussion was the charge that the AJC, like the Alliance Israélite[21] viewed Israelis as kinsmen in contrast to a Zionist ideology that did not "help kinsmen, but only themselves."

Fundamental to the ongoing discussion were important differences about the definition of Zionism after 1948 and, by implication, of Jewish community. While various Zionist leaders continued to work toward maintaining the movement and with it their own positions, both Ben-Gurion and the leaders of the AJC saw the emergence of Israel as requiring adjustments of definition. Ben-Gurion believed that Zionists were defined by settlement in Israel. Already in 1951, he stated that he hoped for "the Zionist Organization [to turn into] an organization of the Jewish people as a whole."[22] The AJC saw itself as one of a number of American Jewish organizations that was providing support for Israel and historically had been more successful than the Zionist movement in the US. Nevertheless, there was understanding that it was in the interests of organizations "not to cease existing voluntarily" and therefore the Zionist movement would continue to work for influence. The AJC issued the following statement: "As a result of this, their attempts to organize a World Jewish Organization have again come to life. As an outcome, we have the Presidents Club, to which an impressive number of Jewish organizations belong. The American Jewish Committee, which was always opposed to a uniform, centralized organization which would be the voice of all Jewry, is not a member." Nahum Goldmann, who was a founder of the Presidents Club, stated in 1957 that "the Committee is of the opinion that there are two Jewish peoples. The Jewish people on the one hand and the American Jewish Committee on the other hand." Goldmann sought to organize and centralize Jewish political life, based on the belief in a transnational Jewish people that had an interest in Israel wherever they lived but also needed non-Israeli representation to protect their interests. The leadership of the American Jewish Committee was committed to firm boundaries and a Jewish identity based on a clear commitment to American citizenship. Institutional differences and leadership competitions were very much a part of the ongoing struggles among different responses to the changing relationships of Israeli and American Jews.[23]

In May 1960, Ben-Gurion made an announcement that was to have significant long-term impact on this domain. He informed the public that Israeli agents had located and captured Adolf Eichmann in Argentina. He was to be tried in Israel for genocide and crimes against humanity. Responses to this news were particularly diverse outside of Israel. Among the respondents was Nahum Goldmann, whose disagreements with Ben-Gurion in June 1960 reflected a combined effort to maintain an independent Zionist movement with a decidedly different perspective on the planned trial of Eichmann. In both cases, Ben-Gurion operated from within an Israeli society/state still in formation while Goldmann viewed developments as one who believed that his position outside its boundaries allowed him an equally valid perspective on its interests.[24]

In a direct confrontation, Ben-Gurion argued that there was no "necessity of further existence of the Zionist movement" (the Zionist Organization of America, of which Goldmann was president) now that Israel had been an independent state for ten years. As he saw it, the most important tasks that needed to be done—organizing immigration to Israel and providing Hebrew education—would not be undertaken by the Zionist

Organization of America. Goldmann, he said, was "neither an Israeli nor an American but a wandering Jew." This was precisely the condition that Zionism had sought to solve and Ben-Gurion felt that by 1960 there was no difference between Zionist Jews and non-Zionists. Other members of his party (Mapai) disagreed with this position, and Goldmann argued that it was wrong for Israeli Jews to believe that Jews outside Israel "are in their pockets"; while the current generation of survivors and those who experienced 1948 felt connected, the next generation might be less so without an international organization to foster relationships between Israel and Jews beyond its borders.[25]

It was during this same period that Goldmann called a press conference to make public his belief that Eichmann should be tried by an international court sitting in Jerusalem. Since the Nazis did not exterminate only Jews, he believed that judges should be invited from other countries whose citizens were exterminated. The press conference was called to respond to Prime Minister Ben-Gurion's accusation that his position was a "blow to the feelings of the people of Israel and to the honor of the state." This disagreement, in tone as well as substance, was one of several in which the two represented very different views on Israel's position in the world as well as in the Jewish diaspora. In this case, Goldmann's views were shared by others outside Israel who worried about how a trial of Eichmann would be seen beyond its borders.[26]

Correspondence over the course of the next year makes clear the ongoing concern of AJC leaders seeking to draw clear lines between the Israeli government and the American Jewish community. At the same time, letters from Moses Bailey of the Hartford Seminary, a Quaker who had taught Palestinian Arabs earlier at a Friends School in Ramallah, first to Golda Meir, then foreign secretary, and then to Gershon Avner, director of the US department of the Israeli Foreign Ministry, serve to document that the concerns the AJC was raising grew out of an environment in which potential charges of double loyalty, or conflict between Israeli interests and those of the US, were present. Such views could arise as a result of earlier experiences in the Middle East, such as those of Bailey among others, or out of American Jewish identities that were ethnic or religious, or both, where people were wary of being viewed as part of a Jewish national movement. Such concern could be based on worries about external reactions, but they also grew out of developments in an American Jewish world that was increasingly integrated.[27]

In 1961, Bailey wrote to question specific Israeli policies and positions that, he argued, could give rise to perceptions that Israel was encouraging dual loyalties and Israeli expectations of loyalty from American Jews. He cited, in particular, the Israeli nationality laws that ensured citizenship to any Jew who wished to claim it, Israeli government protests against the swastikas that had appeared in a number of countries, and the reaction to Israel's claim to represent the Jewish people in its trial of Eichmann. Moreover, Bailey quoted President Eisenhower's caution to an Israeli diplomat in the aftermath of the Suez/Sinai War that he should not expect that American Jews could change US policy.

While Bailey was speaking from outside the Jewish community, the concerns he raised were echoed in a correspondence between Herbert Ehrmann, president of the AJC, and Ben-Gurion in the spring of 1961. At that time, Jacob Blaustein also returned to Israel where he and Ben-Gurion issued a joint statement reaffirming their agreement of 1950.[28] The need for this affirmation had arisen from statements of Ben-Gurion's that were published in the US, but it was also related in some measure to the ways in which Ben-Gurion made clear his views of American Jews. Coming as these did in the context of the Eichmann trial, which was based on the assertion of Israeli responsibility for as well as representation of Jewish victims, the trial marked a new phase in defining a Jewish nation that was not confined by Israeli borders and could not be equated with an Israeli nation. In his responses to Ehrmann, Ben-Gurion clearly articulated his personal views on these subjects.

Ben-Gurion made clear his understanding of differences between himself and those representing American Jews, in a letter to Ehrmann dated March 15, 1961:

> It is my conviction that only Jews living in a free and sovereign Jewish state can live a full Jewish life. . . . my conception of the term Judaism is different from yours. . . . I regard myself as a son of the Jewish people, which has a land of its own, a language of its own, a great past of its own—longer and more illustrious than that of the American people—and all my life has been dedicated to the task of moulding [*sic*] the future of the Jewish people in its own land. . . . Jewishness as I understand it is not what you call Jewishness. . . . Jewishness is for me what Americanism is to an American. . . . I know and esteem American Jewry, and I am well aware of the differences between you and European Jewry.[29]

In another draft, Ben-Gurion stated that he was "fully aware of the entirely different situation of American Jewry from that of East European Jewry" and had been at pains to emphasize this difference. He then further expressed his view that there were in 1961 factors in Jewish life with "tremendous strength and survival capacity . . . These two factors of strength, different as they are in origin, conditions and nature, are in my view Israel and American Jewry. It is on the continued association of these two factors in relation to Jewish affairs that I believe the future of Jewry depends. This appraisal of mine of the historic status and function of American Jewry is made by a man who could not possibly live anywhere except in Israel."[30]

Several points stand out in these various confrontations and expressions of differences. Although Ben-Gurion faced opposition within his own party at this time, he remained a prime minister who fought to impose his own views of the Zionist movement and its outcome in Israeli statehood, in the face of competing voices based on alternative definitions not only of Zionism but also of Jewish community. While believing in the need for American and American Jewish support, he was also asserting an at times belligerent claim to primacy and independence from these alternatives. In his own view he was "a Jew first, and an Israeli only afterwards."[31]

Inevitably, this position contributed to the still unresolved confusions with regard to Israeli boundaries and nationhood. The fact that this blurring of distinctions was occurring as Israel only gradually took shape within a region that was marked by other confusions of political, religious, and national identifications only heightened the tension between establishing independence and the need for external supports.

A key element in all national endeavors remained that of historical narrative with which to provide a foundation to individual as well as collective identities. Ben-Gurion recognized that American Jewry was a phenomenon quite different from Israeli Jewry and from the historical European Jewish communities. In the early 1960s, modern Jewish history was being made in Israel and the US. In Europe and some of its colonies as well as parts of the Middle East, Jewish communities with their own long histories were still reacting to the destructions and fragmentations of the postwar era. In all these arenas, understandings of history were mediated by personal experiences, but it was only in Israel that the state played a major role in developing the narratives of modern Jewish life. From the first, this task was a challenging one that contained a paradoxical quest: creating a unified Jewish community with shared historical understandings in populations that had actually experienced very different histories. Even within the dominant European Jewish groups there were significantly differing earlier histories; in many cases the histories of Jews from the Middle East and North Africa remained obscured. By the early sixties there were, in addition, differences in the way American Jews understood their historical position and role in the context of US citizenship. By then Zionism, which had succeeded in its primary goal of creating a Jewish state, was losing its power to mobilize action in Israel as well as the US. Inevitably, the immediate demands of political and economic development were foremost.

The political narratives in this era grew out of the Cold War and the attendant decolonization that expanded the arena of independent states. As the American Jewish public shared in the effects of the Cuban Missile Crisis, the Kennedy assassination, and the beginnings of the Vietnam War, Israeli Jews were more preoccupied by the ways in which Cold War rivalries played out in their immediate surroundings.

This was an era in which populations in the Arab world bordering Israel were experiencing their own processes of state formation, new leaderships, and mobilization based on Pan-Arab ideologies that were fluid in nature but guided by efforts to legitimate state policies in various arenas. This was also an era in which the Arab-Israeli conflict helped form public political understandings and gave added strength to the equating of security with support for military growth, in both Israel and the Arab world.

While the Arab-Israeli conflict was clearly an outgrowth of the unresolved war over Palestine and the Palestinians, the Israeli Jewish public was concerned more with the growing influence of Nasser and the role of the Cold War powers in the region. In the Arab world, too, Palestinian refugees often found themselves vulnerable and with their political actions often linked to Arab nationalist movements rather than being specific or separate.

Challenges of state formation and political and economic development in themselves were considerable throughout these years. Complicating these, however, were the pressures of seeking external aid and support. While oil-producing states could rely on their value to those who needed their product, this was not true for Egypt, Syria, or Jordan. Nor, clearly, was it true of Israel. As both the US and the USSR made efforts to gain position in the region, the focus was on military rivalries and alliances.

While the Soviet leadership relied on providing rhetorical support for decolonization, the US sought to mobilize alliances geared to containing what was seen as a dangerous, expansionist communist state. In the context of an Arab-Israeli conflict that was driven by regional realities, neither of these frameworks fully matched local concerns. At the same time, it was clear that local rhetoric was geared not simply to the immediate audience but to a larger transnational one that, it was hoped, could provide added legitimacy to one side or the other. In these contexts, building histories that had meaning to broader publics was inevitably a process colored by both the positions of the producers and the lenses available to their audiences.

The years 1960 to 1963 were marked by renewed American assertiveness during the presidency of John F. Kennedy. For our purposes, the most significant developments were those that were to mark the forced French withdrawal from Algeria, the Israeli development of a nuclear reactor in Dimona, and the failed efforts to create closer relations between the US and Nasser. Taken together these shifts were part of a larger moment in which American power clearly replaced and subordinated that of European states in the Middle East and North Africa.

It is then in these contexts, understanding the multiple uncertainties affecting populations in the Middle East and to some degree in the US as well, that the kidnapping of Eichmann and his trial need to be placed.

Chapter 5

Re-creating the Jewish People, 1960–1966

Multiple books on the Eichmann trial and on its historical role emphasize a variety of effects. Hanna Yablonka has written about the ways in which the trial altered Israeli Jewish identity, integrating the Holocaust into a new history for Israeli children, consolidating a Zionist narrative of continuity for Jews, reinforcing Israeli centrality to Jews internationally.[1] Tom Segev earlier had traced the ways in which the Holocaust and survivors helped form the state of Israel in an ongoing struggle to give trauma meaning.[2] Hannah Arendt's report on the trial has remained a subject of discussion, reflecting the changing environment in which it has been read.[3] And Peter Novick's book on *The Holocaust in American Life* seeks to explain how American Jews came to link their identities to the Holocaust, a process in which the Eichmann trial played an important part.[4]

What remains, nevertheless, is to consider the ways in which the trial helped construct a European Jewish history that allowed American and Israeli Jews to see themselves as sharing the past without requiring them to examine the significant differences among them and the conclusions they drew from that history. In this way, the Eichmann trial gave rise to a new version of Jewish community in which Israeli Jews viewed themselves as the dominant party and American Jews could more easily integrate their position as part of a process by which Israel and the US would be seen as partners. It was a process taking shape as the US became involved in the war in Vietnam, explained by the rhetoric of the Cold War, while obscuring its origins in French colonialism; at the same time intensification of the civil rights struggles called attention to an earlier and contemporary American history of racial violence. In Israel, the incompletely assimilated effects of 1948 were similarly now displaced as the Israeli Jewish community found reason to see itself as having power to compensate for the helplessness of earlier generations. Beyond Israel and the US, Europeans struggled with the aftermaths of both World War II and colonial histories that did not easily fit into the bipolarity of the Cold War divisions or its moral framework.

In retrospect, it is more evident that the strivings for national unity that accompanied state-building both in Israel and in Algeria were components of broader struggles to overcome historic ruptures with what would prove to be illusory reassurances of continuity. In the 1960s Israeli Jews saw themselves as redeeming the losses of the Holocaust; Algerian Muslims saw themselves as the vanguard of a revolution that sought to integrate a history of linkage to imperial power with the experiences of subordination to colonialism. For Palestinian Arabs the apparent success of Algerian militancy conveyed a powerful model inspiring hope. In both cases appeals to history played a central role. In both, the efforts of intellectuals seeking to understand their own experiences differed significantly from official ideologies. In both, the formation of new states and nations necessitated exclusions to justify inclusions. And, in both, the role of external forces in impeding resolution of conflicts was obscured by the powerful drive toward independence.

Eichmann Trial Ramifications

In the years 1960–1962, representatives of the Israeli government captured, tried, and eventually executed Adolf Eichmann for crimes against the Jewish people. The trial is considered by many to mark the first mobilization of public attention to the Holocaust, and in particular to its place in twentieth-century Jewish history.[5] In 1967, Israel went to war after a period of weeks in which threats and images of destruction revived fears of Jewish vulnerability and victimization. After Israel's apparently surprising victory, American Jews were among the most avid fans to join the chorus of "never again" that seemed to link the Holocaust to the Middle East conflict. American Jews who had shown little inclination to immigrate were excited by a country that offered power without apology. It is understandable that those who had survived Auschwitz and then the war of 1948 experienced an unexpected relief at the rapid victory of 1967. More complex is the question of how American Jews came to feel that they too belonged to this people from whom many had so often assiduously differentiated themselves. How do we understand the fact that this widespread identification, now evidently based on a common history, coincided with Israel's assumption of regional dominance?

An examination of the Eichmann trial and its aftermath makes clear its critical role in creating the groundwork that allowed 1967 to have the impact that it had. To understand this process, it is essential to place the trial in the context of the Arab/Palestinian-Israeli conflict and to explore the nature of the history that it helped to construct. Critical to both was the changing nature of the Zionist movement after 1948 and, in particular, the relationship between American Jews and Israel. Although at an overt level the trial appeared to reconstruct the experiences of Jews in Europe, its selectivity and focus were designed not only in Israeli national interests but also with a view to generating a common Jewish history, one with which Americans as well as other communities abroad could identify, and which would create an identity between this history and the state of Israel. Central to this process was also the marginalization of alternative understandings as well as of the recognition that this effort to create a unified history was necessarily at the expense of historical accuracy.

The irony of this set of developments is evident in its paradoxical outcome. The trial took place when Israel was just beginning the process of consolidating the military strength, foreign relations, and economic stabilization that would contribute to the victory of 1967. It was also a time of significant immigration from North Africa and of internal tensions arising from the need to integrate a population that was, in today's words, of multicultural background. Hanna Yablonka has argued that the trial played a very important role in the early period of Israeli national identity formation, integrating survivors and connecting Israelis with what their political elite saw as their European heritage; in doing so, the trial also contributed, according to Yablonka, to the pessimism that came to determine Israeli perceptions of the world.[6] Thus the trial, in its emphasis on Jewish unity and historical danger, activated a formidable national commitment that transcended Israeli borders to include Jews everywhere. In the long term, however, its success also inhibited the capacity to adapt perceptions to a changing reality. By shifting the terms of discussion from those of the historic Zionist movement, in which politics and diversity of views were central, to those of national unity and betrayal, and by seeking to unify histories that were in fact quite distinctive, the trial ultimately impoverished the political debate necessary to utilizing the strength it generated so effectively.

Opinions on Planning the Trial

The leadership of the state of Israel in 1960 was one largely formed by its experiences in Palestine, a history of dealing with the British government and Palestinian Arab resistance, leading finally to the war of 1948. Its commitments were shaped by its participation in a movement organized with the goal of breaking decisively with Jewish history in Europe through both physical and ideological separation. This particular attribute, of consciously leaving Europe behind in the search for a new, different life was one that was shared by many American Jewish leaders as well. In other ways, however, the two populations were very different from one another and that difference became the subject of debate and negotiation after 1948. Central to the discussions were questions about the relationship between the state of Israel and the Zionist movement now located primarily in the US, as well as between the state and non-Zionist organizations of American Jews.

Already in 1950, Prime Minister David Ben-Gurion and Jacob Blaustein, head of the American Jewish Committee, had formally agreed to recognize these differences and to establish a boundary between the state and American Jewry.[7] In April 1961 they met to "talk over" the subject once again. The need to do so was linked to a revival of concern within the American Jewish community with regard to Ben-Gurion and members of his government during the preceding years. The result was a recognition of differences of view "on the essence and the meaning of Judaism and Jewishness, both inside American Jewry and between various Jewish communities, in various parts of the world, and in particular between the Jews who live in the independent State of Israel and Jews living in other countries." The meeting ended with a reiteration and reaffirmation of the 1950 Agreement. According to this agreement, Israel recognized "that the State of Israel represents and speaks only on behalf of its own citizens" and that "the people of Israel have no desire and no intention to interfere in any way with the internal affairs of Jewish communities abroad." It goes on to make clear both the interest in the security of Jews outside Israel and the need for cooperation in particular with the Jewish community of the US in order to ensure Israel's success. Moreover, Ben-Gurion spelled out the recognition that cooperation did not depend on the immigration of American Jews to Israel and that such immigration, while desired, was left to individual decision-making.

Blaustein, in turn, emphasized that the "American Jewish community sees its fortunes tied to the fate of liberal democracy in the United States, sustained by its heritage, as Americans and as Jews." Although he noted that "the vast majority of American Jewry" recognized the need to support Israel, he coupled this statement with strong repudiation of any suggestion that American Jews were in exile. "The American Jewish community feels itself bound to Jews the world over by ties of religion, common historical traditions and in certain respects, by a sense of common destiny." Thus, it was recognized that persecution and discrimination against Jews anywhere would sooner or later have an impact on Jews everywhere. However, Blaustein asserted the need for Jewish communities, particularly American Jewry, not to interfere in the affairs of others and welcomed the commitment by the state of Israel to take a similar position. In this agreement, therefore, there was an expectation of separation between the two groups being represented, along with an understanding that their different circumstances necessarily affected their political agendas.[8]

In the years after 1950, the actual relationship between the state and the Zionist movement continued to reflect the contradictions implicit in the fact that the development of statehood occurred while there was no resolution of the conflict with the Palestinians and the Arab states, conflicts that challenged the legitimacy of the Israeli state. As a result, Ben-Gurion's efforts to redefine Zionism as coterminous with Israel as well as his snubbing of American Zionists was accompanied by continuing active efforts to gain support for the state both from the American government and from American Jews more broadly. Underlying this approach was the conviction that while Israel needed support, it did not need the political advice or perspective of those who chose not to live within its borders. In a letter of March 24, 1960, Rose Halprin, acting chairman of the New York executive of the Jewish Agency, wrote to Ben-Gurion after his visit to the US in which he "found it necessary . . . to make derogatory remarks about the Zionist movement." In this letter she made explicit the view of the Zionists of America that their program was "vital for cultural renaissance in the diaspora." In her view, "mutual respect and regard have always been fundamental tenets of Jewish life" and "those of us who have seen them whittled away have also noted with no little dismay that their lack very often undermines deeply the values which we all share."[9] That there might also be real differences in priorities and values was not addressed.

The continuing struggle to establish dominance over those in the Zionist movement who had invested deeply in the efforts to create a state, but whose positions were based outside its borders, became evident in Ben-Gurion's relationship with Nahum Goldmann during the 1950s. In 1956, Goldmann met with Ben-Gurion to discuss whether he should accept the presidency of the World Zionist Organization. His hesitation was based in part on recognition that the office would prevent his being able "to talk frankly publicly about foreign political matters of Israel and eventually also to criticize Israel's foreign policy." The memo of the meeting, which summarizes their discussion and frank acknowledgment of significant differences with regard to Israel's policy, also states that Ben-Gurion had assured Goldmann that if he took the position, which would lead to his being based in Jerusalem, he would be kept closely informed by the prime minister and by his foreign minister, Moshe Sharett. It was evident that central to Ben-Gurion's concerns was the ongoing Arab-Israeli conflict and disagreement with both Goldmann and Sharett on that subject. Goldmann did accept the position, but the relationship remained conflicted.[10]

In 1960 the conflict surfaced with regard to the capture of Adolf Eichmann. Goldmann's critique of Israeli plans for the trial generated an angry response from Ben-Gurion. In return, Goldmann questioned Ben-Gurion's creation of a link between the ongoing conflict over the role of the Zionist movement and what he viewed as his right to make a personal statement: "I stopped expressing publicly opinions not because I feel that I have no legal right to do it but because I did not want to embarrass you and the Government and saw no particular purpose in expressing such dissident views. Therefore, I don't understand why you suddenly want to revive this issue in connection with the Eichmann case which is certainly not part of Zionist business, was never discussed with the Executive nor within the Executive."[11]

American and Israeli Contexts

The divergent perspectives of Jewish leadership in Israel and the US were evident immediately in the response to the announcement of Eichmann's capture in Argentina and plans to try him in Israel for "crimes against the Jewish people." Although there was a range of reactions, there is no doubt that in Israel the event placed state activism into a new context—that of representing Jewish peoplehood internationally and asserting historical continuity with a very specific part of its past. Thus, there was at once a widening of community and a narrowing focus of history.

In the United States the event reinforced concerns that already existed regarding vulnerability to charges of dual loyalty, fears of resurgent anti-Semitism, and questions about the impact of Israeli actions as well as claims on the position of Jews elsewhere. The gist of many discussions is evident in the questions sent by the editor of the *New York Times Magazine* to the office of the prime minister after the latter's interview about the Eichmann case was published on December18, 1960, and in the answers as formulated:

A. You [i.e., Ben-Gurion] state "Eichmann is accused of murdering millions of Jews as Jews. Israel is [the] only inheritor of these Jews. It's only the Jewish State [that] can try him." Does this mean that Israel claims the right to speak and act for all Jews everywhere?

B. You state that "only a Jew with an inferiority complex would hold that since Eichmann's crime was against humanity rather than against Jews as such he should be tried by an international court." Does this set Jews apart from humanity? Does it exempt humanity from responsibility?

C. You state that "moral obligations higher than formal law" conferred the right to take Eichmann from Argentina. Does any other state also have the right, subject only to its own judgment, to seize residents of a foreign country and take them away for trial?

D. How will the trial of Eichmann serve to mitigate anti-Semitism in the world?

The responses formulated were as follows:

A. Israel is a Jewish state in accordance with its Declaration of Independence and in accordance with the decision of the General Assembly of the U.N. on 29 th of Nov., 1947. The government of Israel is chosen only by the residents of Israel and speaks in their name. However, if there are Jews in the world that cannot speak—like the Jews who were killed by the Nazis, or at the mercy of an oppressive regime—Israel sees it as its responsibility as a Jewish state to speak out and protect their honor. Fortunately, most Jews today are found in free, democratic countries and don't need anyone to speak for them.

B. If French or English are injured, does the question arise as to whether they, as French or English, are entitled to defend themselves? Certainly the French and English are members of humanity but they are French or English. . . . Jews in Israel are exactly like Americans in America. They are Americans and members of humanity and we too are Jews and members of humanity . . .

C. The government of Israel did not capture Eichmann. . . . The victims of the Nazis that captured Eichmann broke the law without a doubt but their moral consciousness required them to do so.

D. At the trial it will be evident . . . to where anti-semitism leads and accordingly will increase the opposition of every decent person to the hatred of Jews.[12]

The themes in this interchange make evident both what Ben-Gurion hoped to accomplish with the trial and the fact that there were competing perspectives involved. The issue of Israeli claims to represent Jews everywhere is resolved by differentiation of a collective voice (i.e., that of Israel and those who cannot be heard) from Jews who exist within free societies. It is in the name of this collective and its history that the right to try Eichmann is asserted; Jews who are critical of this position are described as "ashamed to be Jewish" in contrast to proud Israeli Jews. The "higher law" that justifies the capture was initially supported by the pretext that the capture was accomplished by volunteers rather than by the Israeli intelligence services. Nevertheless, the claim served to justify Israeli activism as morally legitimate despite its patent disregard for the law.

Finally, the answers reflect Ben-Gurion's optimistic belief that the outcome of the trial would be to educate and therefore to deter anti-Semitism. Underlying these answers, which speak on the surface to the legitimacy of the capture and trial, are two competing arguments for the legitimacy of the state. One rests on the equation of Israel as a territorial state of the Jews with all other nation-states. The second depends on the singularity of Jewish fate and therefore the appeal to a "higher law." The need to maintain a precarious balance between the two was intimately connected to the ongoing conflict in which the choice of definition had significant implications for the nature of the state and its relationship with its immediate environment.

From the perspective of American Jewish organizations, however, the capture and trial initially posed definite challenges. In the press and in legal circles, debate focused on the right of Israel to try Eichmann for crimes against the Jewish people; those in opposition argued that the charge should be crimes against humanity and that the judges at least should reflect international law.[13] At one level, then, the discussion even prior to the trial served to highlight unresolved questions as to the nature of Israeli nationhood and sovereignty, its relationship to Jewish communities outside its borders, and specifically to the history of Europe. In the United States, as in Israel, the trial was viewed as a vehicle for addressing the destruction of European Jewry. Whatever the differences, there was awareness within both communities that the process of calling public attention to this history was also potentially disturbing and divisive unless it was successfully managed. The steps taken to accomplish this control reflect clearly the fact that while in Israel the trial was part of a national policy, in the US it served to underline the development of a new equation in which criticism of Israeli policies would often come to be identified with anti-Semitism or with self-hating Jews.

Adolf Eichmann was identified and kidnapped by agents of the Israeli state in Argentina on May 11, 1960. By June 14, Teddy Kollek, working out of the prime minister's office, notified interested parties that after some consideration of who should be helped to write a book that "would present appropriately not only the adventurous aspects of the story but the special fields in which we as a State are interested," it was decided to give such help to "Moshe Pearlman, who worked in this office and who is leaving government service to write a book."[14] Such cooperation was contingent on Pearlman's willingness to submit the text for approval before publication. It was taken for granted that this book was to be in English, making evident the intended audience. Pearlman's letter of June 22, 1960 makes clear his eagerness to work closely with the government and to preempt competitive versions by publishing as quickly as possible in the *Saturday Evening Post*, where he promises to "get in as much about the Shuah [*sic*] and about Israel and the fairness of the trial as possible." After summarizing his intentions Pearlman reiterates "the importance of controlling public opinion" and concludes: "Let me repeat that if you agree that I can do it, we can always work out an appropriate formula whereby in no conceivable way will what I write commit the government." Enclosed with the letter was an outline of the book, which suggested inclusion of "possibly a special chapter, if it emerges from the evidence, of the Mufti of Jerusalem's part in the German decision to exterminate the Jews."[15]

Correspondence makes clear the degree to which Pearlman had access to the secret service as well as the prime minister, and the efforts made to present his work as independent while ensuring that it represented the interests of the government. In addition, other publications on the subject were assiduously tracked by the Israeli embassy in Washington. While the legal establishment prepared for the trial, the prime minister's office was particularly concerned with the ways in which it would contribute to broad perceptions of the state of Israel and of the history of the Holocaust, linking the two in a way that had not been generally visible before this time. Implicit in this concern was awareness that in addition to the wanted publicity there was significant potential for unwanted discussion. Thus the efforts to choose a trusted writer and encourage rapid publication of his book were intended to preempt alternative stories. The concern with public relations was shared by some in the American Jewish community. An Anti-Defamation League (ADL) memorandum of February 1961 outlines what were viewed as "Problems of the Eichmann Trial."[16] In taking on the task of interpreting the trial for the American public, the stated premise was the following:

> The State of Israel, not an amorphous group of Jews, is the entity that indicted and will conduct the Eichmann Trial. . . . Jews outside of Israel, bearing no responsibility for Israel's actions, are not required to find excuses or explanations for what the Israeli Government does. . . . On the other hand, it is well that, as an American Jewish agency, ADL be prepared to interpret what occurs from day to day during the course of the Eichmann trial, in terms of American customs and legal traditions.

It would appear that despite the disclaimer, the ADL recognized that the actions of the Israeli government, if not requiring apology, nevertheless required interpretation to make them consonant with American norms. This position can be understood as seeking to resolve a complex dilemma: reconciling the admitted differences between American Jewish and Israeli definitions of the "meaning of Judaism and Jewish identity" in a way that recognized that as a sovereign state Israel now was in a position to act in the name of the Jewish community and that those actions themselves would affect even those who were beyond its borders. It is interesting to note that in supporting the educational value of the trial the ADL memo agrees with the idea of "teaching that Nazism is the ultimate manifestation of anti-Semitism." However, it then goes on some paragraphs later to define the "constructive purpose" of the trial as linked to "the unending Jewish effort to prevent the world from forgetting the incredible dangers of totalitarianism."

Thus, the balancing of universalist with particularist concerns took a different form but echoed the complexities of Israeli self-definition. The context, underlining the consensus on Jewish vulnerability as well as the link between the state of Israel and US interests is evident in the following explanation:

> Also, it [i.e., the state of Israel] believes the Eichmann trial will serve to remind the world of the price that must be paid when nations permit whole sections of mankind to be robbed of their human rights. The need for this grim reminder, says the State of Israel, is evident once again in the current anti-Jewish campaign being conducted with government sanction in Soviet Russia where Jews, native to the land, have become second class citizens in their own country. And the repeated indignities to which masses of Jews in Arab lands are being subjected even today is simply cumulative evidence of the need once again to refresh the world's memory.[17]

In this way, Israeli interests become, at one level, evidence for the moral purpose of the Cold War and, at another, justified in regional terms by linkage to universalist principles. What was emerging here was a new hierarchy of relationships: an organized American Jewish community more clearly dominated by Israeli government actions, but simultaneously an Israeli government more distinctly influenced in its orientation by dependence on American support. This constellation was to be given emotional meaning and historical understanding through the trial itself.

Two themes run through many discussions of the Eichmann trial. One concerns its role as a historical event. This can be seen both in the continued discussion of the trial itself as history and in consideration of the contribution that the trial made to Jewish history, in particular to recovering and recognizing the significance of the Holocaust. The second concerns the tone generated by the trial, that is, its psychological and emotional impact. It has been described as a "catharsis," as traumatic, as part of the process of mastering historical experience.[18] It is the relationship between these two levels of understanding that can be seen to have affected the long-term impact of the trial on Israeli and American Jews, as well as the ties between them. More specifically, the trial both created an apparently shared history and simultaneously established criteria for the right to interpret that history, in part based on "having been there" or representing those who were. Gideon Hausner, the attorney general who prosecuted Eichmann, and Prime Minister Ben-Gurion both saw the trial as an educational opportunity.[19] In line with this perspective, the trial encouraged selected survivors to tell their stories; whether their experience was directly with Eichmann or not, their testimony was deemed useful in communicating the horror of his work.

Although the testimony, as it unfolded, thus contributed to the construction of a collective memory, it remained limited as a historical contribution, among other reasons because of the criteria that determined inclusion as well as exclusion.[20] Many witnesses were survivors who had immigrated to Israel and whose personal histories were illustrative of the "truth" in the Zionist reading of European Jewish history. Some were chosen to counteract the impressions of passivity that had contributed to scorn for the survivors in Israel, and to reinforce the role played by Zionist activists in the resistance to the Nazis. Throughout the testimony, the emotional impact on the Israeli audience was critical to what Hausner and Ben-Gurion saw as the educational task: to teach youth in particular about the historical realities of anti-Semitism and in their view its climax in the Holocaust. The intention was thus to generate a new history, one in which the generation of young Israelis saw themselves as the children and grandchildren of vanished European Jewish communities, whether this was literally accurate or not. In this context, the emergence of the state signified redemption and was thoroughly legitimized by the prescience of Zionists in creating a haven.[21]

Intentionally or not, this construction seemed to elide the reality that the Yishuv had had its own history in Palestine that led to 1948 and in fact to a very powerful military victory. In a state still at war and with a government dependent on a public consensus that there was no alternative to reliance on the military for security, the emotionalism of the trial served to reinforce both the fears for Jewish survival and the need for vigilance. At the same time, subjects that might have triggered serious debate and discussion with regard to this "history" were deliberately excluded or minimized in the trial. These too were determined by the current context. While seeking to awaken understanding of Nazism and its specific destruction of Jews and of Jewish communal life, the prosecution in the trial was aware of Ben-Gurion's interest in emphasizing the distinction between Germans and Nazis so as to protect the relationship developed between Germany and Israel.[22] Separating Nazism from Germany had, however, another advantage from the point of view of Israeli policy. By doing so, it became easier to suggest that Nazism, rather than a product of a specific history, could be equated with any movements hostile not only to Jews but also to Israel, here symbolizing all Jews. In the trial, this point was made by linking the mufti of Jerusalem's actions to his alliance with the Nazis.[23] That this link was contemplated from the start is evident in Pearlman's outline proposed immediately after the capture of Eichmann.[24]

This interpretation had the ultimate result of using historical data in a way that obscured the possibility of generating historical understanding, since in both cases the actions of individuals and movements were separated from their contexts and presented as linked to a perennial, irrational, and thus ultimately permanent danger. Ironically, the Zionism that had been most effective because it was based on an attempt to analyze a specific history and act accordingly was now being argued in a way that undermined the belief that the relationship between Jews and non-Jews could be understood and that conflict could be potentially mitigated if not eliminated.

This paradox extended to another sensitive area intentionally skirted at the trial. This was the question of evaluating the Jewish Councils (Judenrat) and the judgment of Jewish officials, both in Palestine and in Nazi-occupied Europe. Concern that attention focused on these areas would reawaken inclinations to blame those who were victims and distract from the judgment of Eichmann as personally responsible led to deliberate efforts to avoid issues that had already created division to the detriment of the government party, Mapai.[25] What was viewed as essentially a protective effort, however, also eliminated the possibility of addressing the actions of the leaderships involved as part of a complex history, in which the judgments being made were determined not by good and evil but by human beings who were themselves the products of their environments. In the adversarial atmosphere of a courtroom this need for simplification could be understood as contributing to the necessary drama. When placed in juxtaposition to the presentation of the Arab-Israeli conflict as one of right and wrong as well, it suggests that in this way also the trial reinforced emotional community at the expense of both historical accuracy and intellectual analysis. In Israel, however, there were those who had the knowledge and experience to see the trial in all of its complexity as part of their developing national identity.

The challenge of the trial for many American Jews lay both in the general ignorance of much of the European history being presented and the misunderstanding of the Israeli history that shaped it. As a result, it would have been difficult to challenge the new synthesis. Paul Jacobs, a journalist who covered the trial, articulated his view of the dilemmas thus created in particular for those on the left who had been critical of Zionism. His description underlines Israeli suspicion of the non-Jewish world and an atmosphere of pessimism based on fear. At the same time he points out that few of the tensions he observed had been reported to the outside world, "just as so many of the American Jews who visit Israel, in increasing numbers each year, are unaware of the existence of the real strains inside Israeli society. This is especially true for the large group of unthinking American Jews who are far more uncritical enthusiasts of Israel than most Israelis. To these enthusiastic American Jews, Israel is still a state of euphoria; every Israeli action brings a glow of pride, and the Eichmann trial is merely an extension of what they have learned to expect from the tough, brave, fighting Israelis exemplified so falsely and crudely by Leon Uris's *Exodus*. They almost delight in the Eichmann trial because it demonstrates to them, just as Uris's mythical heroes do, that the anti-Semitic image of the Jew, an image they may unconsciously have accepted about themselves, is wrong."[26]

Jacobs acknowledges other groups as well—those who are not identified with Israel in particular. However, what is striking in this passage is the fact that Jacobs is pointing out the way in which a portrait, such as that of Uris's novel *Exodus,* stands in the way of American Jews genuinely comprehending Israeli existence; yet it was precisely Uris who was chosen by Teddy Kollek and his office to write a fictionalized account of the Eichmann case as complementary to the documentary one by Pearlman.[27] This raises the question then as to the implications of creating a trial intended to confront a painful, complex historical reality in Israel while at the same time supporting a presentation that could only further mythologize and distort the understanding American Jews had of that reality. This duality suggests that perhaps the suspicion and pessimism exacerbated by the trial extended further to a lack of trust in the support that would be available even from the Jewish community if it were fully informed. In that light, Hannah Arendt's report, *Eichmann in Jerusalem*, which offered Americans a very different view than that of Moshe Pearlman, could readily be seen not as fruitful for discussion but rather as dangerous competition.[28]

Reporting on the Trial

The controversy that erupted when someone whose own life was decisively altered by the Nazi regime, who had personal experience of the Zionist movement, and who had a taste for keen intellectual critique chose to report on the Eichmann trial was in retrospect inevitable.[29] *Eichmann in Jerusalem* originated in Hannah Arendt's own wish to attend the trial that she described as "an obligation I owe my past."[30] Arendt approached editor William Shawn, who agreed to let her report for the *New Yorker*. The result was first a series of articles in the magazine published in February and March of 1963, and then a book based on the articles, reporting on the form and substance of the trial.[31]

Letters written while she was in Jerusalem reflect clearly the fact that Arendt's experience in Israel represented a continuity of relationships and interests; at the same time the decision to attend the trial was equally linked to wishes to master aspects of her own past and in this sense represented new challenges, emotional as well as intellectual.[32] It is understandable then that Arendt reacted powerfully when her report was most visibly met not with open intellectual debate, but with an attack. In Arendt's view, she faced a "political campaign" that was not criticism and did not really concern her book. It was instead about "a book that was never written."[33] Hannah Arendt could not know that what she wrote seemed to embody precisely that which Teddy Kollek was trying so ardently to avoid: a critique of the Israeli leadership and a historical understanding often contrary to that which was emerging at the trial. The ensuing attack on Arendt distorted her work in an expectable fashion because it was based less on what she said than on what was most feared. As someone who had participated in the Zionist movement but consciously chose not to belong to either the state or the collective it represented, Arendt wrote as the voice of an alternative narrative of European Jewish experience and its implications.[34] Implicit in her stance was a continuity with the position that she described as that of the "conscious pariah," rooted in the European Jewish intellectual experience.[35] As such, she made visible both the continuity of a specifically European Jewish identity and the insistence on an individual right to judgment not circumscribed by community boundaries. The challenge her work embodied became evident in the intensity of anger and fear it triggered.

What was striking about the response to *Eichmann in Jerusalem* was not the debate about its merits or indeed a confrontation with the theoretical and historical assumptions that led Arendt to her observations. The overriding feature of this "controversy" was the organized and emotional attack that sought to place Arendt's work outside the scope of acceptable discussion. In an early review, marked in a personal notation on the clipping by Hannah Arendt herself as "First report before campaign started," the *Jerusalem Post* concludes a balanced and respectful review of Arendt's first article by stating that "her [Arendt's] truth may be commonplace but it will be authentic. *Eichmann in Jerusalem* so far is unique in the literature of the trial. Its New York publication is causing quite a stir in Jewish intellectual circles."[36]

This stir was evident in the ADL memo forwarded to Teddy Kollek shortly thereafter.[37] This memo and another sent to regional offices of the ADL two weeks later outlined a response to those portions of Arendt's analysis that raised questions about the choices made during the war by the Jewish leadership in particular.[38] Arendt was described as "unremittingly critical of Israel"; in the material was also a lengthy quotation from the statement by the Central Council of Jews in Germany, founded in 1950, in which it was stated that "it does not become those who were not there to pass moral judgements on this grim chapter."[39] Thus what was described by the *Jerusalem Post* as commonplace was seen here as "a matter of continuing concern." The ADL was therefore circulating "information for book reviewers" so that when the book appeared it would be met with organized opposition. Similarly, Teddy Kollek became involved in mobilizing opinion. His request to Israel's Washington embassy for further information on the response to Arendt's articles drew an evaluation that suggested that the subject was part of a broader historical debate that probably would go on for decades.[40]

However, Kollek was eager to intervene and wrote numerous critical letters. He also circulated a publication called *Facts* written by an advisor to the prosecution in the trial, with the intent of unmasking Arendt as incompetent as well as incorrect. Finally, Teddy Kollek also wrote to Herbert Friedman of the United Jewish Appeal asking him to endorse the book by Pearlman as a response to "the insidious campaign started by the Hannah Arendt book."[41] Thus, a book that had been planned and in part written long before Arendt went to Jerusalem came to be offered as a rebuttal. Although Kollek could not have known that Arendt would write her book, his earlier support of Pearlman had been undertaken with the clear intent of preempting alternative histories in the public arena. A review in *American Judaism*, published in fall 1963, recognized that the book had been "both willfully misunderstood and all too clearly understood." The author then goes on in an effort to thread his way through "to bring clarity where anger and unreason now prevail." In so doing he points out "for those who get their Jewish history straight from Leon Uris, *Eichmann in Jerusalem* is sure to seem puzzling or mischievous."[42] Arendt's was not a perspective that would reassure those who wanted heroes and villains to populate their history.

Although Arendt was criticized in Israel, efforts to have the book translated and published in Hebrew were unsuccessful. Her correspondence, however, reflects her continued interest in the reactions in Israel. Included in this correspondence is reference to a report on a court decision in 1964 that Arendt interpreted as a "global exoneration of the Judenrate in general."[43] An accompanying letter states that "one of the most astonishing features of this document [the verdict of the Supreme Court in Jerusalem] is that, without mentioning explicitly your name, it is an argument against you and your book."[44] This suggests the degree to which *Eichmann in Jerusalem* could be used to support one of the shifts that the trial had marked—that is, the suppression of further legal efforts to hold Jews responsible for their behavior during the war. Despite such attempts to end the debate and seek relief from painful divisions, however, *Eichmann in Jerusalem* continues to provoke discussion to this day.[45]

It can be argued that it is precisely because Arendt was viewed as an insider that her work provided an opportunity to establish boundaries to permitted debate within the community.[46] It is essential to the irony of this controversy that Arendt, whose deep ties to German culture remained strong, was in some ways attacked in the service of the need to construct an idealized European Jewish community.[47] At one level the controversy, therefore, pitted Arendt's explanations of the European past, undertaken in what she viewed as a quest to know and understand, against the efforts by the Israeli government to publicize aspects of that past in a way that was openly designed to affect the present and future. Where Arendt sought to lay the past to rest, to come to terms with the ways in which the years had diminished those like the Nazis who once were omnipotent, the Israeli government's position was predicated on the need to maintain vigilance and thus to enhance the perception that omnipotent political forces continued to exist. The fact that these forces were now detached from Germany itself and ascribed to Nazism would only suggest greater transportability.[48]

The focus of the Eichmann trial was on the Holocaust, but it can be argued that the testimony about the Holocaust was in certain ways a vehicle to establish a particular perspective on European Jewish history, one that would support the Zionist movement's prescience and retroactively give it continuity as well as unity. The need to create such a dominant narrative can be understood if we see it as serving both to suppress alternative histories and to support the claims of a particular leadership's right to legitimacy. Two themes have been repeatedly cited as the foci for the controversy: Arendt's critical view of the role played by the Jewish leadership in the Judenrat during the Holocaust, and the interpretation of Arendt's subtitle, "The Banality of Evil," as a mitigation of Eichmann's personal responsibility for Jewish suffering and loss. Both subjects served to put in question the assumptions of the trial and therefore, by implication, the historical framework within which it was constructed.

Within the first pages of her book, Arendt directly places Ben-Gurion on trial in juxtaposing his position as "invisible stage manager of the proceedings" with her description of those visible in the courtroom. Arendt's disagreements with the actions of Jewish leadership thus do not remain confined to the overt discussion of the Judenrat; the latter is also to be understood as commentary on contemporary decision-making.[49] Hannah Arendt had been very critical of the Zionist leadership and its emphasis on statehood in the 1940s.[50] Her responses to the trial can be read not only in the context of her work on totalitarianism but equally as part of a perspective on the implications of having been born Jewish in a particular historical time and place.[51] *Eichmann in Jerusalem* has been discussed primarily in the context of Holocaust studies—the trial as the start of a public discussion, and the report as bringing to light painful differences within the Jewish community during the war and afterward. The trial and report did something else, however, because the events that were being uncovered as part of a distinct historical moment were in fact deeply embedded in the complex sociopolitical framework of Jewish life in Europe over centuries.

While it is true that the physical existence of that life had largely been erased or changed beyond recognition during the war, this only complicated the task of understanding its impact on those who carried it with them into new environments. In both Israel and the US, the invisibility of that earlier history in its complexity had interfered with the possibility of integrating that past with the present. The trial thus was much more than an opportunity to bring to light the detailed suffering of the Holocaust. It provided a chance to organize that history. Among the rewards for the Jewish people seemed to be not only survival but a state that could now finally act in their name and provide not only safety but equality in the public arena as an identifiable political presence. If that state was the result of the Holocaust, a necessary outcome of suffering and persecution, then it was also less pressing to pursue the question of how that state came into being as the product of a particular movement. Thus, it can be argued that the Eichmann trial reinforced a particular reading of history—one in which the Zionist movement was proven correct in its pessimism about the future of Jewish life in Europe, and therefore in which the actions taken by its leadership were justified by inevitability, by the need to survive. The cost of this reading was in its suppression of both the activism and the choices characteristic of this history. Hannah Arendt was not an outsider nor was she, as she would have liked to see herself, merely a reporter of the facts.[52] Instead, she was the voice of an alternative historical understanding; her quest was to understand this history in her own search for integration of a fractured past and present. It was precisely in her insistence on choices, her placement of the trial and its content in the context of both European and Israeli histories that she made visible the continuing and unresolved presence of a debate internal to the Jewish community: one about the boundaries of community, the nature of legitimate relationships with non-Jews, and the question of who was to negotiate those relationships, a community leadership (and if so, which) or the individual? While the terms might have changed, these questions had become part of Jewish experience throughout the modern era and, despite wishes to the contrary, were not rendered obsolete by the apparent historical rupture of the war.

Arendt's discussion, located outside Israel and insistent on calling its leadership to account, makes crucial distinctions both in historical time and in political position. In Arendt's writing, the distinctions work to insist both on the differences within the Jewish community and on the ways in which the political understanding of Jews is and must be the product of changing relationships within specific historical circumstances. Arendt understandably viewed the Eichmann trial as intended to legitimize not only Israeli sovereignty but also Zionist constructions of Jewish history. In this framework, the Holocaust indeed could and was seen to justify the earlier arguments by Zionists that the only future for Jews as a community would have to be outside Europe and, for many, that meant in the form of statehood. While Arendt herself supported the assumption of an explicit political definition to Jewish identity, she located that definition in such a way that it entailed recognition of choice rather than inevitability, insisting on the dangers both of imposing apparent continuity on changing historical circumstances and of denying continuity despite a changing context. Thus, Arendt argued:

> It was this conviction [of the eternal and ubiquitous nature of anti-Semitism] which produced the dangerous inability of the Jews to distinguish between friend and foe; . . . If Prime Minister Ben-Gurion, to all practical purposes the head of the Jewish State, meant to strengthen this kind of "Jewish consciousness," he was ill advised; for a change in this mentality is actually one of the most indispensable prerequisites for Israeli statehood, which by definition has made of the Jews a people among peoples, a nation among nations, a state among states, depending now on a plurality which no longer permits the age-old and, unfortunately, religiously anchored dichotomy of Jews and Gentiles.[53]

Aftermath

The war of 1967 made manifest precisely how well Israel had succeeded in becoming a nation among nations and a state among states. The victory made visible an imbalance between Israel and the surrounding states that had not been easily recognized by the general public in the weeks leading to the outbreak of fighting. In the aftermath of a success that left Israel as a dominant regional power, however, internal conflict between a path of "normalization" and that of exceptionalism remained unresolved. The perceived need to maintain the support of the US and of the American Jewish community played an intrinsic role in that conflict. In an article seeking to understand the "outpouring of feeling and commitment" that had characterized the American Jewish community immediately before the outbreak of war, Arthur Hertzberg pointed out that "we [i.e., American

Jews] had to the best of our immediate ability enlisted in the struggle and become participants instead of passive spectators."[54]

This phenomenon was part of a political change occurring within American Jewry. "The pollsters found that 99 per cent of all the Jews in America undeviatingly supported the Israeli position." In Hertzberg's view, the crisis had "forcibly reminded many, perhaps most, American Jews that the posture and destiny of Jews in the world continue to be quite unique and that Israel is not a state like all other states." In seeking to explain the meaning of "this transforming moment . . . for the future of American Jews," Hertzberg hazarded the guess "that the most widespread influence—on Jews in Israel and America alike—was a revulsion against the passivity of the Jewish victims of the Nazis."[55] Six years after the trial of Eichmann, Hertzberg continued to see Israeli and American Jewish mobilization as a way to disavow a mythological passivity that allowed activism to be linked to undoing the past, rather than to changing the present and future. The unity of the Jewish community and its unquestioning support of Israeli policy appeared founded on this common ground of "history." Both the history and the unity were prepared by the events surrounding the Eichmann trial. Less evident in the immediate euphoria of 1967 was the fact that this unity, which appeared to consolidate a national collective identifying the Jewish community with the Israeli state, came at the price of a renewed emphasis on the differences between that collective and others. Thus, the successful accomplishment of gaining the position of a state among states could not be recognized without threatening this newly won unity, and the unity that had been sought to repair a fragmented past now became an obstacle to the adaptation required by a changed present and uncertain future.

Chapter 6

Ruptures and Meaning, 1962–1967

Multiple Jewish, Palestinian, and Algerian Narratives

Jewish history has been marked both by collective experiences set apart by firm boundaries and by integration within various political structures. Throughout that history there has been a tension between the quest of individuals who ventured outside the community and the regulation of community norms. Although the fact that individual Jews played important roles in the world of non-Jewish majorities might at times be viewed as contributing to the benefit of their collective existence, it could equally be viewed as a threat or betrayal. Moreover, differentiation within the community opened it to fragmentation and the risk of having to view Jewish experience not only through the eyes of their own leaders and sages but through the eyes of others, outsiders.

The collective memory of Jewish relationships with non-Jews has had a significant impact on the ways in which this history has been understood and transmitted in the twentieth century. One could go further and say that since the establishment of a Jewish state the conscious construction of this memory has taken on political overtones that have further complicated the task of historians seeking to unravel underlying intricacies of the collective experience over time.

There is little doubt that the coincidence in timing of public recognition of the Holocaust and the establishment of the state of Israel in the years after World War II provided the context in which a Zionist reading of Jewish history could establish what appeared to be an obvious claim to truth over alternative readings that had been at least equally persuasive until the war.

Moreover, the long-standing communities in Europe that had given rise to alternative understandings had been annihilated, while those who had chosen to or felt forced to leave Europe by going to the US and Palestine now had to deal with the sudden decimation of what in fact had been the centers of Jewish life toward which they had had ambivalent feelings at best. A dialogue within the Jewish community was now silenced by the destruction of too many of its members. It may be wondered whether that coincidence also reinforced the association of debate and dialogue with annihilation and communal unity with survival.

The controversy over *Eichmann in Jerusalem* exposed the underlying tensions that accompanied consolidation of Israeli statehood and its drive to represent Jewish history as well as community. Nationally, American Jewish organizations continued to pursue political goals and values as a minority while locally the trial had proved false the initial fears that it would generate an anti-Semitic backlash. The fears that calling attention to Jewish suffering might be counterproductive had a history in World War II, but in fact the attention that the trial focused on crimes against Jews in particular now had a far different effect. It could be seen to reinforce the benefits of statehood as a vehicle for justice.[1]

Nevertheless, the relationship between the state, with its interest in managing Jewish community, and the larger Jewish world remained subject to various strains. On the one hand, there was the ongoing reality of Jewish minorities in multiple states, each with its own conditions. On the other hand was the ongoing presence of Jewish intellectuals, many of whom were survivors of Eichmann's Europe, whose experiences could not readily be reduced to Israeli nationalism, despite their sometimes sympathetic views of Zionism in its origins.

The stakes in the trial of Eichmann went well beyond the guilt of the defendant. In the process of capturing Eichmann and staging the trial, the Israeli government claimed its right to the legacy and history of his victims. Coming as it did at a moment that was giving rise to the multiple claims of colonial victims seeking recognition of their histories, it becomes possible to consider the ways in which multiple narratives began to vie with one another for public attention.

In all these instances, national narratives were serving the needs for unity, visibility, and continuity in the face of fractured and divided populations. As national coherence and in many instances homogeneity became identified with safety as well as continuity, the risks of alternative narratives grew. Ironically, it was precisely the success of the Israeli government and the Eichmann trial that simultaneously underwrote Zionist history as prescient and furthered the view of Israel as an extension of the European history linked to imperialism. These associations in turn limited the space available to those whose personal histories, whether in Europe, Palestine, or elsewhere in the Middle East, saw more complex and cross-cutting cultural networks.

The Eichmann trial offered survivors who had become Israeli citizens a form of integration into both the political and historical significance of their suffering. In a country still developing a national ideology, the trial offered a state-sponsored interpretation of historical experience while seeking to strengthen a particular version of collective identity. The Arendt report on the trial, in contrast, was viewed by many as a threat to that development, offering as it did an alternative set of questions and perspectives on the responses of Jews in Europe to the catastrophe of Nazism, as well as to World War II. Where the Israeli Jewish community was developing a national narrative, Arendt was only one of a sizeable group of secular Jewish intellectuals of European origin who were wrestling with individual efforts to understand and articulate their own histories. These often emerged as counternarratives that challenged a Zionist inter-pretation of Jewish history.

In *The Origins of Totalitarianism*, Arendt made evident her under-standing of the relationship between colonialism and anti-Semitism.[2] Recently, in *Multidirectional Memories*, Michael Rothberg develops this theme to show both Arendt's limitations and at the same time her place in a theory of memory/trauma.[3] Aamir Mufti, in *Enlightenment in the Colony*, links European Jewish experience with that of Muslims in India through a theoretical consideration of minority-majority relationships.[4] Rather than accepting bipolar frameworks that seek fixed boundaries, these explorations underline historical fluidities and contingencies, developments over time as dynamic rather than determined. Like Camus and other existentialists, questions of judgment and action are viewed as reactive to concrete dilemmas rather than ideologically determined. It was precisely the need to understand profound ruptures and devastation accompanying both the Holocaust and decolonization that stimulated intellectual efforts to grasp realities that undermined both certainties and security.

Yet in the aftermath of Israel's independence and American ascen-dance, at a time in which Jews in both locations sought integration, there was a clear, though not always recognized, divide between the sensibilities of European Jewish intellectuals and the emerging redefinition of state and diaspora relations. Where Joachim Prinz and Abraham Joshua Heschel clearly viewed the civil rights movement through their own experiences as Jews in Europe and in the US, the Israeli leadership, as well as American Jewish organizations, was focused on overcoming Jewish vulnerability through state power, Israeli but also American.[5] In the aftermath of the Eichmann trial and then Ben-Gurion's final retirement in 1963, the Jewish history that had most emotional resonance for the dominant Israeli Jewish community was one that could merge the European Zionist belief that Jews remained subject to historical anti-Semitism (wherever they were a minority) with the perception of being encircled by enemies similarly driven by irrational hate. This was an equation supported during the trial by mention of the mufti's time in Berlin during World War II, which made it easy to tarnish the Palestinian national movement with Nazi sympathies. Thus, the search for political and military support from the US was strengthened by an appeal to vulnerability as well as to common moral commitments.[6] It was in this time and context that the emergence of Palestinian Arab activism, modeled on and encouraged by Algerian independence, began to define itself as part of the anticolonial movements and Third World alliance that developed most forcefully in the 1960s. The FLN, which was struggling with its own divisions and competitive leaderships, and its own efforts to redefine an Algerian nation, was nevertheless viewed by many as the wave of the future, a progressive proof that the arc of history was bending toward independence and voice for those long deprived of both.[7]

The Algerian state that emerged and was recognized in 1962 was one that forcefully excluded or lost segments that did not fit with the redefinition of Algerians. European settlers (pied-noirs who were primarily French but included others), Harkis (Muslims who fought with the French against the FLN), and Jews all chose or were forced to leave. Internal divides—Berbers and Arabs, rural and urban, francophone and arabophone intellectuals, Muslim and secular—were largely repressed as an authoritarian military government took shape with a guiding ideology of socialism, Arab nationalism, and Islam as the counter to capitalist imperialism.[8]

In a world defined largely by US-USSR rivalry, the Third World was constructed as an assertion of independent states that defined their positions as revolutionary, neutral, anticolonialist, and socialist. The excitement of movements for transformation and independent power was linked to an emphasis on nation-statehood as the vehicle for success. When that success came, it often allowed little room for the recognition of loss and of mourning the price paid. Yet Algerians came out of their war with a legacy of traumatic violence, rupture, and divided cultures.

Palestinians too had experienced violence, rupture, and divisions. Fractured throughout the era of the Palestine mandate, they were unprepared for the war of 1947–1948. Largely abandoned by those they had reason to expect would support them, they emerged into a world without place for their voices. Splintered into multiple minorities among various states, Palestinians were divided by class, family, citizenship (or statelessness), and resources. Whether they remained on their own land or were displaced, their claims for self-determination were shattered.[9]

Without any form of state apparatus or unifying structure, Palestinians found themselves in a newly fractured political world. Legally, their communities were divided among states with different, sometimes conflicting, international positions. While those officially recognized as refugees were defined by the UN and served by UNRWA (the United Nations Relief and Works Agency for Palestine Refugees in the Near East), others were faced with new political authorities requiring a variety of choices. Among the challenges now facing them was that of self-definition and response to external, often hostile redefinition. In the face of traumatic ruptures that were experienced by individuals and families, immediate responses had to ensure survival as well as to maintain hope of undoing and redoing shocking events. That hope required recognition and international responsibility.[10]

UN Resolution 194 provided a basis of hope for some measure of relief but it did not address the need for a political voice or representation of Palestinians other than as refugees.[11] This was reflective of the broader expectation that Palestinian Arabs could readily be assimilated either in neighboring states with which they shared language, culture, and history or in an Israel that had declared itself a democracy with equal citizenship for all.

Following the armistices of 1949, neither Resolution 194 nor various diplomatic efforts could resolve either the material effects of displacement or the attendant loss of political recognition. In the years that followed, powerful currents of Pan-Arabism instead required Palestinians to respond in the context of specific state conditions and to see their own history largely submerged or politicized, or both.[12]

During the construction of Cold War alliances and an Arab world torn by diverse regimes, each with its own external supports, Palestinians largely remained subject to local conditions and material constraints.

Construction of Palestinian history was necessarily also the product of multiple strands—oral transmission, collection (preservation) of documents, journalism, literature, and scholarship. Lacking any organizing framework, it was an endeavor strengthened by experiences of loss and commitment to preservation. Although largely unseen or denied in Israel, Europe, and the US, these efforts preserved the foundation for a distinct Palestinian identity and history.[13]

The framework for the reemergence of distinctly Palestinian political movements, however, can best be understood in an international context. In the years between 1959 and 1967, key elements of a Palestinian national movement began to emerge. They were generated in a regional world of Arab states still struggling with the aftermath of foreign control, a geographically divided Palestinian population, a Cold War of superpowers competing to gain support in the Middle East as elsewhere, and, entwined in all these, competing ideological frameworks charting the past as well as prescribing the future.

For Palestinian activists the goal of recovering from and reversing the defeat of 1948 was clear, but the alternative routes to arrival were colored by multiple immediate challenges. Depending on Arab states that had already failed them and seeking to stabilize personal as well as communal existence, Palestinians were faced with choosing to join existing political organizations—tying their specific aspirations to a broader state or Arab framework—or to formulate a particularist view, rooted in the distinctiveness of their experiences. Whatever the decisions, Palestinians in the Arab world were negotiating layers of obstacles to the emergence of a clear Palestinian voice.

From the first, the Palestinian national movement was divided in its analysis and hence its strategy. Before 1964 the most notable claimants to leadership and mobilization of Palestinians were represented by the Arab National Movement (George Habash in particular) and Fatah (Yasir Arafat and a small circle as leaders). With differing views of what Nasser's ascendancy in the politics of the Arab world might mean for Palestinians, the two groups also were distinguished by ideological differences and their formulation of Palestinian priorities. While the Arab National Movement saw a need for transformation and unity of Arab states, Fatah emerged from a group committed to Palestinian nationalism and separatism. In the years from 1957 to 1964 these groups lived through ongoing periods of Arab state unity and conflict that underlined the tension between needing to sustain Palestinian life in multiple states and the need for recognition of particular trauma that transcended political boundaries.[14]

It was only in 1964, with the creation of the Palestine Liberation Organization, that an institution intended by some to control Palestinian activism unwittingly created an arena for Palestinian political life that eventually integrated various movements under one umbrella. Palestinian political life in these years (1957–1967) was characterized by a drive to enable effective military action as well as political debate on the relationship between Palestinian needs and Arab state capacities. While the Arab National Movement pursued transformation in the Arab states as a requirement to act effectively against Israel, Fatah began to seek both support and enlistment for direct entry into the battlefield.

In 1961 and 1962 two events helped to prod further Palestinian consciousness and mobilization. With the breakdown of the United Arab Republic, which had briefly united Egypt and Syria, strength through Arab unity was subject to greater questioning.[15] In 1962, Algerian independence heightened admiration for a movement that had struggled long and hard, via guerrilla warfare and in the international arena, to claim its independence and freedom from colonial control. In an era of multiple anticolonial conflicts, the Algerian revolution took on symbolic and practical significance for Palestinians and, in particular, the Fatah leadership.

There was another element also playing a role. The long-term nature of France's control, in addition to cultural elements of its dominance, had contributed to divisions within the Algerian population and disruption of historical identities. The Algerian revolution was a fight against French and settler control, but it was also explicitly an effort to create an Algerian nation with its own voices. The depth of French penetration gave rise in turn to a revolutionary drive that sought to integrate revival with re-creation of traditional identity markers such as Arabic and Islam.

Independent Algeria, like the FLN before it, identified with other revolutionary movements and saw itself as part of a Third World. As such, Algerian president Ben Bella and others offered Palestinians material support and training. It was Fatah—an explicitly Palestinian separatist nationalist movement—that based its hopes for success against Israel on the Algerian model of struggle. Although the circumstances were very different, it is not hard to understand the attraction. Palestinians needed practical help and sought to build a guerrilla movement that could use existing frustrations and anger, particularly those of refugees, against Israel. Yet the anger and frustration of the post-1948 era was fueled not only by Israel but also by Palestinian experiences in the Arab world. The leadership of Fatah in particular sought to assert a need for specific recognition and to be supported, but not controlled, by Arab states.[16] Palestinians too had experienced deep penetration by outside forces. Although this had been a much shorter experience than that of Algerians, it was followed by displacement, loss, and the need to resist an integration that would have been at the expense of finding a reflection of their own difference.

As the era of European colonial empires drew to a close, the language of expansion and control shifted. Where the French had believed in the value of their cultural exports and the British had been proud imperialists, Americans utilized a language of freedom, anticolonialism, and self-determination while supporting an expansion theoretically predicated on defense against communism. In parallel fashion, the USSR identified itself not only as anti-imperialist but also as revolutionary. For those who sought external support, the shift from a world dominated by Europe to that of US-USSR rivalry also entailed the construction of their own political narratives to fit the perspectives of those with the power to provide. Israelis, Palestinians, and Algerians sought international legitimacy through appeals to postwar norms as understood by particular patrons. Where Palestinian Arabs and Jews contained in the mandate addressed primarily the British, both now had to consider the impact of bipolarity on their conflict. Similarly, the triangle of Algerian settlers, natives, and the French state shifted during the war to recognize the role of the global community.

These shifts, taking place before 1967, were accompanied by actions on the ground and by literary formulations that were building histories and buttressing and explaining developments. In retrospect it is clear that the effects of war in 1967 were conditioned not only by preceding military and diplomatic shifts but also by the ways in which Arabs and Jews had come to construct their conflict. Absent the direct interchange and contact of the pre-1948 era, differences were further magnified, fears intensified, and reliance on military effectiveness strengthened.

These were also important years for the development of historical narratives and generational transmission of earlier experiences. It was not insignificant that there were also now new audiences to be addressed.

Material Contexts, Changing Lenses

The Suez/Sinai War of 1956 marked the end of long-standing French and British roles in the area.[17] At the same time, it served to consolidate further a perception in the Arab world of Israel as an imperial project and increased wariness of US policy (despite American intervention to force British, French, and Israeli withdrawal from Egyptian territory). In the next years, the focus on defense and military buildup was formative for both Israel and Egypt (as the primary actors in the conflict). The arms race that followed inevitably brought the Cold War further into regional relationships; it was a development ironic in its juxtaposition with the power of nationalist ideologies insistent on self-determination.[18]

In Israel the years 1961–1967 were marked by political strains, socio-economic challenges, and a weakening of ideological mobilization. The Eichmann trial underlined that strain of Zionism that viewed Jewish life in the diaspora as fragile and Israel as the logical outcome of European Jewish history. Almost imperceptibly, Zionism as an ideology of active transformation and will was now shading into a state ideology of defense in the face of historical persecution. The ingathering from the diaspora, many from the Arab world and North Africa, was viewed as essential to the Zionist mission, but less acknowledged was the need for such ingathering, whatever the price, to further strengthen a new, fragile state.

Isolated in the region, Israelis continued to depend on external supports—economic as well as military. At the same time, US policy in the region continued to be driven by efforts to maintain useful relations with major Arab states while ensuring Israel's territorial integrity.[19] In this uncertain environment, Israeli policy focused on gaining increased US military and political support while simultaneously developing greater independent resources, including nuclear energy. Among the narratives mobilized to generate US government and American Jewish support were those that linked the Jewish population of Israel to victims of the Holocaust, as well as those that represented Arab nationalism as committed to annihilation of the Jewish state.

The prime visible threat to Israel's security appeared to come from Egypt and the force of Pan-Arabism led by President Nasser. Seen from Israel, Arab nationalism fostered unity among adversaries committed to its erasure. For the general public in Israel, Arabs were a category into which Palestinians could easily merge. Thus the paradoxical outcome, which favored the disappearance of Palestinians but viewed as threatening the possibility of actualizing the promise of Arab nationalism. In this era of national liberation movements, the mobilizing power of nationalist ideology was mirrored in the Arab-Israeli conflict.

In retrospect, it is much easier to discern the ways in which this powerful appeal could hide the complexity of actualizing its promise in secure and functioning states. In the Arab world independence came in the form of various regimes, resources, and historical experiences. The hopes for unity had force both at a popular level and at a more elite level, in which it seemed to have the potential to support regional power. In the aftermath of 1948, the Arab states and Israel pursued their own development but did so with the insecurity of an unresolved war that made them all the more dependent on outside patronage.

In those years, American policy was based on assumptions that support for modernization and reform in the Middle East could act as counterweights to the appeals of revolutionary nationalisms, which threatened economic and military interests. Projecting itself as a defender of freedom against communist totalitarianism, the US hoped that it could separate itself sufficiently from the history of British and French imperialism to gain credibility with newly emerging regimes. In some cases, such as that of Iran in 1953, Americans hoped to help this process along by direct intervention. In others, such as Turkey, historical conflicts with Russia contributed to an alliance with the US. In the Arab states still experiencing political instability and experiment, however, US initiatives largely failed to elicit trust.[20]

US ties to Israel nevertheless remained limited and cautious, shifting gradually after 1961. At the same time, American focus remained on existing states and the ongoing unresolved status of Palestinian refugees. In line with broader American assumptions, efforts had been made to utilize economic means as well as political persuasion to foster refugee integration and to dissolve the continuing effects of 1948 in the region.[21] Such initiatives were predicated on hopes to achieve broader regional goals and ongoing fears of being caught in a conflict that showed little evidence of moderating. Palestinians in fact were among those who, along with other Arab activists, were hopeful of the promise seemingly contained in revolutionary nationalisms. History, it seemed, was on their side.

Alternative Zionist/Jewish Memories and Definitions

While governments and military leaders focused on concrete activity geared to the future, writers and artists sought to link past to present. As the Cold War settled into a state to state contest that saw decolonization as an opportunity to mobilize support, populations newly endowed with national states had to make significant adjustments in shifting from the mobilization of fights for independence to navigating complex domestic, regional, and international conditions.

In 1960 prominent sociologist Daniel Bell published *The End of Ideology*.[22] A controversial book that was variously interpreted, the title itself signaled a turning point. (Other titles that have unintentionally become shorthand beyond the author's control include Arendt's *The Banality of Evil* subtitle as well as Francis Fukuyama's *The End of History*.) Bell argued for the waning power of ideology in the context of the US and Europe, but he did so in the beginning of a time marked precisely by the emergence of new movements with their own formulations of ideology and commitments. As such, Bell was one who shared a past and presumed a future based on specific intellectual and political contexts.

In contrast, we can juxtapose on the one hand Jewish intellectuals of European origins, whose writings are situated in personal experiences of historical engagement and its consequences, with the emergence of writers experiencing decolonization also and inevitably affected by the immediacy of traumatic violence. Those experiences finally ruptured any promises of equal inclusion in European empires whose cultures were premised on the contradictions of a secular humanism married to capitalist expansion. In the sixties, the relationship between articulations and mobilizations remained fluid, with significant gaps that expanded and contracted over time. Underlying the shift from the fifties to the sixties (in Bell's terms from the appeal of utopian ideology to that of modernization/reform) were the increasingly visible, emerging redefinitions of collectivity and freedom. While Jewish writers were exploring the aftermath of escapes from violence, Palestinians and Algerians were dealing with the ongoing and unresolved effects of achieving distinctiveness that made evident the continuing need to master internal differences as well as to rely on external sources of support.

While the United States was moving past the red scares of Senator Joe McCarthy, the global battlefield took on more significance. The Marxist ideology that Bell discounted was rooted in a presumed scientific historical analysis. Herzl's Zionism, growing out of European perspectives as well, based itself on an analysis of European power relationships and priorities, With the loss of belief in such understandings also came efforts to use history to bolster newly developing political movements; decolonization was accompanied by rewritings of history characteristic of nationalism.[23] Increasingly, fragmentation of perspectives gave rise to competing narratives, to incomplete yet powerful searches for meaningful expression of experiences and appeals for recognition.

There were several threads that took shape before 1967 and contributed to the new constellation that emerged in its wake. Israeli Jews wrote about a newly emerging Jewish nation with multiple histories seeking security and unity while struggling with integration. These were years in which Zionism no longer had the force of earlier years, with decreasing immigration and more uncertainty of direction. At the same time, stabilization of national institutions created the context for a dominant Israeli identity based on common experience, education, and Hebrew culture.[24]

In the US and Europe, refugee European Jewish intellectuals continued to reflect on their own varying trajectories and relationships to national identities, cultures, and political life.

American Jews were increasingly identified with the American state that had allowed them to thrive while their co-religionists—often including families as well—had perished. At the same time, the civil rights movements, as well as intervention in Vietnam, contributed to new divisions.

Largely invisible to any of these, Palestinians too were responding to both their own fragmentations and to displacements that were psychological as well as physical. Writers and poets had begun to respond by giving voice to painful realities, as well as histories, that necessarily mired the majority in considerations of survival, through adaptation to dramatically new circumstances.

An independent Algeria, now demographically transformed by the exodus of Europeans, Jews, and Harkis, came to life as a new political arena while France had to begin dealing with the separation, adding complexity to the questions that had surrounded its wartime actions.

What all these had in common, despite insistence on the uniqueness of each, was the fact that in the sixties they were experiencing the layering of new violence and division onto older traumatic events that had not been absorbed, let alone integrated into new national and political constellations. Moreover, these challenges were occurring in an international framework that endowed some with power while others continued to be marginalized. This could only intensify the struggles to define who belonged where and to draw borders/separations. Throughout, the pressure of nationalisms that defined the collective was challenged by voices that crossed boundaries and recognized alternative forms of political organization. Yet in the years 1960–1967 the density of action largely obscured the competing narratives.

In all these cases the ways in which nationalism demanded separatism gave rise to ruptures and resistances, to contradictions between individual life experiences and longing for collective belonging. Among Jews, this was an era in which the Zionist bifurcation of homeland and diaspora, with the attendant ideologies, created the context in which various writers struggled with defining the meaning of the past in order to imagine a future. Nahum Goldmann, remaining the quintessential insider/outsider, recognized ongoing contradictions within Zionism and sought to create frameworks that linked Israel with the diaspora without merger. Operating as president of the World Jewish Congress and from outside Israel, Goldmann felt free to analyze Zionism in its historical goals and limitations, to speak of the dangers that accompanied successes, and to question its ongoing viability. For Goldmann, disaffection among Israeli youth, assimilation of American Jews, and the loss of secular Jewish education all contributed to the importance of maintaining an active, substantive, and critical Jewish diaspora.[25]

Goldmann's roots in the intellectual world of secular European Jews generated a form of personal continuity that became evident in his efforts to transcend the historical and physical breaks that accompanied his development. Although he understood the growing differences—prewar and postwar—between the US and Israel, the USSR and the US Jewish populations, Goldmann argued for positions he believed would support an ongoing transnational Jewish people. The key elements, in his mind, were the strengthening of culture and education, along with efforts to prevent Israeli entanglement in Cold War alliances. For Goldmann, the Jewish collective required a distinctive cultural existence even while navigating interactions with multiple others.[26]

Goldmann was speaking during a time in which Israeli Jewish culture was very much in a formative stage and internal relationships among Jews were fraught with tensions. At the same time, Goldmann's analysis was supported by privileges that remained implicit. In Israel, the dominance of European Jews continued and the categories in which Goldmann conceptualized Jewish life were easily understood. Despite a measure of military and economic insecurity, this was an era in which statehood and American Jewish assimilation provided opportunities that dramatically contrasted with conditions only twenty years before. When Goldmann spoke of the need for education he did so in the context of existing institutions and resources. The peoplehood that he wanted to see continue was one in which Jewish life was distinctive yet buttressed by integration into one of European culture and American power. This vision was furthered by the outcome of Goldmann's earlier negotiations to ensure German reparations, which provided both material support and the basis for a relationship in which the responsibility for the destruction of European Jewish life was recognized.[27]

In Israel, however, other writers spoke from very different vantage points to offer alternative narratives about an Israeli Jewish culture that was in process of formation. S. Yizhar (Yizhar Smilansky) had written of the price and pain that accompanied Israel's experience in 1947/48. Writing from a soldier's point of view, describing the expulsion of Arab civilians through a lens that likened them to Jewish experiences in Eastern Europe, Yizhar placed the moral price of victory into discussion. In a time that allowed little doubt that the war had been unavoidable and defensive, the novel was read as a positive reflection of sensitivity. Less than twenty years later, the story was seen as dangerous to the nation.[28]

A writer less widely known, Jacqueline Kahanoff, brought to her observations of Israel in the fifties and sixties a cosmopolitan history very different from that of Nahum Goldmann. Kahanoff was born in Egypt to Jewish parents whose families originated in Iraq and Tunisia. It was a family well integrated into a Middle Eastern world that consisted of multiple cultural communities coexisting in an era of European dominance, with various hierarchies defining relationships. While sharing both knowledge of and respect for European languages as well as histories, Kahanoff chose to live in Israel beginning in 1954. There she wrote her stories, essays, and newspaper commentaries published largely in Hebrew. Particularly interesting to recent writers has been her cycle on the generation of Levantines, and her insistence that Israel could never be at peace until its leaders and population understood that they existed in the Middle East.[29] She "presented the Israeli cultural elite with a radical theory of cultural identity that was appealing to all Israeli communities equally: Levantinism."[30] She "conceived of Levantinism as a uniquely multilayered cultural matrix."[31] Her articles on "The Levantine Generation" were published in the journal *Keshet* in 1959.

Kahanoff came from a family that understood the national liberation movements of North Africa in particular. In one essay, she describes their relationships with the Tunisians as well as a personal effort to help an Algerian that they knew under a pseudonym, but eventually learned was the FLN leader Ahmed Ben Bella.[32] Personal experiences, as well as those of her family, enabled Kahanoff to see the Israeli world as one that internalized aspects of the colonial experience in its response to Mizrahi Jews (Jews from the Muslim world). What she failed to recognize, at least in her writings, was the ways in which the relationship of Israeli Jews to Arabs constituted a deeper, more challenging divide that could be defined in the colonial terms that were self-evident to Palestinian Arabs.

The interpretations of Goldmann and Kahanoff were examples of narratives offered in the context of an unfinished Zionist/Israeli project. Their engagement contrasts sharply with the various shades of distance adopted by exiled European Jewish intellectuals who remained in the US, Great Britain, or, for some, had returned to France or Germany. Their constructions of Jewish identity, history, and the future remained rooted in adaptations to rupture as well as skepticism toward nationalism.

Hannah Arendt largely left behind any writing on Jewish concerns after the controversy over her report on the Eichmann trial. With Israel taking shape as an arena for Jewish politics—one she was not a part of—her writing, teaching, and political engagement continued to address a larger world of European and American concerns. As Jews now had political recognition as well as safety, Arendt's need to participate in the world of specifically Jewish politics lessened. At the same time, her own history continued to shape her understandings, and her reactions to school integration in the South, for example, was formed by projecting her own, very different experiences as a member of a devalued minority.[33]

It was precisely as thinkers that European Jews, who had escaped the European wartime destruction, continued to make their contributions to analyzing and understanding the ruptures of their own lives (and those of their communities) in contexts that saw their own identities as multiple—linguistically, educationally, historically. Viewing their Jewishness from varying vantage points and with different political consequences, these intellectuals represented the lives of destroyed communities as well as failed promises. After World War II Jewish intellectuals wrestled with their own complex experiences on the borderline between colonizer and colonized.

Certain individuals, whose personal and intellectual histories were formed within Europe prior to Nazi control, came to embody a counter-narrative, either through their own survival or through the survival of their writings. Specifically, it was a counternarrative of the relationship between Jewish collective existence and, on the one hand, internal argument about the meaning of that existence, and, on the other, interaction with non-Jews both as majorities and as minorities. In the modern history of Jews in Europe the relationship between collective memory and historical understanding can clearly be seen as one of complex reciprocity.

A collective national memory as consciously constructed to master history—to deal among other things with the redefinitions of surrounding collectivities—took on a life of its own. Historical understanding, in turn, has come to be challenged by the replacement of conscious construction with the assumption of national life by significant sections of the collective. The subtheme of relationship between collective memory and territoriality thus becomes critical in determining claims of legitimacy for particular historical understandings.[34]

Precisely the success of Zionism, both in its ideological and in its experiential physical forms, has given rise to profound recent revisions in the memory of collective experience. Thus, in recent Israeli historiography there is a growing critical effort to grapple with a history of Arab-Jewish relations—both in the creation of a Jewish state with clear self-definition as apart and in the internal construction of an Israeli society dominated by groups of European/American origin—that integrates memories earlier unspoken. It is no accident that this effort has simultaneously focused on the origins of the state of Israel and on the Holocaust.[35]

Efforts to understand modern Jewish history, in a way that places the Holocaust and the state of Israel in its center, have served a critical role in the construction of a collective national memory for American and Israeli Jews. This selective emphasis, while appearing to derive from efforts to master an overwhelmingly painful past, can be viewed as part of the effort to create a new community that could not yet permit itself to know publicly the costs involved. The relative significance of the need for survival, as opposed to the drive for dominance involved in this process, might be variously understood depending on one's perspective. What appears less uncertain is that what is seen at one level as the retrieval and integration of traumatic memory can be seen at another as displacement from the actual experiences of many of those involved in the remembering. From this point of view the very real differences in relationship to European Jewish experience in the twentieth century were profound between those Jews who chose to leave Europe for an alternative future and those whose leaving was pervaded by the loss of the future that they expected to have.

The "memory" of the Holocaust in Israel was necessarily colored not only by the distance of the Jewish settlement in Palestine from its occurrence, but by its role in suppressing that memory of the immediate aftermath in the war of independence, which was experienced memory. Thus, it is possible to argue both that the working through of one set of memories diverted from acknowledgment of the other, and that indeed one necessarily prepared the way for the other. In a somewhat different but related manner, the "memory" of the Holocaust for American Jews appeared to re-create a link to their own premigration history, while still avoiding a confrontation with the ambivalence and rejection that had characterized their experienced memories of life in Europe.

Tom Segev, writing on Israelis and the Holocaust, argues that, in the aftermath of the war, survivors and Israelis arrived at an "ideological-emotional compact" that united them during 1948. This compact was based on an assumption that "the rest of the world—literally every nation—was hostile and had done nothing to save the Jews during the Holocaust" and that "the less everybody talked about the Holocaust, the better." Thus, according to Segev, a silence was born.[36] In an essay on "Trauma and Transference," historian Saul Friedlander notes that, particularly in the United States, fifteen or twenty years of "latency" followed the war "in regard to talking or writing about the Shoah'"[37] In both cases, the silence was followed by an increasingly intense focus on public remembering. Many cite the 1961 Eichmann trial in Jerusalem as a turning point in this process.

The writings of Hannah Arendt, whose name has become attached for better or worse to the Eichmann trial, and the history of the controversy attached to some of those writings are among the best-known evidence for the persistence of alternative narratives. Although not alone, Arendt's oppositional stance within the Zionist movement is among the clearest examples of the way in which European Jewish émigrés expressed the duality of profound awareness that they were a part of a collective, and yet resisted belonging to any collective.[38] Arendt's insistence on the problematic nature of the relationship between the collective and history, the demand for the intervention of critical, moral judgment by the individual, maintained a precarious balance of engagement with detachment. This balance was evident in the evolution and form of her writing over time; from the thirties onward Arendt participated in Zionist politics, but the nature of her involvement changed significantly after the establishment of the state of Israel.[39]

It was only with the controversy over her report on the Eichmann trial (published as *Eichmann in Jerusalem* in 1963), however, that she was made aware of the degree to which her effort to remain attached while protecting her status as an observer would make her vulnerable—not simply to intellectual or political criticism but to personal attack and charges of betrayal that interpreted her position as that of an outsider.

This reaction highlights a central paradox: Arendt's insistence on the need for resistance to what she viewed as the danger of collective identity was never separated from the importance of finding an acceptable relationship to it. Her response to the controversy over her book appears to reveal her own difficulty integrating the emotional drive to understand personal experience with the intellectual, rational search for historical meaning.[40]

In the aftermath of the trial, Arendt found that a number of those who had shared aspects of her history and culture reacted with anger as well as pain to her report. The best-known example lies in the published exchange of letters with Gershom Scholem, which appeared in *Encounter* magazine in 1963.[41] Scholem's public denunciation was particularly difficult for Arendt in view of their earlier cordial relationship. At the same time, she found that others from whose writings she wished to separate herself supported her. For example, Arendt's response to being connected with Bruno Bettelheim appears to have been ambivalent at best.[42] The controversy, which was in part at least about significant differences within the European Jewish community during the war, now became the occasion to make evident the continuing fragmentation among Jews and, with it, a renewed effort to impose unity.

From our point of view, over fifty years later, this event affords the opportunity to explore the absence of collective memory, the insistence on the fragmentation of memory, as the object of historical understanding. Friedlander talks about the ongoing failure, in the face of more and more information, to incorporate the Holocaust into "any compelling framework of meaning."[43] In another essay, he links the nonintegration to the discontinuities (formulated by Lawrence Langer) inherent in the disparity between an ordinary memory, which reconstructs realities surrounding the Holocaust, and the deep memory that survivors carry but cannot integrate.[44] George Steiner writes about his own being "out of touch with his own generation" as an émigré whose origins were the same as those who did not survive, even if he himself left Europe before the war.[45] His writings and others point to the continuing wish to understand unbearably painful ambiguities and confusions, while resisting at all cost the sacrifice of complex experiences that sabotages all such efforts.

The tension between experience and meaning unfolds in a series of relationships with the émigré intellectuals at their center. The Nazi regime utilized Jews as the vehicle for its own effort to master history. Intellectuals such as Arendt, in turn, insisted all the more on their own drive to make meaning, to attribute an active impact on history to that capacity to perceive accurately the political forces at work. And yet it is precisely the failure to do so with regard to the Zionist movement and the development of the state of Israel that reveals the degree to which Arendt's vision could not help but be determined by her own evolution—that which she acknowledged and that which remained hidden.

The extraordinary tragedy of that community of which Arendt was a member (which Steiner describes as defined by its secular humanism) was located in the effort at once to live within history and outside it. Their European secular education, including the philosophical training of some (such as Arendt), had taken place during a particular moment of Western dominance that contributed to the illusion that thought could provide a mastery without guilt. For European Jewish émigrés it was possible to carry this torch as if it were the authentic legacy of a culture gone sour. Arendt indeed understood many of the political forces at work in Zionism and the state of Israel. What she could not tolerate was the subordination of historical explanation to the drive for survival, security, and revenge. To have done so might have been to forfeit the only, fragile claim to control over destiny afforded by intellect, and to have had to contend with the potentially disorganizing impact of her own experience.[46]

In the individual, memory serves to constantly shape responses to the present, but the present also serves to determine the content of recalled memories. The individual is located within a set of relationships that contribute to the nature of those memories as well. Where the trauma of the past may prevent development in the present, lack of memory may also serve to prepare the way for its eventual return. Interpenetration of past and present helps shape the self-understanding that eventually creates the groundwork for conscious and unconscious anticipation of a future.

What we understand as collective memory shares with that of the individual in interrelating past with present, as well as serving to organize experience in hopes of better understanding. It may mean a shared memory of the collective, expressed in rituals, monuments, textbooks, or institutions, which perpetuates selected aspects of experience. In this sense, it is a clearly constructed phenomenon. It may, on the other hand, also mean the memory of experiences that bind individuals to the collective that is based less on the need to create a collective identity and more on the urge to give meaning to its history. In either case, collective memory presumes an "other" or "others" that do not share in its history. As in the case of the individual, memory simultaneously reinforces separate identity and creates a narrative of relationship to those who contribute to that identity while remaining outside of it. The creation of this narrative, with its own dynamics, supplies a way of understanding with the purpose of containing difference and avoiding vulnerability. When the acknowledgment of interdependence in itself threatens survival, then memory may be mobilized as a source of reassurance that continuity can be maintained in the face of isolation.

The European Jewish émigrés who were displaced by the Nazi victory could never again count on that continuity. Thus, memory and remembrance took on new significance; the maintenance of language and friendship embodied the drive to reconstruct relationships with a world beyond the individual. Personal feeling often remained carefully separated from the public statements, but the intensity of personal relationships was not unrelated to this division. The intellectual émigrés who insisted by their existence and decisions on the continuity of the individual nevertheless were characterized by a common belief in the importance of transcending individual existence through politics and culture. The individual's resistance took on significance in the context of relationship to a collective, not in its absence.[47]

During the war, physical distance did not yet threaten this construction and the émigrés' intimate connection to German/European culture could be maintained because its complexity remained known, while the degree to which Jewish life was decimated was not yet fully evident. In the aftermath of the war that intimacy created a difficult, painful dilemma that surfaced over and over again in the conflicts over collaboration, in the differences between public and private discourse, in the political support for a Jewish state, and in the personal decision to remain apart from it. Individually, the émigrés had to contend with the fact that they had been shaped irreversibly by their love and admiration for a world that was also the source of their deepest rage and hatred; to forget or rewrite that relationship was to lose touch with the sources of their own continuity. At the same time, the destruction of European Jewry altered that world beyond recognition and eliminated the context in which these intellectuals had developed their secular humanist views. There was no longer any one world in which they could express all aspects of themselves and feel understood.

Zionist and American Jewish readings of European Jewish history could now find overwhelming justification for their own choices—the emphasis on necessary separation, on the danger of interdependence in Europe, and the permanence of specifically European anti-Semitism.

These readings in turn strengthened the already existing drive to create a new collective, one based in significant measure on its definition of itself as different from the European Jewish communities, determined not to suffer as they had or ever to be as vulnerable. Necessarily eliminated from this picture was the degree to which both Israeli and American Jewish communal life drew and depended on its European origins in the creation of its collectivity, while simultaneously building it on the illusion that this could be done without incorporating those aspects of European interdependence that were being rejected.

It was precisely this victory for a particular reading of their history to which émigré intellectuals could not assent without losing all hope of recognition for their own experience. Yet they were caught in an unresolvable dilemma. Their life had taught them that politics is a daily accretion of evaluations and decisions; that survival requires will and choice in the face of the unknown; that the survival of some is at the expense of others; and that the survival of the individual does not automatically provide continuity. Survival only enhanced the need to justify, to utilize the past, to find a meaning that could once again reconnect the severed ties. In this search, Arendt was at odds with the Zionist insistence on inevitability, precisely because it appeared to erase the need to consider moral dilemmas and the meaning of survival as well as collective existence.[48] For European Jewish intellectuals such as Arendt the collective as created, shifting, and historically constructed was not in doubt. At the same time, however, the idiom in which the debate on Jewish history and politics took place, as well as the territory on which the history was now being lived, undermined Arendt's ability to succeed. The idiom was often one of the righteous against the evil, in which Arendt's efforts to challenge the drama as misleading faltered as much on her stance of detachment as on the substance of her position. This divide was in fact rooted in an inherent contradiction that she could not grasp. The understanding she sought to convey was based on a daily personal engagement, but that engagement had been disrupted, and the pain of that disruption had helped give rise to an altered understanding in which continuity had to be protected by resisting the replacement of earlier attachments by new ones. If the two (past and present) could not be linked, they could be maintained by remaining equidistant from both.

The debate about Eichmann and the Holocaust, however, took place on a territory in which a new collective entity had established roots, and the primary players in its unfolding were caught up precisely in that daily engagement to which Arendt no longer had access. Moreover, their relationship to the trial was driven by the need to create a new collective memory—one that would serve the present and future by establishing a useful past, one that would eradicate the discontinuities and ambiguities, the fragmentation and loss, the possibility that geographical separation brought with it only the illusion of putting the past behind them. No wonder then that Arendt's hope of making meaningful her experience by transmission was so bitterly disappointed.

The twentieth century has given rise to repetitive experiences that appear designed not only to sabotage the quest for historical meaning but to undermine the belief in a meaning beyond survival itself. Disappointment in the illusion that memory in itself can free the present and future can too easily lead to discounting of its significance entirely. Recognition that memory itself is not simply the rediscovery of the past, but its reconstruction in the present similarly appears to undermine the possibility of ordering the relationship between past and present with a view to influencing the future. The experience of the modern European Jewish community—in Europe and in its extension to the US and Israel—has given rise to alternative narratives of the relationships between its members and those of other communities. The degree to which some of these narratives become dominant and suppress others can be understood as the outcome both of wishes to establish inevitability in history and the resistance to it.

Moving Toward a Dominant Narrative

Jewish life in the Western world was transformed during the twenty-two years following World War II. The experience of recognition for earlier suffering—whether through the acquisition of statehood, German reparations, Vatican II, or integration into American society—took various forms and had multiple impacts. Individual responses varied. The bittersweet aftermath could generate expectation of compensation; the rage of helplessness could remain or take new forms; recognition could help foster a new view of self and history as age-old victims requiring capacities to ensure that "never again" would history repeat itself.

Largely absent was recognition of the ways in which the activist Zionism of Herzl, itself based on an analysis of history and power, was gradually shifting to a Zionism of "no choice," not of normalization and integration in the world, but of regional isolation viewed as forced on a small country struggling to survive. As a new generation came to maturity, their focus was on managing rather than heroics, accepting the centrality of security and the military as a pragmatic need, continuing to look to Europe and the US for support as well as example. Among the dominant elite Kahanoff's views would not be responded to with favor.

In an environment newly acknowledging the particularity of Jewish suffering, Palestinian Arabs found little room for recognition of the losses they were experiencing and very limited avenues for empathetic response. Anger and determination, as well as humiliation, contributed to the emergence of Fatah and the Palestinian sections of the Arab National Movement. Existing ideological frameworks helped frame emerging politics; the drive for relief helped fuel the understanding that only the acquisition of power could help restore a measure of self-determination.

Beyond these developments, however, the sixties also gave rise to Palestinian creativity in writing or documentation. Mahmoud Darwish, known as a national poet, wrote "Identity Card" in 1963 while still resident in Israel. Its insistence on recognition as an Arab reflected the terminology in an Israel that sought to control and tame the Palestinian Arabs who had remained within its borders. Darwish was speaking at that time to Jewish authority as well as to his own community, demanding recognition as well as respect.[49] Darwish was to leave Israel in 1970 and to write with power about his losses, as well as the Palestinian exile more broadly, for the rest of his life. His words had fallen on deaf ears in Israel where he had made some efforts to function in the Communist Party; his imprisonment only further alienated him. After the war of 1967 and its outcome, Darwish left for Cairo and then Beirut.

Ghassan Kanafani, who was twelve years old when he became a refugee in 1948, intertwined a life of political activism with the transformation of Palestinian Arab experience in exile through writing. His stories and novels had the dual effect of recording the continuity of Palestinian Arab life and recognizing its redefinition as refugees became Palestinians in the Arab world. Kanafani, a Marxist and Popular Front for the Liberation of Palestine member, wrote in the fifties and sixties of those who struggled to survive despite the harshness of their lives in the Arab world.[50]

Fawaz Turki, a younger refugee whose experiences in a Lebanese refugee camp for Palestinians marked his early development, wrote of the bitterness, rage, and deprivation that he attributed to the Palestinian refugee experience in Lebanon; Palestinian refugees there were largely unwelcome and had little access to paths that would allow them to integrate. There was no possibility of achieving citizenship, work permits were scarce, and the camps were dependent on UNRWA for education, food, and emergency support.[51] These three writers, each with his own history and experience, wrestled with finding the means to articulate the effects of their losses, in language and format that transcended the personal, within varying fates of Palestinian Arab families in the aftermath of 1948. The results of writings such as these, as well as documentations and oral history, was to complement the simultaneously emerging political movements that sought to define Palestinians as both apart from and intrinsic to the larger Arab world.

Before 1967 these writers and others were formulating their unsettled existences in the context of Arab states emerging only gradually from a range of external controls, none of which fit the clearer and defining structures of colonialism that marked Algeria, for example. Nevertheless, for secular intellectuals among Palestinians as for the FLN, Marxism and revolution held promises that history would ultimately help to overcome injustices and bring recognition of painful losses as well as legitimate claims. Like many early Zionists, hope was based on mixed expectations of the need to mobilize and articulate while seeking support to act. The bipolarity of the Cold War, however, provided choices unavailable when Zionists were seeing their historical analysis seemingly fulfilled in the aftermath of World War II.

In the sixties, Palestinians were beginning their struggle while Algerians soon learned that gaining independence could not provide the unity or security that nationalism promised. While creating a new political entity with borders—physical and legal—that redefined community and legitimate belonging, independence also created a new context for ongoing competitions as well as the need to face a new reality. Defeat of French colonial control and the exodus of French settlers along with those who were identified with them (Harkis, Jews) could not uproot the effects of a deep cultural penetration that was manifest in linguistic divides, among others. Through literature and history, cultural production by Algerians, and in particular those who wrote in French about Algeria, make clear the internalized struggles submerged by nationalist discourses.[52]

Michael Rothberg's discussion of multidirectional memory takes for its subject the ways in which coinciding developments, such as the emergence of Holocaust memory into public view and the Algerian struggle for decolonization, far from being coincidental, can in fact be viewed as constructing a different understanding of collective memory and history.[53]

Rather than placing various experiences of violence and victimization in competition with one another, he offers a more complex analysis in which the emergence of testimony to the Holocaust is placed in relationship to decolonization conflicts in France. Referring to this as multidirectional, Rothberg can suggest relationships that cross boundaries rather than insist on difference and uniqueness. Particularly relevant to our discussion is Rothberg's focus on literary and cinematic evidence showing the year 1961 as exemplary of this process, which is only evident in hindsight. While the Eichmann trial was ultimately linked to insistence on the uniqueness of the Holocaust, and Fanon's work underlined the particularity of Algerian experiences, Rothberg's lens can encompass both in ways that suggest mutuality of influence and construction.

Recently, a number of literary and cultural scholars, as well as historians, have drawn attention to the potential fruitfulness of placing aspects of Jewish identity in conversation with postcolonialism. Yet notably absent from such studies is the historical context in which the relationships between Jewish and postcolonial studies diverged, and then seemingly have newly converged for some. Consciousness of this context is critical to understanding the possibility for transcending boundaries that were the products of a specific time and arc. Earlier works that serve Rothberg as evidence are largely the product of years before 1967. In some cases, they became more visible in recent years. The timing is suggestive of a historical periodization that begins in 1967 and ends roughly in 2000.[54]

There are two axes along which to view these shifts. The first marks the ways in which Zionism as embodied in the state of Israel came to be identified with colonialism, particularly after the war of 1967 and solidification of the alliance between Israel and the US. The second assesses the ways in which Zionism and postcolonial nationalisms constrained recognition of cultural work that challenged dominant historical narratives.

It is striking in light of recent scholarship to consider the ways in which searches for home, and experiences of exile, are central to the narratives of all those being discussed. While intellectuals and writers used words—in stories, poems, essays, reflections, or otherwise—to work through painful experiences and conflicts, seeking meaning in the suffering, they also struggled with a time characterized by the construction of collectives out of groups with disparate life experiences and, often, cultures. Seeking to capture their time, they nevertheless stood apart from the majority, constituting a different form of minority, one that could survive without the rootedness a majority requires.

Before 1948, Zionists in particular adapted a long-standing religious system of belief to accommodate both the demands of European nationalisms and the fears of annihilation. A traditional narrative of exile and return thus emerged as an ideology in which diaspora life appears doomed or, in religious terms, moving toward return to a past home. In the sixties the creation of a collective Holocaust memory emphasized Jewish suffering and victimization. At the same time, however, something different was beginning to take shape. Jews in Israel and in the US were coming to feel very much at home as citizens in territories where recognition of historic anti-Semitism was gaining more attention; in addition, barriers to integration in the US were falling while in Israel the military gained strength in conventional weaponry and in Dimona a nuclear plant created the possibility of a far more serious deterrent power. In both the US and in Israel, Jewish leaders and institutions were working to achieve effective participation in a range of political settings. While some continued to identify Jewish identity with that of the outsider, others were increasingly comfortable identifying with the power of states and national collectivities.

Before the war of 1967 echoes of prewar Europe and the Holocaust intersected with recognitions of colonial repression and decolonization. Among Jewish and non-Jewish writers, the fluidity and contingency of movements to disentangle national cultures and to recapture historical continuity or authenticity could still coexist with recognition of the effects of state violence on multiple populations. This era came to an end in June 1967.

Part III

Making Meaning After Violence

Chapter 7

The War to End All Wars, 1965–1967

In 1965 the French sociologist Georges Friedmann published a book entitled *The End of the Jewish People?*[1] It was based on his visits to Israel in 1963 and 1964. Friedmann was a French citizen whose connection to his family's Jewish history was tenuous. As he relates in his preface, he had witnessed anti-Semitism in the Poland he visited in the thirties but it appears that he had little expectation of being threatened in France. It came as a shock when he was deprived of his teaching position after France was occupied by Nazi forces, but his ultimate response remained consistent with his identification as a Frenchman. Friedmann joined the Resistance, where he felt entirely accepted. Thus, Friedmann's observations of Israel must be understood as those of a European whose Jewishness was defined by external circumstances and experienced at some emotional distance. This vantage point helped define his perspective as that of an academic interested in social developments, in his findings, and the questions he was asking. These are spelled out in his preface, where he acknowledges the ways in which his observations came to be part of a new engagement with Judaism as it was being lived in the modern world. His first chapter then sets the stage for his observations of Israel as a transformative crucible.

Friedmann began with an interest in the social experiments that Israel represented. Throughout his study he recognizes that Israel is undergoing transitions at multiple levels. Kibbutz life is altered both by integration into a new state and the pull of a developing economy that undermines the egalitarian ideology of early Labor Zionists. In addition, the generational shifts from Yishuv to state give rise to a crisis that he understands as the outcome of success. As the generation of "pioneers" cedes to their children, Friedmann identifies the challenge of "what next?" Impressed as Friedmann is by Israeli accomplishments, he also understands the very real challenges emerging after 1948. Central to these is the Third World line that runs through the Israeli population, creating the significant differences and inequalities between immigrants from the Arab world and those who had come from Europe. Use of the term "Third World" makes clear the author's internationalist view, taking account of the context in which Israel was taking shape. Finally, Friedmann comments on the ways in which Israeli political and social structures are affected by linkage to Judaism.

What Friedmann saw throughout his experiences was the emergence of an Israeli nation that was distinct from Judaism and Jews in the diaspora. Central to this development was the complex relationship between American and Israeli Jews. He understood that for Ben-Gurion and those who subscribed to his definition of Zionism, it was not enough for Israel to be the "center" for Jews in the diaspora. Rather, there was a need for American Jews to immigrate and participate in a common project. "Thus the 'centrality' of Israel is a fundamental principle, closely linked to that of the 'unity of the Jewish people.' American Zionists admit that this double principle is not generally accepted by Jews in the United States, who might well point out, as Nahum Goldmann does, that it is not accepted by the new generations of *sabras* either."[2]

Friedmann recognized the ongoing impact of Israeli needs for American support while simultaneously seeing themselves as the only bulwark against the anti-Semitism that had strengthened the claims of Zionism. For the Israeli elite, the legitimacy of, and need for, their state rested on playing an ongoing historical role ensuring Jewish survival as well as unity. What Friedmann saw, however, was something different. "The 'Jewish people' is disappearing and giving place to the Israeli nation."[3] He recognized the ongoing role that anti-Semitism played in linking Israel with diaspora communities, generating continuing feelings of interdependence. At the same time, he pointed to diverging trajectories and therefore implicitly suggested that the focus on common danger, rather than a united project, was the more powerful force maintaining the unity of a historical Jewish people. "In the land of Palestine, in a sum-total of geographic, climatic, social, cultural and political conditions profoundly different from those that formed it, the Jewish personality is disintegrating. The 'Jewish people' is disappearing and giving place to the Israeli nation."[4] For Friedmann, there had been something that could be identified as a Jewish personality and it was clearly the product of historical conditions in Europe where

Zionism had originated. Thus, the irony of a "homecoming" to Palestine where Jews from the Middle East were being integrated with the European Zionist migration, which, in Friedmann's view, resulted in the creation of a distinctive Israeli nationality.

Friedmann wrote as a secular French citizen whose historical experience led him to believe that diaspora Jewishness depended on the sense of Jewish interdependence. "It is because of that sense and the name I bear that I, a citizen of France, who recognize no homeland but France, accept and will to the end of my days continue to accept my Jewishness as a fact of my life, without pride or provocation but also without the slightest embarrassment or shame."[5] This statement bears resemblance to those of Hannah Arendt and other secular European Jewish intellectuals.

Friedmann briefly noted current threats to Israel as well. Recognizing the effects of ongoing emphasis by the government, the press, and the radio on threats to Israeli security, he acknowledged the ways in which this reality acted as background to the developments he was studying. Noting the rhetoric of Arab states, he also recognized the recent development of a Palestinian movement aimed at national liberation and defeat of what it saw as Zionist imperialism.

Without minimizing the very real possibilities of new confrontations, he noted both the existence of internal differences with regard to efforts at negotiation and distortions in official Israeli narratives with regard to the origins of the Palestinian refugee population. Friedmann's critique was leveled at the wholesale denial of Israeli responsibility and the limitations to claims of Arab equality within Israel. At the same time, he believed that the "Jewish-Arab" conflict was not entirely without advantage to Israel where the possibilities of normalization and the "good life" might lead to the loss of an earlier spirit of mobilization and collective idealism. Reflecting ongoing preoccupations with Jewish survival and continuity, Friedmann mentioned the urgent plea of Nahum Goldmann to the second World Congress of Jewish Youth in Jerusalem, in which Goldmann urged Jews in the diaspora to resist conformity. Friedmann, in turn, claimed that the same plea might well be addressed to Jews of Israel to "put them on their guard against their conformism to western mass culture."[6] Rather than recognizing common challenges, however, Friedmann saw growing differences and an Israeli Jewish population that was harshly critical of diaspora Jews, seeing them as useful primarily to serve Israel.

Forty years later Tom Segev, Israeli historian and journalist, wrote of the period preceding the war of 1967.[7] Citing personal letters as primary sources from the period, he noted the strong identification that the dominant group of Ashkenazi Jews felt with the state. A continuing sense of collective identity helped fuel ongoing anger at the Germans and those, like Nahum Goldman, who voiced what were viewed as critical comments on the state, even when the statements attributed might well have been apocryphal.[8] Like Friedmann, Segev described the internal fractures that differentiated various ethnic groups of Jews whose relationship to the state was directly affected by their differing experiences of recognition and benefit. The recession that developed in 1966 only further accentuated these differences while forcing greater recognition from those most privileged of "the extent of their self-delusion, forcing them to recognize that Israeli reality was different from the pictures projected in Ascot cigarette ads, and less homogenously Ashkenazi. . . . And there were Israeli 'others' who were Arab or who lived on kibbutzim. These people lived different lives."[9]

Although Segev described elements of Israeli life that Friedmann had studied, there was a different tone to Segev's much lengthier study. In this work, the author recognized the emotional effects of divisions, the ways in which varying definitions of Jewish life and history colored relationships in a very young state. While Jacqueline Kahanoff wrote of a Levant that was valued for its tolerance and multiplicity, Segev saw the fears that European Jews had of dangers to Israeli culture from Levantinism, which represents a cosmopolitanism that is of the Middle East.[10] The new Jewish state contained many competing definitions of what it meant to be Jewish, and its mission to gather in the diaspora remained in tension with the need to depend precisely on American Jews, the largest of those diaspora communities that was developing its own strengths while being integrated into a very different whole.

Segev, like Friedman, understood the multiplicity of internal struggles that Israelis were dealing with in the sixties, but his perspective gave him the knowledge of outcomes that had been obscure at that time. Segev could note the skepticism of Ben-Gurion and other Israelis about the possibilities for minorities to achieve equal rights, whether Arabs in Israel or Jews in the US. But Segev also made clear the tension that was emerging as more Israelis left Israel and emigrated, many to the US, seeking individual satisfactions. Like Friedman, Segev also described the effects of an underlying contradiction generated by a Zionist ideology that accorded Israelis responsibility for world Jewry, while simultaneously deepening the divide between Israelis (or Hebrews)[11] and Jews. Friedman expected that decreasing anti-Semitism and danger might in fact erode the unity of a Jewish people. Segev was writing with the knowledge that these expectations had not materialized forty years later. Nevertheless, both conveyed recognition of the lively discussions with regard to fundamental elements of the now successful Zionist project to create a Jewish state.

Segev's descriptions of the years 1965–1967 were darker than anything that Friedman saw only two years before. Both saw the impact of generational change and the weakening of Zionism as an effective ideology. Segev lists the headlines of this period, reflecting a pessimism and moods of mourning or loss. Like Friedman he also notes the ways in which the US and American Jews were the object of ambivalent interest. While the fears of Levantinism were linked to the identification with European culture as superior, American power and material culture were exerting attractions and gradually altering an earlier collective ideal.

Friedman could only see the beginnings of other forces that were surrounding Israelis, however. Segev's hindsight and access to historical documents could incorporate the external context in which the Israeli-American relationship was being shaped. Among the most significant were, on the one hand, the emergence of a Palestinian guerrilla national movement and, on the other, a drive for deterrence via nuclear weapons status. As Israelis reacted to growing border threats in addition to economic challenges, the political transition from Ben-Gurion to Levi Eshkol in 1963 was also creating new strains on a political system in which identification with the state was colored by perception of the military as in many ways its embodiment.

Zionism arose in Europe to solve the "Jewish Question." This was a problem for nation-states and for Jews. In Western Europe, Jews could not redefine themselves as a collective to be integrated, and assimilation had provided neither safety nor survival. In Eastern Europe, multiple efforts to ensure the continuity and richness of Jewish culture, as well as Jewish life, eventually foundered on the powerful ideologies of communism and fascism combined with nationalisms that incorporated earlier anti-Semitisms. In the modern era, therefore, earlier strategies did not work as well and survival became cultural and political as well as physical. Relationships between Jews and the non-Jewish world were complex; Zionism, itself made up of varying definitions, offered one route to hope.

By the 1960s, the Jewish Question that Zionists had sought to solve no longer existed. European Jews had been largely annihilated and remnants irredeemably scarred. In the US and Israel, newer questions arose as to the nature of Jewish community and survival. In contrast to Europe, where being Jewish was largely not a matter of individual choice, in Israel and the US there was increasing opportunity for choices of identity as well as its meaning. At the same time, the world within which choices were being made was variously conceived as continuous with the European cultural heritages of migrants or as representing the "new Jew" in a new world, or both.

Both Segev and Friedmann recognized that before the war of 1967 Israelis were struggling with conflicts that threatened to undermine both domestic confidence and external support. The successes of a society seen by most Europeans and Americans as modern, progressive, egalitarian, democratic, and heroic in its survival relied on the marginalization of narratives telling the stories of recent life in the Middle East and North Africa, whether Arab or Jewish. It also relied on identification with a Western modernity that had to be separated from its history of colonialism and fascism.

By the mid-sixties, both Israeli Jews and the American Jewish community were facing internal divisions that mirrored to some extent the rapidly changing international structures in which colonialism and racial discrimination were actively fought. Within each, there were those who identified Jewish identity with opposition to racial hierarchies and oppressive colonial authorities, but there were also those who saw the new Jewish future as requiring physical power, competitive political position, and national/ethnic solidarity above all. Friedmann and Segev noted the developing interdependence of Israeli and American Jews while also recognizing the ambivalence of the relationship. Israelis looked increasingly to American Jews for support, but they also sought recognition of the role they felt they played for Jews everywhere. In this light, the fact that few American Jews were interested in immigrating, or in participating in the developing secular Hebrew culture, added to questions about who belonged in what community.

Michael Staub writes of American Jews in this era as also deeply divided.[12] As they increasingly felt secure and American, Jews responded to major events in a variety of ways. The civil rights movement attracted support but also challenged Jews to consider their own place and interests in a US that was expanding globally. While simultaneously reexamining their own history of discrimination, Jews responded to these challenges not with unity but with divisions that were class, education, age, and geographically based. How being Jewish affected political decisions was neither direct nor uniform, but competing views mobilized deep feelings.

Staub writes of ongoing debates about the "correct" stance Jews should adopt toward the fight for civil rights and integration. While Jewish liberalism has sometimes been assumed from the visible presence of many Jews in these movements, Staub shows the ways in which these subjects became arenas for disagreement about protecting Jewish interests and particularism. While Israeli Jews were concerned about physical survival, American Jews debated avenues to ward off feared versions of assimilation and loss of boundaries. At the same time, powerful spokesmen made an argument for defining Jews and Judaism based on differentiation from African Americans or others making historical claims for recognition. Where Jewish activists grounded their participation in the civil rights movement on definitions of a prophetic Judaism demanding social justice, an emerging conservative position viewed this as damaging to the particularism of Jewish history and culture. Thus, precisely as Jews were attaining status as white, there were significant divisions as to the desirability of identifying with the white majority, as opposed to maintaining the stance of outsiders whose perspective was that of critics able to see from that position, competing with other victims versus identifying with them.[13] Assimilation could be defined as being absorbed into the American majority, conforming with its middle-class, consumer values, or it could be defined as being swallowed up by universal causes that were not Jewish.

The historically negative view of assimilation could easily be weaponized as a way of excluding others as insufficiently Jewish. However it was defined, the fears and conflicts spoke of transformations that threatened to turn desirable accomplishments into new dangers. What then, some asked, would ensure survival? And survival for what?[14]

By 1966 these internal debates were shifting. No longer focused as much on civil rights, Americans (including Jews) were responding to the developing intervention in Vietnam. Put in the international context, disagreements within the American Jewish world were now taking on new meanings. As the Vietnam War expanded, with increasing casualties and conscription, the frameworks within which citizens responded were variable. Where some viewed the war in the Cold War context as legitimate containment of communism, others saw it as an attempt to destroy a national liberation movement, the outcome of a long, painful colonial history. The implications of these very different lenses further divided American Jews, by generation as well as political analysis. While the preponderance of American Jews continued to view themselves as a religious group—whatever its denomination—the American Jewish leadership was reshaping the arena of Jewish institutions in accordance with the possibilities now offered by the national and international worlds of politics.

As opposition to the war in Vietnam grew, this too became a location for debate about the role of Jewish students, activists, and intellectuals who joined others in defining the US role as an aggression fighting a legitimate national liberation movement. In fact, we now know that US presidents from Dwight Eisenhower to Richard Nixon as well as other military and political leaders were well aware that the war could not be won, and that the conflict needed diplomatic resolution. Yet they feared the consequences of acknowledging this reality publicly, continuing to label military action as essential to US interests.

The war took on meanings that led Americans to examine their own ideas about the legitimate use of force, inevitably linked to considerations of what the US as a state represented. For Americans who had experienced World War II as the epitome of a moral struggle, Vietnam brought a far more complex question and not one that was necessarily reassuring to those willing to examine it. Jewish Americans were largely no different in their reactions than other citizens. And yet there were those who began to make analogies that they hoped would change opposition to support. Anxiety about the future of Jewish life broadly was manifest in debates about the lessons of the Holocaust and the teachings of Judaism that had political implications. For some, these dictated support for others who were suffering, including Vietnamese and Palestinians. For others, there was alarm for Israel and fear that Jewish opposition to the war would undermine US support for that country. As a result, some Jewish leaders made the analogy between Jewish suffering and that of other national groups seeking self-determination, while others likened the Viet Cong to totalitarian regimes and equated them with Palestinians. Implicit in these discussions were views on how and why Jews in the US should express themselves politically.[15]

Viewing the US war in Vietnam through the prism of the Middle East and Israel inevitably created a bipolar framework that blurred significant differences. The fact that American Jews adopted these stances at a moment when Palestinian guerrilla groups had their own reasons to claim links to other national liberation movements contributed to the ways in which each perceived the other. Before June 1967, however, this coincidence of developments went largely unremarked. Palestinian life continued to be determined by the various state contexts in which it was lived, ranging from Jordan (which relied on American support) to Syria, which underwent multiple coups adhering to increasingly radical positions while reliant on Soviet patronage. Egypt, under Nasser, which controlled the Gaza Strip, claimed regional leadership underpinned by a Pan-Arab nationalism that could never function to create effective trans-state unity.

It was in this environment that Fatah, with Syrian support, began to make its presence felt after 1965, undertaking actions against or across the borders of Israel in hopes of provoking broader conflict to reclaim Palestinian land. Not less significant was the effort to mobilize Palestinians of the younger generation to overcome the shame of earlier loss and to identify with a specific Palestinian history.

In very different ways, Palestinian Arabs and Israeli Jews were continuing to wrestle with the image of older generations that they imagined had been passive victims of history, unable to resist or to stand up and fight for their own communal survival. Israeli Jews now had a well-armed and trained military but there were those who believed they needed nuclear capacity in order to deter the attacks that they expected in light of the unfinished war of 1948. Palestinians had been deeply disappointed with the failure of Arab states to protect them in that war, but the leaders of Fatah believed in their own abilities to use an altered international environment to win recognition as a legitimate national presence.

Historians can now disentangle the threads that resulted in the 1967 war, a war most agree was unwanted and unexpected at the moment of its occurrence. A number of recent books have examined the international, national, and regional dynamics that contributed in the end to the violence. While the record remains incomplete because some relevant archives are not yet accessible, it is clear that the unfinished outcome of war in 1949, the isolation of Israel in the region (along with the lack of contact between Arab and Jewish populations), and the competitive Cold War dynamics that fueled the buildup of arms throughout the region all generated ongoing expectations that war would come. In all the states ultimately involved, strengthening military capacity (which overshadowed ongoing political efforts and conversations) was linked to both the security of political power—independence and regime—as well as dependence on external supply.[16]

In the late fifties it was France, not the US, that had supplied Israel with equipment and furnished the means to create a nuclear reactor in Dimona. Viewing nuclear weapons capacity as a necessary deterrent for Israel, Ben-Gurion was a primary supporter of this development, which was known to relatively few and opposed by a significant number of those who were aware.[17] At the same time, preparations for a coming confrontation and the unfinished business of 1948—Palestinian refugees, undefined borders, the status of Jerusalem—continued to support the military as likely to be decisive. While political activists differed in their views of desirable solutions, regional militaries had to prepare for the possible uses of war and its outcomes, political as well as territorial. In Arab states, these entailed consideration of intra-Arab conflicts as well as the rhetorical commitments to eliminating Israel. In Israel, those who believed in political solutions or compromises had difficulty winning support in a society with substantial traumatized populations hungry for security. The ongoing Arab nationalist movement, in which the Palestine Question was a central vehicle for mobilization, fueled the fears of extinction for Israelis while maintaining Palestinian hopes of reversing the losses to Zionism that they experienced as having given rise to their own national extinction. The reality of power balances and imbalances could easily be obscured on both sides as a result. The emergence of the Palestine Liberation Organization (PLO) and Fatah only added to the perceptions of existential conflict on both sides. As tensions intensified, the likelihood and appeal of action in hopes of relief grew.

Despite the complicated network of conflicts that Arab states and Israel navigated before June 1967, there were also forces that acted to delay confrontation. The leaders of both Egypt and Israel, the two major military powers, were challenged by economic problems and domestic rivalries. In addition, multiple intra-Arab conflicts (including war in Yemen) contributed to regional instability and unpredictability. In these circumstances, the Cold War context further complicated military and political calculations. Where good relations with Egypt remained an objective for both the US and the USSR, this was a period in which US efforts remained largely unrewarded while Soviet military supplies, combined with anxiety about German missile scientists aiding Egypt, heightened Israeli concerns. In contrast, despite ongoing American concerns about the purposes of the nuclear plant in Dimona and the risks of closer ties with Israel, US-Israeli ties grew warmer once President Kennedy had been replaced by Lyndon Johnson.

By 1966/67 border incursions and retaliations generated more heated military confrontations. A new Syrian regime, moreover, supported actions that were met with escalating Israeli responses. While the question of who was the aggressor and who the defender has always been open to debate in the Arab-Israeli conflict, there was little question that the specific

Syrian-Israeli dimension of conflict was becoming more volatile. At the same time, it was clear that the Syrians alone did not have the capacity to fulfill their rhetorical goals. As a result, the pressure on Egypt's president, Gamal Abdel Nasser, leader of the radical Arab states, to act began to build. And yet the timing of the crisis when it came was unanticipated, unplanned, and managed largely with short-term goals for response. It was the three weeks from May 14 to June 5 that became critical in shaping the war that followed, the perceptions of its meaning, and the long-term effects on Palestinians and Israelis, Americans and Arabs, and the Middle East as a whole.

For the public that paid attention, the crisis began on May 14 when President Nasser put Egypt's armed forces on maximum alert and sent troops into the Sinai Peninsula. These actions were explained as necessary to protect Syria, which was, according to Soviet information and in light of ongoing border tensions, in danger of Israeli attack. Two days later, on May 16, President Nasser requested that U Thant, UN secretary-general, remove the UN Emergency Force from the Israel-Egypt border where they had acted as a peacekeeping force since the withdrawal of Israeli forces in the aftermath of the Sinai/Suez War of 1956. The UN Emergency Force had prevented direct engagement on that border, and U Thant's decision to heed the Egyptian request inevitably increased the possibility of war. Nasser's intentions remained unclear, however, and the initial steps could be viewed as efforts to strengthen his own regional credibility without requiring the outbreak of hostilities. It was only several days later that the likelihood of war escalated while the options for avoiding it decreased. When Egyptian troops took over Sharm el-Sheikh on May 21 and closed the Straits of Tiran to Israeli ships, as well as to ships bringing strategic goods to the port of Eilat, the crisis entered a full-blown stage. All the participants were aware that this action was considered a casus belli by Israel and that it was reversing agreements made in the aftermath of the withdrawal in 1957. Yet both Egyptian and Israeli authorities had reason to seek nonmilitary means to defuse the situation. Given the lack of normal diplomatic relations, however, communication tended to be based on inference, interpretation, and mediated interchange. The US and the USSR both had formal diplomatic representation in Israel and Egypt; neither had an interest in direct conflict, but both had significant patronage ties—the USSR with Syria and Egypt, the US with Israel.

While we do not have all the necessary information as to the full role and cause of Soviet interventions, we do know that initial suggestions that Israel was planning to attack Syria came from representatives of the USSR to Egyptian authorities. The Soviet Union had definite interests in strengthening Egyptian-Syrian military cooperation and in warding off the realization of Israeli threats in the form of a significant attack on Syria. Whether Soviet concern about developments in Dimona contributed to the USSR's actions cannot at this point be established with any certainty.

The US, which had in the past expressed concern about Israel's nuclear potential, was now deeply involved in the war in Vietnam, which was not going well. Despite a past understanding that Israel would view the closure of the Straits of Tiran as a casus belli and despite US commitments to free shipping, President Johnson did not find partners to challenge the Egyptian blockade. It quickly became clear that Johnson's stated support of Israel's position, as well as long-standing US commitments to the territorial integrity of states in the region, were unlikely to be translated into a political solution to the crisis.

By May 22, Nasser had made a public shift in explaining the reasons for Egyptian actions. Speeches on May 25 and 26 appealed to widespread Arab hopes for victory over Israel, the restoration of Palestinian rights, and the defeat of imperialist powers. Not long before, Nasser had cautioned against any premature confrontation with Israel and had hoped to contain Palestinian activism. His troops remained in Yemen fighting for what were labeled progressive forces against those viewed as reactionary, such as the Saudi monarchy. Yet, in his claim to lead a progressive Arab nationalism, Nasser was vulnerable to attack from both the right and the left in the region. His caution with regard to Israel generated provocations not only from Syria but also from Jordan, seeking to highlight the gap between promises and fulfillment. Stimulated by excited public response to mobilization, he shifted from a focus on defending Syria to promises to eliminate Israel. By May 26, other states were eager to participate in this promised battle against imperialism, with Algeria and Iraq among those sending troops.

In Israel, mobilization of military reserves had immediate and very different effects than those in the surrounding states. The Israel Defense Forces (IDF) had been constituted to be a nation in arms. For Jewish citizens, conscription was mandatory for both men and women, with active service followed by decades of service in the reserves. Beyond this shared reality of experience, in these early years of the state identification with the military was widespread, and trust in its functioning exceeded that granted to politicians. At the same time, it was precisely the structure of the IDF that contributed to its limitations in responding to Egyptian actions in 1967. As the government moved to mobilize reserves, there was general awareness that the country could not maintain this heightened state of readiness for an undefined period of time. Manpower that was being sent to the front was being taken out of the economy; mobilization had personal as well as national ramifications that would mount with time.

While Prime Minister Levi Eshkol was hoping that diplomatic efforts would bring relief and restoration of Israeli shipping, President Nasser was embarked on efforts to maximize the political gains of his initiatives. While Eshkol dealt with military leaders increasingly eager to act with a view to restoring their deterrent capacities, Nasser relied on his minister of defense, Abdel Hakim Amer, who expressed confidence in the capacity of the Egyptian military, whether in an offensive or in absorbing a first blow. And, in the very significant background, both Eshkol and Nasser consulted their superpower patrons with a view to ensuring the protection they feared might be necessary. President Johnson, wrestling not only with the war in Vietnam itself but also with growing public opposition, proved unable to organize a material challenge to the blockade. Yet his known sympathy for Israel as well as a final visit by the head of the Mossad, Meir Amit, to Washington conveyed acceptance of Israeli decision-making. In contrast, Soviet responses to Egyptian representatives, which had contributed to the initial mobilization, were finally firm in discouraging any attack. On both sides of the border, leaders were left to assess their positions without adequate information about the internal dynamics of their foes that would ultimately decide for war.

As tensions grew after May 22, publics on both sides of the conflict also began to play a role and to narrow the space for peaceful resolution. In the Arab world Nasser's bold moves and speeches aroused excited expectations, widespread admiration, and belief in success. In Cairo and Damascus demonstrators showed their enthusiasm; leaders in Algeria, Iraq, and Kuwait committed to sending troops to participate. Palestinians in many parts of the region believed that they would now have their land and lives restored. Nasser appeared to be the leader of all Arabs who could succeed and thus erase the humiliations of 1948, in addition to defeating that reminder of a painful imperialist past, Israel. On the surface, it seemed that the Arabs were united.

In Israel, this period of waiting with full mobilization that directly affected most families, and with sufficiently ready access to the gathering storm of emotional threats around them, led Israeli Jews to feel that a noose was tightening around them. Evoking memories of 1948 in those who had lived through that war (one that had been turned into a narrative of being encircled by hostile Arab states), Israelis experienced their situation as one of existential danger. Layered onto their memories, or stories, of 1948 were the testimonies that had emerged in the Eichmann trial of just seven years before. Here, the memories of participants in the pre-1948 Zionist project began to merge with those European Jewish survivors of the Holocaust to reinforce fears of annihilation, and to give realistic force to the rhetorical threats now spoken by Nasser as well as by Palestinians.

We know now that those who understood the realities of the military balance were aware that there was never an existential danger to Israel.[18] In the State Department documents of that time there is clear evidence of US assessments; more recent work supports the view that Soviet assessments were similar. What was realistically at issue in Israel as the crisis developed had to do with judgments of Egyptian intentions and the potential repercussions of a first strike, as opposed to reliance on diplomatic efforts to achieve resolution. US support was sought, but in contrast to Nasser's beliefs there was no expectation of American engagement. Obviously, the assumptions of Israeli victory could not predict what the price of military conflict would be in terms of casualties. For the military, increasingly, the concern was the price of inaction.[19]

By June 1, two developments effectively ensured war. On May 30, King Hussein of Jordan signed a treaty of common defense with the United Arab Republic. Jordanian forces were now to be under Egyptian command and Iraqi forces would be permitted to enter the country in support. The initial contest between Israel and Egypt had now been transformed into collective Arab action that seemed to override earlier divisions. Ahmad Shukeiri, head of the PLO, represented the official Palestinian voice, reinforcing the shift that had already taken place: this was to be a war to gain justice for Palestinians and end the imperialist Zionist project that had displaced them.

On the next day, June 1st, the Israeli government of Prime Minister Eshkol yielded to multiple pressures and became an all-party coalition with Moshe Dayan as minister of defense. Replacing Eshkol, who also held the post of defense minister and was seen as weak and hesitant, Dayan represented an admired military and the willingness to act. Four days later, the Israeli Air Force struck Egyptian airfields and destroyed its air force. Despite the long wait and the growing tensions, the strike came as a surprise; the devastating outcome was initially hidden from the public and even the Israeli public did not know at first what had happened.

As the next five days unfolded it was clear that the Israeli military was moving rapidly to occupy Gaza and the Sinai, take advantage of King Hussein's inability to remain on the sidelines by entering East Jerusalem and then taking the West Bank; finally, on the last day Dayan decided on conquering the Golan Heights from Syria. Despite concerns about Soviet intervention, the Israelis succeeded rapidly before accepting a final ceasefire with Syria. These conquests were the results of decisions made in the course of the fighting and without defined plans for the future. Some, like Jerusalem and the West Bank, contained places with significant resonance in Jewish history as well as in the lives of those who had lived in Palestine before 1948. Israel now controlled the entire territory that had constituted the Palestine mandate and, with it, restored the conflict between two national claims and two narratives of history. Nineteen years after the forced disentanglement between them, the difference in power was boldly illuminated and the one subjugated to the other, seeming to confirm the already longtime fears of an expansive, imperialist Zionism.

In the course of six days, Israeli Jews (and with them many American Jews as well) experienced a sudden, unexpected relief that quickly turned into a euphoric response that in turn gave rise to conflicting readings of Israel's position in the Middle East and a deepening dependence on the US. Rather than resulting in the desired use of territorial gains to ensure security, this war was followed by intensified conflict and an occupation that has over time endangered Israel from within. This set of developments has been intimately linked to the definition of US interests in the region.

On the surface, Israeli victory on June 11 signaled a dramatic transformation of the Middle East regional state system. Israel's geographical reach extended to the Suez Canal, Sharm al-Shaykh, the Jordan River, and the Golan. Prewar fears based on physical vulnerability (such as the narrow center of the country, civilian centers lying below the Golan, or the division of Jerusalem) seemed to have vanished miraculously. Once the war began and the IDF was as successful as it was, the impetus to take advantage of opportunities grew. This inclination did not end with the ceasefire. Despite earlier Israeli assurances that this was not a war of expansion, by June 27 the Israeli government declared the unification of Jerusalem. The power and effectiveness of the IDF could no longer be dismissed or attributed to Western powers. The reality of the state could not be denied, and to many Israelis the victory seemed to offer relief from fears of war and hopes for recognition and greater security. In the Arab world, there was shock at the defeats but also hope that, as in 1956/57, Israel would have to withdraw from the conquered territories.

But 1967 was not 1957, and the elements contributing to stabilization in 1957 were no longer in place. The UN Emergency Force had been removed rapidly at the start of the crisis and American commitments to safe passage through the Straits of Tiran had not held up under new conditions. War in 1967 was precipitated by failures to deal with the unsolved issues of war in 1947/48; the outcome of the war only deepened these, in addition to creating new layers of conflict while obscuring further the experiences of those directly affected.

The Israel-Arab conflict, which had since 1948 been largely defined as one between states, was now on its way to dividing into, on the one hand, conflict over territory between Israel and the surrounding states and, on the other hand, a continuation of what was articulated as an existential conflict between Israel and an emerging, nonstate Palestinian national movement.

Equally critical to the longer-term impact of the war was the ways in which it decisively shifted the international framework within which Israeli and Arab governments would now function. Until 1967, the US government operated to support the integrity of all states, including Israel, in the region. At the same time, the US had also put pressure on Israel both with regard to solving the refugee problem and the development of nuclear power. Until 1967, US supplies of arms to Israel were also limited, with France and Germany having been important supporters.

Although not immediately obvious, the US-Israel relationship was shifting to one in which Israeli military success helped consolidate the perception of mutual interests in the region. As soon as the war was over, this potential was evident in President Johnson's refusal to support UN pressure on Israel to withdraw from the occupied territories. Instead, Johnson agreed to Israel's insistence on using its victory to win political and security gains that would alter the map.

The United States was still heavily involved in the Vietnam War, with its divisive impact on the public and growing debate about its purpose as well as the chances of military success. As opposition grew, the challenges often took the form of questioning the legitimacy of US intervention and the suggestion that it was linked to imperialist aspirations rather than to the defense of American freedom and democracy. World War II had generated a heroic narrative of American power and benevolence. Vietnam and an American intervention that could be viewed as continuing the French colonial project now called the use of the American military based on conscription into question. The continuing policy of investing more troops and resources without any positive outcome was a significant backdrop to the American response in the Middle East in 1967.

The Israeli victory on the ground was exciting for many not only in Israel but also very much so for American Jews, whose pride derived from an intensified identification with the state of Israel. During the initial crisis, American Jews had participated by donating significant sums of money and there were those who volunteered in positions on the ground. American Jewish organizational life was gaining confidence in its ability to play a role in national politics and, again not coincidentally, the coloring of Jews as white was proceeding as well. This was therefore a time in which the relationship between American and Israeli Jews as communities was significantly supplemented by the movement of the relationship between Israel and the US in new directions. While the USSR broke off relations with Israel and President Charles de Gaulle in France condemned Israel's strike in terms that had a suspicion of anti-Semitism attached, the US government now supported Israel's refusal to withdraw from occupied territories without a comprehensive settlement of the conflict. This goal came to be embodied in Security Council Resolution 242, which was the product of lengthy negotiations and contained a deliberate ambiguity resulting in obfuscation of important differences among the states that formulated it.[20] Beyond the specifics of this framework, moreover, it became evident that the US would become the major supplier of the IDF and would come to see its relationship with Israel as strategically useful, now that Israel had become a dominant power in the region.

The irony of 1967 lies in the fact that military victory—intended to generate security and leverage for negotiations—resulted instead in increased threat (particularly in the form of Palestinian terrorist actions) and paralysis with regard to achieving a negotiated settlement. The paradox of its result is that gaining control of the West Bank, which some had sought since 1948, led not to a solution of the Israel-Palestine conflict but rather to its acquiring renewed salience and impact. In addition, the national unity seemingly created in the anticipation of conflict—with a national unity government being formed—came to be challenged by new divisions that were in part the outcome of the war's impact. While there were those who saw victory as proof of religious beliefs, which now fueled a more militant nationalism, others saw it as providing needed security and enhancing the status of the military's role. In contrast, there was also a minority of voices who supported alternative solutions and warned about the dangers of long-term occupation in territories with approximately a million Palestinians.[21]

Putting the war of 1967 into the context of two longer-term realities can also enhance understanding. Israel was a state with significant challenges in aligning its ideology with its citizenry. The state was defined as belonging to the Jewish people but made up of Jews with very different experiences, as well as of Palestinian Arabs who had been displaced in a variety of ways. It was also a state with no fixed written constitution because it was still very much a work in progress. Crucially, it was an Israeli state that did not recognize the existence of Israelis as nationals territorially based, sharing national culture and citizenship.

Jewish Israelis were categorized by Jewish religious/ethnic identity, and Arabs were separate even when holding citizenship rights. The resulting manifold contradictions of what before 1967 looked like part of an ongoing set of developments that were actively debated were largely suppressed after June 1967.

Israel was also a state that from the first required outside support from international powers. While Jewish migration to Palestine and the Zionist movement antedated World War I, it was the installation of the mandate with British governance that crucially lent international legitimacy to the project for a Jewish homeland, and ultimately of a state. Between 1948 and 1967, European sympathies for Israel were enhanced both by its self-definition as a socialist society that was transforming European Jews in the image of Western modernity and by a post-Holocaust commitment to restitution. After 1967, the primary support came from the US and was viewed in light of this increasingly strong relationship that came to color not only political and military developments but also cultural shifts. Although described often as based on common values and beliefs, the nature of the Israeli-American cooperation in many areas must be viewed in the context of the Cold War and American political, military, and strategic interests in the Middle East more broadly.[22]

In the aftermath of war, it seems possible to evaluate what was accurate in earlier analyses and what seems faulty or disproven. After World War II and the Holocaust, the political Zionist analysis of European history was much more widely accepted. Prophecies of doom for Jewish life in Europe and the need to leave it behind seemed to have been proven correct, while alternative projects for meaningful diaspora life appeared lost. In the aftermath of the War of 1967, it was inevitable that there would be reevaluations of the Pan-Arabism that had promised that unity would bring victory, and there would be redefinitions of Zionism to incorporate what seemed like new opportunities for recovering the historical Land of Israel.

In the US, too, the war had multiple effects. Where American Jews felt liberated from fear but also from stigma, suddenly proud to see Jewish power respected, Arabs in the US also reacted to the sudden, dramatic end of the war. In his memoir, *Out of Place*, Palestinian scholar Edward Said mentions an article he had written while a student at Princeton about the Suez/Sinai War from the Arab point of view. He reports that the article was published without provoking the kind of response that it might have had it appeared after 1967. For him, as for many others from the Arab world and in particular Palestinians, 1967 was another watershed. He describes his own transformation in the memoir as follows: "Until 1967 I succeeded in mentally dividing U.S. support for Israel from the fact of my being an American pursuing a career there and having Jewish friends and colleagues; . . . I all too uncomfortably remember the shock of the total Arab defeat of 1967."[23]

As a student Said was well aware that his understanding of Palestinian history incorporated a perspective that was foreign to most Americans. In response to a remark that the war of 1948 was six against one, he was shocked to discover the gap between his view of having Palestine stolen by Europeans and that of another student articulating the more common American perception. Yet it was not until 1967 that earlier dislocations and losses seem to have been subsumed by this newest one. "I was no longer the same person after 1967."[24]

For Said, 1967 proved to be transformative, professionally and personally. Yet his subsequent work might not have evoked the powerful resonances and creative interchanges had it not been for the fact that others were also increasingly aware of the ways in which the expansiveness of American interests were built upon decolonization in many parts of the world. Said's work contributed in particular to the newly emerging literature and scholarship dealing with the Middle East. And Middle East studies, one of numerous university area studies fields that also reflected the global expansion of US interests, now developed in ways that were intertwined with the changing world.

Just as earlier wars legitimized particular narratives and contributed to suppressing others, the war of 1967 provided distinctive support to the views of those who had understood Zionism as a colonizing project tied to imperial interests and inherently expansionist. Where the period from 1948 to 1967 was one rife with competing views and alternative perceptions of both Israel and Zionism, and open to constantly changing realities, the War of 1967 signaled the beginning of an era that would redefine these terms and create increasing partisanship as well as polarization. In Israel as elsewhere the meaning of success and how it should be dealt with quickly made evident that assumptions that had governed the period before June 1967 had disappeared. In place of an emphasis on survival, recognition, and peace as wished-for outcomes, the war was quickly followed by altered definitions of security, competing proposals for the future of the West Bank, and a strengthened religious nationalism that could successfully link its settlement ambitions to the nostalgia of those with emotional ties to that area as belonging to their own histories. The immediate claim of a unified Jerusalem captured the beginning of these transformations.

The first year after the war brought contradictory developments and policies. At a meeting in Khartoum, the leaders of Arab states issued a statement that was easily interpreted as closing off opportunities for a negotiated resolution.[25] In that context, Jewish groups intent on settling in the occupied territories continued an earlier Zionist project of creating facts on the ground, whether legally supported or not. Despite American efforts to formulate a plan based on indirect negotiations between Israel and Egypt, Syria, or Jordan, there was little willingness in Israel to give up gains, and in the Arab world there was opposition to any territorial compromise or abandonment of Palestinian claims. Although there were Israelis and Americans who foresaw the danger of long-term occupation, this was far from the predominant mood, which continued to see the war as having brought relief, expansion, and economic benefits. At the same time the USSR as patron to Egypt and Syria provided substantial resupply of arms and had little interest in encouraging any agreements that would further undermine their interests. As a result of the ways in which the US and USSR continued to engage in their own rivalry, the Middle East as a whole and the Arab-Israeli region in particular remained a locus of significant emphasis on military preparedness as well as multiple rivalries.

Israeli and American attention to immediate challenges, as well as the formulation of political plans in the context of existing states, tended to minimize the centrality of Palestinians as a national group with its own particularity.[26] Viewing Fatah and eventually the PLO as terrorist groups, on the one hand, and the Palestinians living in the occupied territories as quiescent, on the other, there were only a few voices that spoke for the distinctive needs of this population. Even fewer trusted that the reincorporation of Palestinians into territory governed by Israel could lead to mutual recognition and formulas for peaceful coexistence. More, among Israelis, feared that becoming an occupying power would have destructive effects, political and moral, on their own state.

As June receded and control over territory neither prevented ongoing violence, including a war of attrition on the Egyptian border in addition to terrorist attacks, nor gave rise to policies based on confidence in the altered position of Israel in the region, political debates shifted in their terminology. In Israel the secular Zionist project was taken up by religious nationalists who saw it as having served to make way for their commitment to redeeming sacred land. At the same time, the Greater Land of Israel Movement, which advocated settlement of the occupied territories, included members of Labor and others on the left. By 1977, when the Likud Party displaced Labor, there was substantial support for the movement of settlers into Gaza and the West Bank. Another war in 1973 had destroyed any remaining euphoria; the emergence of an active, visible Palestinian national movement succeeded in staging dramatic terrorist attacks. Prime Minister Golda Meir, who succeeded Levi Eshkol in 1969, was famously quoted as saying that there were no Palestinians, and the American government joined the Israeli government in denying the PLO any legitimacy.[27] In Israel, there was room for debate as these years unfolded and Israelis had to deal with rapidly changing circumstances and their own cultural shifts.

In the US, however, these were years in which the discussions about Israel, the Palestinians, and the Arab-Israeli conflict were becoming more contentious. Jews who had experienced 1967 and then 1973 as incorporating them in an Israeli-American alliance were drawing new boundaries and creating new definitions of loyalty and betrayal.

Chapter 8

Timing and Defining

Too Many Cooks Spoil the Broth, 1967–1975

The June War, otherwise known as the Six-Day War, did not result in either peace or resolution of the problems created by the war of 1947–1949. Instead, it exacerbated some problems and created new ones. Palestinian refugees did not regain their homes, Arab nationalists gained neither political unity nor freedom from external interference in the region, and Israelis failed to achieve either formal recognition or regional integration. Despite Israeli euphoria and relief, as well as the perception of greater safety due to expansion and economic gains, the challenges of these successes were accompanied by the onset of a period in which military strength and victory led not to peace but rather to conflict on multiple fronts. Such developments in turn contributed to political divisions as well as diplomatic stalemates. Zionism as the basis of the state had been losing its mobilizing force in the years prior to war; now it took on new meanings both inside Israel and on the international stage.

The period from 1967 to 1973 was critical in opening boundaries, physical as well as theoretical. It was also a time in which multiple players sought to set the agenda for developments in the Arab-Israeli conflict as central to the Middle East. Tensions over who would control land and resources were intertwined with struggles over who would make political decisions and exercise power in the region. Both the US and the USSR now embraced client states in an expansion of Cold War confrontations. These developments, which included the fueling of an arms race, were consequential for all the states involved, as well as for the nonstate

Palestinian movement. While attention centered on maintaining a military equilibrium, the more profound effects were evident in economic priorities and technological competitions that altered the shape of the various states as well as the region. Understanding this period is thus complicated by the multiple players involved.

These would include an Israeli government reacting to the unexpected ease with which the IDF conquered substantial territory and thus altered military goals in the course of war. A political leadership already viewed as weak and indecisive was unprepared to recognize the possibilities (and limits) that became available in the aftermath. As fear gave way to euphoria and arrogance, a leadership molded by the Zionism of the prestate era failed to adjust to the evidence of its own power as well as the responsibilities it now held.

A Palestinian national movement barely taking shape prior to the war emerged to offer alternatives to the Pan-Arabism and Arab states that had been so badly defeated. Fatah and other guerrilla groups mobilized around an armed struggle against what they saw as Israeli occupation of Palestinian land, making no distinction between 1948 and 1967. Within a short time, Fatah's leader, Yasir Arafat, also became president of the PLO, now clearly claiming to represent the Palestinian people. Overall, Palestinian activists worked to organize their national claims in a way that mobilized their own population and strived for recognition on the world stage.

The Arab states that bordered Israel and took part in the war—Egypt, Jordan, and Syria—were forced to deal with a new reality. Loss of substantial territory removed the possibility of supporting Palestinian claims rhetorically while focusing on domestic political interests or regional ambitions. Instead, each state government now had to define its own path to removing Israeli occupation and navigating more fully the engaged international forces.

The UN had passed Resolution 242 in November 1967. The resolution provided for withdrawal of Israeli forces from territories occupied in the war, but it did not specify which territories and its call for a just settlement of the refugee problem did not recognize Palestinian claims. This resolution was the outcome of negotiations among the Security Council powers and continued to address the conflict as one between states. Its deliberate ambiguity in the call for withdrawal from occupied territories was intended to bridge differences. The ceasefire that ended the fighting in June was followed by a period in which differences as to what was to come next surfaced, not only among the combatants but crucially also in the international arena. As a result, the resolution that was finally passed contained key ambiguities. It could pass primarily because it was open to multiple conflicting interpretations while still formulating the principle that became "land for peace."

The US and the USSR supported the resolution but were at odds with regard to final status goals. The war had resulted in the severing of diplomatic ties between the USSR and Israel as well as between Egypt and the US. In contrast to 1956, the US government now supported Israeli unwillingness to withdraw from conquered territory without gaining recognition as well as what they were to define as secure borders. The USSR responded to the losses its client states had experienced by providing arms to replace those that had been lost. In both the US and the USSR, the aftermath of the war was viewed through a global lens.

A substantial literature has been devoted to developments from the war in 1967 through the war in 1973. Initial reactions on all sides have been followed over time by memoirs, historical accounts, publication of documents, and political analysis. Given the variety of interests and responses, the literature has come to include studies of military strategy and action, political decision-making, cultural transformations, and leadership responsibility. On a broader scale as well, there have been studies in international relations and global developments. Less explored, however, are the effects of multiple frameworks defining the visions of those involved. These perceptions in turn helped redefine goals and actions, identity and morality. Most importantly they served to include as well as exclude those considered legitimate or illegitimate participants in the region.[1]

In the prestate period, the leaderships of both the Zionist movement and the Palestinian Arab community had largely addressed themselves to Great Britain as holder of the mandate. After 1948, European states continued to play roles that made them the focus of Israeli/Jewish and Arab/Palestinian hopes, wishes, and anger. Despite the fact that the US had already sought largely to replace France and Britain as imperial powers in the Middle East, it was not until after the war of 1967 that the triangle decisively shifted once again. With European states largely playing more peripheral roles in a decolonizing world, the US and the USSR now competed actively for power in the Middle East. Inevitably, then, they became the focus of hopes and fears in the region.

Immediate Views and Concerns

Israeli responses to victory ranged across a spectrum of emotions. Euphoria and relief were immediate, releasing tensions that had built up over preceding weeks. Excitement mixed with pride, welcoming the rapidity of IDF success as well as the relatively small price paid in deaths. Conquest of Jerusalem carried its own symbolic weight, whether for the secular population that had experienced the divided city since 1948, or for the religious for whom it was a sign of divine support. In a country in which the military was identified with the nation and military service was close to universal, there were few families that did not have an intimate connection to the ways in which the war had transformed those who fought.

Yet the Israeli population was made up of many different communities and the conquests affected some more than others. For individuals who had lived in pre-1948 Palestine, the conquests of 1967 appeared to restore an access (particularly to Jerusalem and the West Bank) that they had lost. Whether that possibility was understood in religious terms or in definitions of security or in the reawakened emotional connections, it meant that the future of historical Palestine was now in the hands of just one of its communities. In less than a week, the outcomes of 1948/49 were potentially again open to debate.

The vast majority of Israelis knew of a Palestinian Arab population that had lived in the territory that they now inhabited. They were aware of Arab refugees who had been displaced and they were familiar with the "Israeli Arabs" who were citizens and yet clearly not equals. They knew too of militants who crossed borders and perpetrated attacks prior to the war in 1967. What most did not yet recognize was the transformative effect of 1967 on Palestinian Arabs in particular.

In the immediate aftermath of the war and ceasefire, the Israeli public was happy to travel into Jerusalem and the West Bank, to shop and revisit with little awareness of their impact as representatives of conquest. Others focused on plans to re-create earlier settlements and "return" to locations of historical meaning without considering the political implications of acting on these impulses. Very rapidly, the acquisitions of land that had been beyond the armistice lines accepted as a border now reverted to contested territory in which settlement could, as during the mandate, create facts on the ground.

In the government and among political or military leaders, however, there were those who understood that they were now responsible for a large Palestinian Arab population and had to assess competing priorities. While some proposed the option of working with local Palestinian leaders to develop an autonomous entity, understanding that they were facing the relatively new phenomenon of an organized, activist Palestinian nationalist movement, the value of pursuing such a policy was quickly submerged in the drive to ensure control over territory now defined as necessary for national security, when it was not held to be a sacred Jewish heritage.[2]

The policy of the Israeli government could soon be defined by Dayan's statement of waiting for a call from Arab states and direct negotiations, combined not long after with Golda Meir's deciding not to decide.[3] In the first flush of victory there was fear of international pressure to withdraw, but little focus on the longer-term implications of Israeli power for others in the region. Most important in the long run was the absence of any clearly defined proposal for a diplomatic resolution to the conflict.

Viewing the war at a distance, most American Jews reacted to its end with wholehearted pride and excitement. American reporting reflected public identification with Israelis and uncritical acceptance of a black and white narrative with Arabs perceived as the aggressors. In contrast to the news from Vietnam, this was experienced as a rapid and just end to dangerous conflict. Zionist American Jews had a history of denying any possible contradiction between their identity as Americans with commitment to American political values and their Zionist Jewish support for Israel that did not necessitate physical movement. As a much larger segment of American Jews came to identify with Israel after 1967, there was greater need to avoid any potential contradictions.[4]

Despite this dominant narrative, however, there were voices offering more nuanced responses. In the US, moreover, immigrants from various Arab states had to grapple with their own reactions to a war that was making visible the connections between Americans and Israelis, while contributing further to the lack of Arab American presence in the public discourse. The establishment of the Association for Arab American Graduates in 1967 was one of many indicators that the Arab-Israeli conflict was coming to the US in new ways.[5]

The war had increased the number and nature of stakeholders in the conflict that had been defined as between Arab states and Israel. The shock of a ceasefire that created new borders (ostensibly temporary but without steps to alter them) generated no clear path to any resolution. A war that began with Israeli assertions of acting in self-defense and not with any intent to expand ended with quick assertion that Jerusalem would remain united. Soon after there were statements that made clear official Israeli conditions for negotiations, which included expectations of altering borders as well as insistence on face-to-face negotiations (which were viewed as conferring legitimacy on the state) and final peace treaties. These positions were predicated on assumptions that time was on the Israeli side and that there was no likelihood of war for quite a long time.[6]

The Israeli positions were also the product of an American stance that supported the view that, unlike the situation during the Suez crisis in 1956, there was no reason to force withdrawal until the situation yielded political results. The immediate diplomatic breaks in relationships—Israel and the USSR, Egypt and the US—made evident a new constellation in which each superpower was clearly becoming a participant in its own direct interests and hoping to use the opportunity to strengthen its own position.

Immediate Aftermath, 1967–1970

In Israel, according to Shlomo Ben Ami, the "orgy of political drunkenness and military triumphalism" that followed victory blinded the leadership to the real opportunities now available, preventing the formulation of meaningful diplomatic proposals.[7] A process of mythmaking contributed, according to scholar Dalia Nur-Gavrieli, to the prevention of "an open debate regarding the real costs of war, supported rejection of peace initiatives and an ongoing situation of 'No peace-no war.'"[8] In the early years after the war, Jewish Israelis lived a paradox—feeling safe from war, and yet maintaining a long familiar underlying vulnerability that stood in the way of acting on their proven military power to take the risk of trusting a process of uncertain negotiation with those they had defeated and humiliated. The most recent government efforts to generate an Israeli identification with diaspora Jewish history through Holocaust education combined with the 1967 prewar anxieties to underline the perception of a non-Jewish world as inherently unreliable and an Arab world impervious to change in its enmity.[9] At the same time, somewhat in contradiction, this period saw the beginning of a new, developing reliance on the US. Despite disagreements that developed over various UN and US plans to implement UN Resolution 242, the Israeli government continued to focus on maintaining military superiority and deterrence while the American government became a primary provider of the arms required.[10]

Internally in Israel, competing groups represented various ideas as to what kind of state would best exemplify the Zionist project under very new circumstances. Messianic ideas vied with the pragmatic, beliefs in democracy and inclusiveness vied with insistence on Jewish survival as paramount. The political environment enabled those who chose to act, beginning a settlement project that was to grow over the years. The same environment limited the impact of voices that called for recognition of alternative possibilities opened up by victory but which required a variety of risks. As the status quo seemed comfortable and there appeared to be little danger of a new war, it became easier to react against proposed resolutions that required compromises than to hold on to positions generated in a different era. Although political discussion continued to be vibrant, the ongoing perception of environmental danger inhibited full recognition of choices being made, not only in actions undertaken but as importantly in the lack of initiatives. The war had produced far more powerful feelings of Jewish unity that crossed borders and enhanced the reluctance to explore paths that might make differences more visible.

Given these conditions, the Israeli government headed by Golda Meir after the death of Levi Eshkol in 1969 was much more focused on gaining American support in the form of arms as well as diplomacy than on exploring or exploiting the differences between Arab state interests and the Palestinian movement. This orientation could only be strengthened by the development, on the one hand, of the War of Attrition with Egypt and, on the other, of multiple attacks undertaken by Palestinian activists. Both served to support the Israeli narrative of defense, the need for deterrence, and pessimism about any negotiated settlement.[11]

In 1970, disagreement between Golda Meir and Nahum Goldmann was indicative of the ways in which two individuals who had played major roles in the Zionist movement were now signaling much broader shifts as they each sought to maintain personal power. Goldmann, now president of the World Jewish Congress, operated as a cosmopolitan diplomat in the European, American, and occasionally Israeli worlds that he inhabited. His perspective, however, continued to be marked by a commitment to the importance of the Jewish diaspora and by a capacity to engage with multiple leaders, not in any way limited to the Jewish world. His Zionism, far from being delimited by a national border or identity, was rooted in a culture that historically transcended political divisions. Golda Meir, in direct contrast, had been shaped by her early years in the US, which she used very effectively in her later communications with Americans, and by the Labor Zionist movement deeply rooted in the provincialism of Yishuv culture. While neither one had particular knowledge of or connection with the Arab Middle East, their outlooks on this subject were in large part determined by, on the one hand, Golda's fears and underlying mistrust while, on the other, Goldmann's self-confidence or perhaps arrogance in navigating the world.

As prime minister, Golda Meir was immersed in the daily requirements of governance while also managing a cabinet of national unity consisting of parties with historically divergent views on the state and its policies. She claimed that her goal was peace and that she was willing to go anywhere to attain this outcome. Her definition of this policy, however, included insistence on direct negotiations with Arab leaders without any Israeli prior indication of a willingness to withdraw from the territories conquered during the war. While this position had the advantage of seeming logical to general publics in the US with little understanding of the conflict, it was in fact a policy that protected the status quo that was now viewed as in Israel's interest.

In March 1969 the War of Attrition on the border with Egypt provided an ongoing reminder that military victory did not result in peace and its absence continued to exact a price. At the same time, Palestinian guerrilla actions called attention to a movement asserting a direct challenge to Israeli national legitimacy by providing an alternative narrative of its history. The PLO, now headed by Yasir Arafat of Fatah, pursued a seat at the table of any effort to resolve the Arab-Israeli conflict. Having conquered all of what had been mandatory Palestine, Israeli leaders were now faced with resurgence of the unfinished business from 1948.

This regional situation could easily be interpreted in contradictory ways. On the one hand, in the context of continuity, ongoing violence reinforced the need for military strength as well as a focus on arms and vigilance. All could readily be linked to the idea that there was no choice involved nor was there any "partner for peace." At the same time, a competing interpretation—seeing June 1967 as altering earlier balances decisively—could reassess the same events in a different framework. Such a perspective provided more room to recognize significant differences between Arab states as well as between those states and the PLO. Analyzing those differences, and including confidence in Israeli military power, opened up questions as to the benefits of formulating Israeli initiatives as well as the longer-term advantages of the risks involved.

These differences were clearly evident in what came to be known as the Goldmann Affair. [12] For our purposes many of the details and ambiguities of this incident are largely irrelevant. The outline consists of the following developments: As a man with considerable diplomatic experience and a history of leadership in Jewish as well as Zionist settings, Nahum Goldmann had been seeking a way to meet President Gamal Abdel Nasser off and on since the mid-1950s. In 1969, his contacts with President Josip Broz Tito of Yugoslavia generated the possibility of success in this effort. As a result of preliminary contact with an Egyptian envoy, Goldmann traveled to Jerusalem in order to notify the prime minister and to seek her agreement to his acting on this invitation to meet with Nasser. For a variety of reasons, the prime minister refused to take personal responsibility for the effort and, instead, brought the request to her cabinet. It was clear to both Meir and Goldmann that this action would result in a denial of his initiative.

In the aftermath of the cabinet decision and the resulting publicity, several developments made clear that Goldmann's initiative was linked to his effort to precipitate debate about Israeli foreign policymaking. An article of his was published *in Foreign Policy* during this time, as was a series of articles in *Ha'aretz*.[13] In these forums, Goldmann articulated views that challenged the assumptions of Israeli policy as well as the value of the state as it had taken shape. His argument was based on a view of Zionism as necessary for Jewish cultural survival in addition to its function for Jews in need of refuge. It was also based on a reading of world politics that was extremely pessimistic about the future of a small state that could not integrate itself into the region of its location, but more optimistic about the possibility that it could gain international security under particular circumstances. In his mind, these could be created with the proposal to neutralize Israel in the Cold War as well as to limit any arms race.

Responses to Goldmann's initiative took a number of forms. The prime minister reacted to his efforts with the suggestion that he move to Israel, which presumably would give him the legitimacy to express his views. At the same time, she saw him as no longer a Zionist. Among the public, and in particular some of the youth, there was initially more positive response to the possibility of a meeting between Goldmann and Nasser. In this case, the response was clearly due to the frustration with a government that appeared to remain stalemated. In the long run, however, public and media opinion was largely critical of Goldmann and minimized the likelihood of any success from such a meeting. Critical to this episode is the way in which it illuminates the changes that 1967 bought about at various levels and the transformation in definitions of Zionism that were included.

Zionism in its origins had been a movement and ideology that took shape first in aspirational terms, building on historical continuities while seeking to transform them. During its early years it could easily include a wide variety of definitions and expectations. Over time, in the period of the British mandate, party development gave concrete form to a range of competing interpretations. In 1948, with the establishment of the state, it became more important to translate ideology into specific structures and commitments. This was done in the context of international expectations that were not entirely aligned with the particularities of creating a Jewish nation-state, and one with a significant religious heritage that dictated legal norms as well as daily obligations for those who accepted it. In addition, the existence of a diaspora included in the community with which the state was identified further complicated the process of state and nation articulation.

While the Israeli Declaration of Independence stated that the state would be "open to the immigration of Jews from all countries," it also stated that it would "promote the development of the country for the benefit of all its inhabitants"; it would be "based on the principles of liberty, justice and peace as conceived by the Prophets of Israel," but also "uphold the full social and political equality of all its citizens." Implementation of these norms was to be codified in a constitution that was never written. As a result, the potential for internal contradictions in the nature of the state as well as differences of interpretation with regard to its constituency—whether it would be territorial, religious, or ideological—remained subject to political developments and reactions.

In 1967 the failure to make earlier choices further complicated the process of state formation. This abstraction can be seen in a very tangible symptom: the physical boundaries of the state remained legally undefined while the political system similarly remained suspended between formal secular democracy and the reservation of significant areas of public interest to religious authority. Democracy and citizenship were territorial while special privilege accrued to Jewish communities, whether local or diasporic. Before 1967 there was no obvious pressure for political leaders to clarify certain limits or make difficult choices. The 1949 armistice boundaries were generally accepted but the lack of peace treaties also allowed continuing attachments to territory not within them, such as the old city of Jerusalem or the West Bank. The majority of the Israeli Jewish population was secular but religious authorities dominated with regard to personal law, and without a written constitution it was possible to avoid taking positions on the relationship between religious and political domains. Perhaps most complex was the fact that Israel, the state of the Jewish people, did not recognize an Israeli territorial nationality; although its Palestinian Arab population had Israeli citizenship, nationality on passports was listed as Arab or Jewish. Here once again was a practice that enabled avoidance of clear choices with regard to the nature of the state and its constituency.

After the war in 1967 there were groups in Israel that had clear aims and views about what should follow. Religious nationalists and secular believers in the Greater Land of Israel wanted to see settlement in the occupied territories. At another pole, critics who held to the compatibility of Zionism with a democratic, liberal, and tolerant state were more cognizant of dangers from maintaining control over territories with a substantial Palestinian Arab population. Claims on the definitions of Zionism were not lacking, but recognition of its inherent contradictions, which now became more obvious, was more limited. This was, at least in part, due to the ways in which Zionism was linked to moral claims that had been bolstered by the Eichmann trial and then by the buildup to the war in 1967.

Nahum Goldmann may have been the last major figure to make an argument for Zionism that combined the political analysis of Herzl with the cultural and spiritual values of Ahad HaAm. In his article in *Foreign Affairs,* published in April 1970, Goldmann offered his critique of the Israeli state as it had developed in its first twenty years and made what might be called a utopian suggestion for its future.[14] In his opinion, Zionism could not be seen as a success if all it did was lead to "a small state like dozens of others . . . , living continuously in peril of its annihilation, bound to remain mobilized and armed to the teeth, and concentrating its major efforts on physical survival."[15] Nor did he believe that world Jewry would permanently support such a state. At the same time, Goldmann believed that policies based on the belief that military strength would ultimately force Arab leaders to capitulate to Israel's demands were likely to lead only to more violence rather than an end to conflict. In Goldmann's views, the Arab view of Israel as a "foreign element"[16] in its midst had to be understood, as did the fact that Israel's future in the long term would be determined by, on the one hand, its relation to the Arab world and, on the other, with the Jewish people. At the same time, he was aware of the ways in which Israel's international position was becoming vulnerable to attacks from those who once saw the state as a progressive force while its new position as a military power increased its appeal to "reactionary, nationalistic groups."[17] The article thus carried forward Goldmann's focus on the nature of the state and its relationships to its surroundings.

In the context of this critique and of his own diplomatic experiences, Goldmann offered a radical suggestion: making Israel a neutral state protected by broad international commitments. His analysis was based on the perception that the USSR now had a stake in the region, no interest in further conflict, and a preference for stability. Agreement between the US and the USSR to guarantee Israel's existence while also ensuring the security of all other states in the region seemed to Goldmann within reason. A bit more difficult, he acknowledged, would be gaining Arab support for such a plan, but he understood that it would have the advantage of assuring them that Israel would not expand its borders or play a role in international power relationships. Although he recognized that such a solution might require an international force to ensure its effectiveness, he also argued that this outcome could permit Israel to maintain its military without requiring an arms race in the region. For Goldmann this outcome was an important element in allowing Israel to become the kind of creative Jewish center that he believed was the true goal of Zionism as he understood it.

As a European Jew by background and education, Goldmann did not react to the realities of Nazism and the Holocaust with an inclination to withdraw. On the contrary, his various positions were based on a comfortable interaction with Jews and non-Jews over large geographical areas. His understanding of Arab perspectives on Zionism combined with acceptance of the interdependence that Jewish communities necessarily experienced outside of Israel. It was from this external vantage point that he related to Israel while feeling a profound attachment to what it signified. It was also a long-term perspective that he could afford to take. That insider/outsider role that Goldmann took helped undermine his ability to have influence after 1970.

In contrast to Goldmann, Golda Meir may have been the first Israeli leader to operate with a singular focus on the US as critical to Israeli survival. Her comfort with Americans and her knowledge of the American Jewish environment, where she came to be admired, helped structure her policies as prime minister. Her reactions were deeply colored by her years in Mapai (the Zionist Labor Party) and the moral universe that was constructed during her work in the Yishuv. This perspective and experience in turn did not allow her to view the Palestinian Arab claims and narrative as legitimate.

The Goldmann incident brought to the surface differences between the two individuals that went well beyond personal conflict. It signaled a fork in the road for Zionism and those who defined themselves as adherents. Where Ben-Gurion had argued that Zionists were those who moved to Israel while all other American Jews could provide welcome support for the state, Goldmann continued to believe that there was a place for diaspora Jews to go beyond support to participating in the work of state formation, which could include critique of state policies. By 1967, however, the bifurcation between Israeli Jews and American Jews was supplemented by the growing role and interest of the US in the region. For Israelis now seeking to benefit from their military strength, the US was an important factor in determining their future, and the role of American Jews was viewed in light of this emerging relationship. The nature of the state was to be determined by Israeli Jews and their domestic differences. For most, the diaspora was valued at best as a source of support, but with suspicion of any efforts to offer advice or alternative views.

The Nahum Goldmann–Golda Meir disagreement occurred while violent confrontations were continuing on the Israeli border with Egypt, and in the form of terrorist attacks that served to heighten awareness of Palestinian claims to be heard. The episode itself reflected an ongoing tension between political analyses focused on decreasing conflict and military assessments that assumed ongoing confrontations to be managed.

Central to these differences were the responses of Palestinians on the one hand and the US on the other. Although the victory in 1967 confirmed a military imbalance that underlined Israel's status as a major regional power, it also widened the chasm between Israeli public narratives of self-definition and that of Palestinian Arabs. Most Israeli Jews viewed themselves as the object of historical enmity with no rational foundation, let alone requiring recognition of responsibility on their part. American Jews, whose understanding of the pre-1948 era and its aftermath was generally limited, could easily identify with this perspective. It was a framework that allowed for pride in accomplishment without questions about the costs involved.

This situation inevitably gave greater force to Palestinian Arab efforts to gain attention for their own very different experience and point of view. After 1967 and especially in 1968, the PLO acted to strengthen its own power to attract international attention, to stimulate a national movement, and to offer alternative narratives as well as political projects.[18]

The brief period between 1967 and 1970 was characterized by competing struggles internal to each state or movement, with a stake in either altering the outcome of war or entrenching its effects on regional power relationships. In Israel, a framework dictating that the victors in war had legitimate claim to its benefits meant that there was broad agreement on the need to improve borders, unite Jerusalem, and expect formal recognition from the defeated states. At the same time, minority voices supported policies that expressed significant differences with regard to the moral as well as political implications of the war. Where some, including some officials in the Labor Party, argued for recognition of Palestinian national identity, others began a process of "return," creating new facts on the ground while clearly ignoring any Palestinian collective presence in occupied territories now controlled by the Israel Defense Forces.[19]

Among Palestinians themselves, the results of earlier divides became more salient in an environment that seemed to have some promise of redress, but also introduced new dangers. While Palestinians living on the West Bank and Gaza were now subject to an Israeli authority that had no clear time limits or future plans, Palestinians in Jordan, Syria, and Lebanon were reacting to a transformed PLO now headed by Yasir Arafat of Fatah, and now dominated by guerrilla groups. Although Arafat had hopes of stimulating active guerrilla resistance in the West Bank and Gaza, these plans were largely defeated by conditions on the ground. In spite of the 1968 Battle of Karama's message of Palestinian fortitude, the movement remained internally divided and lacking a reliable territorial base. While the constituent groups of the PLO continued to attract activists, to train fighters, to develop cultural resources, and to energize Palestinians living outside the boundary of Palestine, its success was accompanied not only by Israeli reprisals but also by the anxiety of Arab regimes about losing control within various states.[20]

The revolutionary models to which Palestinians appealed were those of Algerians and Vietnamese, as well as others who then seemed particularly effective in fighting imperial power. Casting Palestinian actions within this framework had the effect of winning support from a variety of postcolonial states, in addition to the left within Europe and the US, thus linking the Palestinians to other sources of support while conveying a model of national identity to their own constituencies. Not less important was the hope of gaining international mobilization in an era of UN expansion to include numerous new states. At some levels, the initial post-1967 years were successful ones for the PLO. Whereas UN Resolution 242 had taken account only of "refugees" (not Palestinians) displaced in 1948, the PLO after 1967 undertook military, terrorist, political, and cultural initiatives that asserted a national identity transcending historical fragmentation. New generations were finding reflections of their own experiences in multiple sites, each with its own implications for the Palestinian national project.[21]

At the same time as they were gaining momentum, Palestinians also articulated a variety of desires, expressing varying points of view and intents—where some acted in support of transformation throughout the Arab world, others stayed close to a more conservative nationalism, and others found themselves having to navigate an occupation that was still in its early stages. Despite a rhetoric of unity, the PLO was hampered by its efforts to incorporate multiple political groups with their own positions under one umbrella. Operating under substantial external pressures, there was limited opportunity to achieve genuine integration or to work through important conflicts in political analysis. Existing, moreover, within an Arab world that both provided support and contained elements seeking to control Palestinian actions that affected them, the PLO leadership was navigating multiple challenges.[22]

One factor that helped maintain both hopes and fluidity for Palestinians was the international context within which they were acting. Ongoing struggles for decolonization and revolutionary nationalisms created hopes for transnational partnerships sympathetic to Palestinian aspirations. It was an environment in which both the US and the USSR sought to build their own client bases while avoiding direct conflict between themselves. In the US, the Vietnam War and its domestic repercussions heightened divisions that affected foreign policy. In the post-1967 period, the PLO's identification with Vietnamese forces resisting the American military made it easy to see Palestinians as anti-American radicals while Israeli actions could readily be viewed as rationally responsive to provocation.

How the US should respond to Israel's expansive victory was very much an open question, particularly after the election of President Richard Nixon in 1968. Although there appeared to be a framework for negotiations agreed to in Resolution 242, American policy was still in process of formation. President Lyndon Johnson had set an initial tone with his statement in June 1967, making clear that the US would not demand, as it had in 1956, that Israel withdraw from occupied territories before an agreed-upon end to conflict. Critical to policy decisions on the Middle East was the ongoing impact of the Vietnam War, which provided a background to the ways in which Americans had responded to Israeli military success in 1967. What this would mean for the US position long term, however, remained unclear.[23]

When the UN passed Resolution 242 with its provision for a mediator, the mechanism to resolve conflict appeared to achieve consensus among the major powers. Its ambiguity and failure to recognize Palestinian claims, however, only further ensured continuing struggle on the part of all those directly affected, as well as the US and the USSR. Although the resolution did not explicitly speak to Israeli claims, the failure to include a Palestinian voice or recognize one did set a precedent that left the primary parties to the conflict clearly on an even more unequal playing field than that between Arab regimes and Israel.

In the US and in Israel reactions in 1967 were clearly affected by memories of 1956. President Johnson himself, while clearly sympathetic to Israeli positions, had concerns both at home and abroad that took priority over the Middle East. Once he had expressed his initial position, he did not see any urgency to American intervention, and conditions in the region also favored US acquiescence in Israel's wait and see policy. This was further justified after an Arab state summit in Khartoum in August 1967 resulted in the three No's: No Recognition, No Negotiation, No Peace.[24]

When Nixon took office, however, the development of foreign policy came to be divided between the National Security Council and the State Department. Despite the continuation of the war in Vietnam, the Nixon administration was free to develop broader assessments of global American interests and policies. Initially this process included competing positions represented by Secretary of State William Rogers and National Security Advisor Henry Kissinger, with the former attributing greater importance to local factors in the Middle East, and the latter viewing conflict through the Cold War lens of US-USSR rivalry. However, it quickly became clear that when it came to the Arab-Israeli conflict, President Nixon would not be supportive of a Rogers plan that was designed to achieve Israeli withdrawal from occupied areas, and to define agreement to nonbelligerency as an end point. Although neither the US nor the USSR was interested in a revival of warfare, both sought to profit from the new postwar conditions.

In the case of the USSR, this situation entailed not only military and other support to its clients but also an ideological stance in which anti-Zionism came to be absorbed into domestic as well as foreign policy, intended to underline Soviet support for Arab "revolutionary" forces in contrast to US identification with Israel. Until 1970 these conditions as well as those on the ground allowed for both ongoing insecurity and continuing optimism for both Palestinians and Israelis. Precisely the fact of continuing violence underlined the expectation that there would be resolution, while at the same time the nature of such hoped for resolution took widely differing forms for all those involved.[25]

By 1970/71, new constellations of power were emerging, although their implications for Israelis and Palestinians were only to become evident over time. As the US and USSR operated at a global level, utilizing their resources to ensure links to states in the Middle East, conditions within those states were shifting in ways not always visible or understood. The war had resulted in conditions that required states bordering Israel to work toward regaining territory they had lost, as well as recovering from the deep shock that accompanied a defeat to Pan-Arabism as an ideal, whatever its limits in practice. The Palestinian cause was implicated in the ideals of Pan-Arabism, with its promise of unity and strength to right the historic wrong of 1948. While some Palestinian activists supported Nasser's leadership, others were committed to revolutionary change in the Arab world and particularly in Jordan. Palestinian groups gaining adherents before 1967 were just beginning to differentiate their movement from the Arab states more clearly, while also relying on various state territorial bases as well as financial support. After 1967, it was the Palestinians, knowing that they could not win their struggle militarily, who claimed the mantle of success in challenging both Israeli legitimacy and the role of imperialist powers in supporting Zionism. In Israel, reactions to the reality of an expanded territorial space largely populated by Palestinian Arabs, who had been rendered politically invisible after 1949, were varied. The new situation allowed Israelis geographical access that included the pleasures of tourism without travel to other countries. At the same time, it allowed resurgent claims to rights of ownership in the lands they believed to be a rightful Jewish heritage. Relatively few had any interest in learning more about Palestinians and their experiences, or facing the realities of a new coexistence in which they were the powerful controlling others.

In September 1970 several events combined to alter and limit possibilities for political transformation in the region, or a genuine movement toward peaceful outcomes. After the US secured an agreement to a ceasefire and commitment to new negotiations in July, several weeks later a series of hijackings by members of the Popular Front for the Liberation of Palestine highlighted the multiplicity of groups with a stake in the outcome of any agreement. At the same time, the hijackings brought tensions between Palestinian activists and Arab state regimes to a head. In the aftermath of this crisis, American policy contributed to maintaining the historically complex interdependence between the Jordanian regime and Israel. Although Yasir Arafat had not supported the international hijackings and opposed actions against the Jordanian government, the

PLO as a whole paid a heavy price as the Palestinian movement was displaced from Jordan in the succeeding months, requiring reconstitution in Lebanon. These developments were accompanied by the unexpected death of President Nasser in Egypt, with the attendant loss of his capacities to navigate between the Palestinian movement and state regimes.[26]

President Nasser's successor, Anwar Sadat, viewed the Arab-Israeli conflict from a very different perspective. Taking control after the apparent failure of Pan-Arabism to defeat Zionism, Sadat gave priority to the interests of the Egyptian state. It did not take long for President Sadat to take initiatives that made his priorities clear. In February 1971 Sadat made public his interest in finding diplomatic solutions that would restore Egypt's control over the territories occupied by Israel. Operating in the context of Soviet military aid and presence in Egypt, it became clear that Sadat saw the United States as more likely to provide the political help he sought. Given the US support for Israel, Sadat hoped that his willingness both to compromise and ultimately to remove Soviet forces would produce diplomatic movement with American encouragement of Israeli compromise as well. To his dismay, it became clear that Prime Minister Golda Meir remained firm in her unwillingness to accept a step by step process. Although Kissinger was not yet secretary of state, his consistent prioritizing of global issues, particularly the need to exclude Soviet influence, as well as belief in the usefulness of Israel's stalemate, contributed to an American policy that lacked singular focus on the Middle East or clarity with regard to Israeli redefinitions of national security. In the two years immediately prior to the war of 1973, Golda Meir continued to focus on ensuring US support without pressure as critical, while Sadat acted in hopes of American willingness to be evenhanded and to help Egyptian recovery of land without another war. Both Israel and Egypt operated according to the presumption that nation-states represented primary legitimate international actors.[27]

In the aftermath of September 1970, however, Palestinian activists and in particular the PLO leadership had to contend with new challenges. While consolidating their position in the Third World/Non-Aligned bloc of states, gaining Soviet support and moving their primary base to Lebanon, they continued to live with internal divisions and differences. In contrast to the Algerian FLN, Arafat was not in a position to enforce internal discipline and unity. While Palestinians in the diaspora could be mobilized by appeals to solidarity and action, Palestinians living on the West Bank and in Gaza were not in a position to launch guerrilla warfare. The Algerian and Vietnamese models therefore were inspiring but limited in practical effect. Instead, they functioned to reinforce American and Israeli stereotyping of Palestinians as radical terrorists without legitimate claims. As the US-USSR rivalry became integral to regional power relationships, Israeli preferences for a new status quo were aligning with American interests in ensuring Israeli military dominance in the region. Palestinians, in contrast, could hope that a movement appealing to social justice in a period of decolonization would gain the international supports necessary to achieve recognition, legitimacy, and liberation.

By the time the war of 1973 broke out, the likelihood that either the PLO or the Israeli government would find a way to deal directly with their conflict was slim indeed. The war itself, which exacted a significant price for Israelis while enabling the opening of an Egyptian-Israeli negotiation, strengthened the American position in the region. It also reinforced the asymmetries between an Israel now with nuclear weapon capabilities and a nonstate Palestinian movement with a vulnerable territorial base in Lebanon. At the end of the war, the US—in the person of Secretary of State Kissinger—took on the role of mediating and managing the start of a gradual process that would return to Egypt the territories that had been lost in 1967 and would finally lead to a peace treaty between the two countries in 1979.

These developments were variously interpreted and continue to be the object of study. What is clear, however, is that they contributed to strengthening the positions of two American client states while further marginalizing Palestinian representation. In making the US appear to succeed, this process also obscured a role that has since been labeled that of a dishonest broker or one charged with duplicity. It raises the question as to why it was believed the US interventions were or could be neutral or, alternatively, that they were intended to serve one side of conflict, when the significant question concerned how the US government was coming to define its interests in an increasingly complex and conflict-ridden region. [28]

American Views, 1967–1973

In the six years from 1967 to 1973 the structure of conversations in the United States about the Arab-Israeli conflict, which now gradually took the shape of a Palestinian-Israeli conflict, changed substantially, reflecting major shifts in the multiplicity of political conflicts characteristic of those years. The war of 1967 was over in six days but it was preceded by weeks in which most Americans as well as Europeans saw Israel as surrounded by enemies intent on destroying the Jewish state. That perception was enhanced by the relatively short period that had elapsed since World War II and the emerging, growing recognition of the Holocaust as a distinctly Jewish event. For Americans and Europeans, then, Israel existed as a refuge and as recompense. Once the threat feared before the war in 1967 proved to be ephemeral and Israel emerged as a newly powerful, expansive state, reactions to it were linked to broader political commitments and, in the US, to the changed American role. As 1968 unfolded with broad and transnational conflicts—cultural as well as political—the Arab-Israeli conflict took on different meanings for specific groups that felt personally affected. At the same time, the ongoing, if sporadic, efforts to end the continuing state of hostilities came to be redefined as a peace process. Debates about who should participate in this process added a new layer of conflict to an already daunting set of challenges, making it difficult to separate out the ways in which multiple players were defining peace, national security, and justice from different perspectives, with various interests. In the US, Kissinger's insistence on excluding the USSR, however, finally came to dominate American policy with wide-ranging implications for populations in the region.[29]

In Israel, political debate about the outcomes of war was overshadowed by a pervasive impression that there was no urgency, since there could not be another Arab attack in the near future. Simultaneously, however, those who sought to begin settlements did operate with urgency to establish facts on the ground. Understanding this movement as an extension of historical Zionism (adopting its tools in a new context), these developments served to redefine Zionism and its claims, emphasizing both religious and historical grounds while minimizing the secular and contextual elements of settlement before 1948.

Among Palestinians, the need to make use of opportunities created by the defeats of 1967 drove action as well as discussion and institution building. Crucial for Palestinians was the need to gain recognition and understanding of their national specificity of experience, which in turn drove the need for inclusion in any new diplomatic and political arrangements. Closely linked was the need to establish legitimacy for the Palestinian voice in the international arena. This priority contributed inevitably to entering into competition with an Israeli Zionist narrative that had obscured, if not erased, the communal, material bases of the mandate era leading to 1948.

Operating at cross-purposes, Palestinian leaders, intellectuals, and activists were working to raise consciousness of their own history, while the Israeli government was moving toward suppression of suggestions that 1967 marked the return of the repressed in the form of Israeli-Palestinian conflict. While the younger generation of Palestinians was seeking to recover and correct a history of loss, Israeli Jews were increasingly identifying with the history constituted by the Eichmann trial and now linking them with American Jews, as well as an earlier European history. Schoolchildren were taught a Jewish history linking the distant past with the national present, but the period of the Palestine mandate was largely absent.

A singular example of the process that redefined an earlier era for a new generation was evident in the fate of S. Yizhar's novel, *Khirbet Khizeh*. A short but powerful narrative told through the eyes of a young Jewish soldier in 1948, the novel described an action in which Israeli soldiers followed orders to empty an Arab village of its inhabitants, forcing them over the Jordanian border. Disturbed by this process and associating it with the forced movements of Jews in Europe, the narrator reflects on his experience during a war whose necessity he does not question. The book was read in the fifties as one that showed the complexity and moral sensitivity of its main character. It was included in the literature offered to high school students and not viewed as in any way dangerous. Yet, by 1977, when the Israel Broadcasting Authority planned to show a film based on the book, it provoked a significant conflict and the danger of censorship from the new Israeli government. By that time, the story it told was one that could be interpreted as challenging the legitimacy and morality of the IDF's actions in an earlier era. History, as always, was being shaped by the renewed presence of the past and, more specifically, by the ways in which Israeli-Palestinian conflict was focused on competing claims with regard to legitimacy and morality.

In the United States, the war of 1967 also brought the Israel-Palestine conflict home as various groups felt personally implicated and concerned about American policy in the region. Whereas the Vietnam War had generated heated debate and critique at various levels, its domestic ramifications were largely due to the effects of a military draft and to ideological differences rather than ethnic conflict. In the seventies, however, the conflict helped shape emerging American constituencies responding to the perceived and growing American role.[30]

The American Jewish community already had numerous organizations and institutions with significant political presence. This established network, which had already developed both domestic political visibility and links to

Israel, had helped to mobilize substantial financial and moral support for Israel in the weeks preceding war. In the aftermath, the relationship between organizations representing American Jews and the Israeli government shifted decisively, with the strengthening of government-to-government relations that relegated communal leadership to supportive roles.

Among the broader American Jewish public, however, earlier differences continued to exist but were now accompanied by the heightened significance that Israel had gained in the minds of many. For Jewish political activists—in particular left-wing radicals—the war of 1967 made visible more urgent questions about the nature of the Israeli state and its regional relationships. At the same time, the broad majority found itself newly proud of an Israel that appeared to embody a successful "new" Jewish culture, assertive and unapologetic. By 1973, the emerging alliance between Israel and the US furthered the perception that American Jewish identity was safe in its apparently harmonious ties to Israel and the US. Only the few who were familiar with the longer history were in a position to grapple with the radically changing nature of the Israeli state and its new challenges. These included internal and external stressors that interacted in ways that ultimately reformulated the Zionist project, intensifying competing arguments. Over a relatively short time, new efforts to exclude and delegitimize those who did not subscribe to the emerging, dominant narrative emerged.

These developments intersected with the increased assertiveness of Americans of Arab background, many of whom felt blindsided by the ways in which media responses to the war of 1967 brought out clear identifications with Israel and denigration of Arabs in the aftermath of a humiliating defeat. Responses reflected drives both to correct perceived distortions and mobilization to attain a public presence in a United States that was viewed as increasingly instrumental in the Middle East. New organizations from this time period include the Association of Arab American University Graduates and the National Association of Arab Americans. In addition, this was a period of significant shifts in the academic world of Middle East studies.[31]

Prior to 1967, Zionism, Israel and the Palestinians were the subjects of various conversations in Europe, the Arab world, and the United States. These conversations, dealing with ethical questions, international law, ideological commitments, and the Arab-Israeli conflict, took place largely at a distance from policymaking or direct action. In Israel, the relevance of Zionism was subject to question as the existence of the state seemed to have fulfilled its goals. In the United States, relations between Israel and the diaspora remained subject to discussion. In Europe, particularly France, the conflict was embedded in broader colonial/anticolonial debates as well as in the Algerian War. In the Arab world, the exclusion of Israel as a topic for study meant that political and intellectual developments were anchored in the ongoing experience of, and separation from, European dominance.

After 1967 this situation changed. As the United States moved toward taking a more active role—providing arms and engaging diplomatically—a new triangle gradually took shape. While support for Israel was being incorporated into US policy, it also seemed that such support could be used to influence Israeli policies. In a Cold War setting that identified an Israeli democracy with US freedoms, appeals to moral justifications of policies helped obscure the role that the change in regional power relations played. Arab American political activism took shape in this context just as Palestinian militant actions did. What could not be controlled by activists was the way in which appeals to international law and fairmindedness missed the deeper fit between US and Israeli interests in sustaining the status quo achieved after the war. More significant still were the effects on intellectual life of an environment in which competing views were rapidly turned into action, with less and less space for reflection. Political formulations increasingly served particular interests in an intensifying competition for control over the Middle East.

At one level the US and the USSR moved toward direct interventions through the supply of arms and diplomatic actions. At another level, Arab states and Israel sought to establish firmer lines without compromising perceived core interests. And, beyond these visible debates, a deeper, more enduring struggle was taking place between an Israeli state that claimed after 1967 the right to "secure borders" and a Palestinian movement that claimed a right to reparation. It was at this level that the dangers of history were felt.

Between 1967 and 1974, it is possible to read the effects of a short period in which various conversations could and did take place. In the first three years after the war, immediate reactions were supplemented by writing and conversations that sought to make sense of its significance. In Israel, a number of prominent individuals immediately focused on the risks of a lengthy occupation as well as on the need to recognize the claims of the Palestinian Arab population.[32] In certain ways, these views represented a return to much earlier Zionist debates about the priority of working with Palestinian Arabs as opposed to relying on outside powers. While specific arguments were varied, this position was based on the recognition that military strength could not solve the ongoing conflict and that what was at stake was the nature of the state that Zionists had built. Underlying political arguments was the revival of competing responses to the return of the repressed communal conflict between Palestinian Arabs and Jews that had resulted in the 1948 war. The new territorial gains thus reopened barely suppressed historical divides in a very different context. Among these were the following:

- Zionism as necessary to rescue Jews at risk versus Zionism as a vehicle to rescue Judaism in the modern era. Either and both of these strains foresaw an eventual Jewish state but neither foresaw the emergence of a state that would require Jewish immigration to fortify it in a hostile environment.

- Zionism that was presumed to be a vehicle for "normalizing" Jewish life by adopting Western European political structures, that is, assimilating via statehood, versus Zionism based on assumptions of inherent Jewish separatism combined with historical messianism.

- Jewish settlements established to enable the life of an immigrant population to survive in a difficult environment, ultimately coming to be seen as necessary for defense of a nationalist project, versus the utopian socialist view of to build and be built by.

- Those who viewed military strength as having priority, versus those who believed in diplomacy as essential for long-term security.

- The belief that Israel could not survive without the support of a major Western power, versus those who saw survival as ultimately dependent on effective integration in the Middle East.

- Views of the Diaspora as requiring negation, representing Jewish absence from history, versus expectations of a permanent diaspora that would remain interdependent with a Jewish state.

And, finally, the post-1967 period, in which all of the Palestine mandate territory came under Israeli control, was colored by the ways in which the Holocaust had been adopted by the Israeli state as central to modern Jewish history, while the history of Jewish communities destroyed by the Holocaust was not yet a major focus of study, and the impact of 1948 on Palestinian Arabs was largely suppressed.

Among Palestinians also, competing views were debated as they faced a new situation from different vantage points. In the occupied territories the renewed direct contact with a historical adversary brought home dramatic changes in their respective capacities, power, and daily existences. There were a few local leaders who saw opportunities for resolution and coexistence, but their voices were largely obscured both by disinterest on the Israeli side and PLO militancy.[33]

Ongoing ideological differences and goals led various groups to adopt a variety of direct actions. Where Fatah leadership was committed to a strategy of guerrilla warfare as well as actions within the territory controlled by Israel, and noninterference in other Arab states, the Popular Front for the Liberation of Palestine undertook international actions and was governed by an ideological commitment to transformation of Arab states.

Palestinians living in Jordan, refugees and others, were now in a position to mobilize in the renewed struggle for self-determination, but the ultimate meaning of this goal was not uniformly defined. The relationship of Palestinians to the Hashemite monarchy of Jordan was historically complex; the territory of Jordan was originally separated from the Palestine mandate by Great Britain in 1920; between 1948 and 1967 it had included the West Bank of Palestine now occupied by Israel. As a result of this history, the Palestinian drive to return reawakened an earlier ambiguity in Hashemite-Palestinian relations as well.

As the Palestinian movement worked to create and re-create its own history and as writers and intellectuals articulated a national culture, the centrality of the Naqba in 1948 served as a pivotal event, helping to organize many different experiences around a shared loss.

For Israelis and Palestinians, 1967 not only opened up a physical border that had been closed, but it brought back a history that had polarizing effects. Israelis saw 1948 as an accomplishment that formed the base for thinking about the future. Any renewal of questions about that history seemed to threaten their legitimate existence. Palestinians, however, were now re-creating their own experiences, history, and narratives. As they built a movement dedicated to return and recovery, they seemed to Israelis to be driving toward a reversal of history.

In the US the distance from Israel/Palestine was not just territorial. It was emotional and political, as Americans viewed events through lenses created by the intense domestic conflicts that characterized the second half of the sixties, from civil rights to the Vietnam War as well as the ongoing impact of the Cold War. This was evident in the July 1967 issue of *Ramparts*, the progressive magazine, responding to the war of 1967. Following an editorial that explicitly cautioned against the dangers of US and Soviet interventions, three articles offered analyses outlining the complexities of postwar conditions.

Paul Jacobs, drawing on earlier experiences in the region, offered a historical introduction to the context in which war had occurred.[34] Understanding the intensity of feeling on both sides of the border, he traced the ways in which military success had been accompanied by political failure, and raised questions that would accompany any effort to avoid further violence. In doing so, he pointed to the fears and humiliations that were regional, but also to the potential impact of extraregional powers that could undermine the risky search for compromise due to interests that would fuel the conflicts.

In an essay titled "Israel Is Not Vietnam" political scientists Michael Walzer and Martin Peretz addressed an ideological question that took on a life of its own in this period.[35] In it, they sought to disentangle the US war in Vietnam—which was interpreted variously by those adhering to a Cold War perspective and those viewing the conflict as one of intervention against a legitimate nationalist movement entitled to self-determination—from the Israeli-Arab conflict in which they supported US action to protect Israel. Visible here are the challenges that the Israeli victory created for many supporters of a political left, who had earlier experienced little contradiction between that position and support of Israel. In addition, the essay makes evident the shifting considerations interfering with capacities to maintain sympathy for Third World nationalisms, while also supporting an Israel now occupying territory populated by Palestinian Arabs. Walzer and Peretz make the case for a Zionism that could be viewed as itself a movement against an imperial state, but this would be increasingly difficult in the years to come.

Finally, I. F. Stone wrote about "The Future of Israel."[36] Stone, who had reported sympathetically on Israel in 1948 as it became a state, understood the earlier history. Now he addressed the problems he saw facing that state, first and foremost the likely pressures coming from the US and the USSR. Stone outlined the ambivalence of US policy, seeking to protect interests both in oil and in arms production. Under these circumstances, he argued for the importance of seeking peace directly with the Arab states, avoiding errors of the past such as allying with France during the Algerian War. Stone, like others, viewed 1948 as a moral tragedy but was very aware of the dangers threatening a lengthy period of no peace in the aftermath of June 1967. These dangers were not those that were coming to be associated with the need for secure borders; these were dangers that would lead to loss of moral credibility and support in the Third World, resulting from failure to understand changes that had occurred since 1948. *Ramparts* spoke to an audience sympathetic to New Left positions. By 1974, it reflected the shift from commitment to Israel's existence, which made clear the assumptions of its vulnerability, to more concern about the challenges of a new war in which Israeli military strength required supply from the US and gave further evidence of the ways in which the region had become intertwined with broader global developments.

Commentary was a prominent Jewish journal that was shifting from earlier voices on the left to growing conservatism. In August 1967, contributors spoke to concerns in the American Jewish world, offering particular explanations of what had occurred in June.[37] Arthur Hertzberg, noted rabbi and scholar of Zionism, wrote of "Israel and American Jewry" in an attempt to explain the outpouring of resources in support of Israel during the run-up to war.[38] Hertzberg attributed the response to fears for Israel's survival and identification with the state. In contrast to earlier American Jewish ambivalence towards Zionism, 1967 appeared to have created broad unity, as Hertzberg noted.

> Very large numbers of American Jews now feel their Jewish identity more intensely than they have for at least a generation and they are less worried than before about what the rest of the world might be thinking of their feelings or of the actions through which they have been expressing these feelings. . . . I would say that the most widespread influence—on Jews in Israel and America alike—was a revulsion against the passivity of the Jewish victims of the Nazis.

Hertzberg might have added that these reactions made evident the changes in an American Jewish community that had largely felt unable to demand

US support for Jewish refugees and victims during World War II. Israel, he noted, "evoked more in American Jews than a sense of moral reparation for the memory of the passive victims of mass murder." It was now generating a sense of belonging to the worldwide Jewish people. Whether this intense identification would last was impossible to know, but this appeared to be a transformative moment that coincided with significant generational change.[39]

Theodore Draper, an academic historian and political writer, contributed a lengthy article on "Israel and World Politics."[40] In it he says that the real casus belli was a struggle against history, a history now laden with myths and legends.[41] Specifically, Draper sought to answer claims that Israel was the creation of imperial power by pointing out the joint role of the US and USSR in supporting the UN resolution for partition in 1947. While noting that 1967 was a continuation of the violent conflicts in 1948 and 1956, Draper pays no attention to the Palestinian Arabs as actors in the conflict. Focused on intrastate relations, his analysis directly holds the USSR responsible and recognizes the development of "wars by proxy" as the context for 1967.

In 1968, Amos Elon reported on "The Israeli Occupation" already taking shape.[42] His description includes recognition of the fact that the "unexpected seizure of the 'whole of Palestine' as well as of sizable chunks of Syria and Egypt, has given rise to a national debate of an intensity that has not been seen here since the earlier, more fervent days of Zionist colonization. An impressive number of writers, poets, and others has joined in the 'Movement for the Whole of Eretz Israel.'" This was a movement dedicated to the annexation of all the land understood to be part of historic Israel, which meant minimally all the territories of the West Bank and Gaza. As part of this commitment, adherents believed in the necessity of creating large numbers of settlements. Elon captured the impact of this development:

> The appearance of this movement has thrown the intellectual community here into its first really heated debate in years. The old questions arise once again: "Who are we?" Why are we here and not in Uganda or America?" Are we here by right or by sufferance?" The annexationists argue that Israel has a historic right to all the lands once promised by God to His chosen people. This right, they say, supersedes the rights of West Bank Arabs to national self-determination. They tell

their critics: If you do not recognize our right to Nablus, you cannot recognize our right to Tel Aviv. That being the case, you must emigrate. [43]

Elon cited the novelist Amos Oz as one of those offering a rebuttal to this argument. In "The Meaning of Homeland," Oz expressed an attachment to secular Zionism and to Israel that relied on both personal experiences and historical understanding. Unlike those who elided the differences between settlement before 1948 and after 1967, Amos Oz argued that logical consistency was irrelevant when considering facts on the ground:

> The Six Day War has once more given birth, all along the political spectrum, to "mighty" geopolitical formulas: total annexation, mass settlement, a Semitic or Palestinian Federation or Confederation, a Palestinian protectorate, an Ottoman-style Jewish empire, Kurdistan and Druzistan, by the grace of the Israel Defense Force. . . . What all these old-new formulas have in common is the attempt to shift our range of view beyond the fact of the existence, under our rule, of a considerable Arab population with—small or not so small—beginnings of national consciousness. All the geopolitical ideas that sprouted so hastily and abundantly after the Six Day War clearly have a common denominator: even when they want to shower the Palestinian Arabs with marvelous benevolence, resettle the refugees and set the Arabs on the road to progress, they all try to bypass the elementary need to consult those they are dealing with.[44]

Oz does not offer solutions here but he is making a critical point in the larger debate that Elon was describing. Within Israel and without, the war of 1967 shifted not only the ground being discussed but equally the terms of discussion. Central to the discussions were questions about legitimacy and rights to have a voice.

In 1970, Robert Alter, scholar of Hebrew literature, addressed the question of "Zionism for the '70s."[45] His discussion makes clear both continuity in the conversations about Zionism and the fissures brought about by developments after 1967. To begin with, Alter points to a series of interviews with prominent Israeli intellectuals that had been conducted by Ehud Ben-Ezer under the general title *The Price of Zionism*, which were being published prior to the war. The interviews included, among other subjects, references to the "moral wrongs perpetrated upon the Palestinian Arabs, Israel's betrayal of world Jewry, the capitulation of the Israeli intelligentsia to the blandishments of the governing clique."[46] Alter understood this as taking stock of Zionism at a time of Israeli malaise and questioning. Although publication of the interviews was interrupted before the war, the questions remained afterwards in a new context.[47] Recognizing well the limits and paradoxes of Zionism, Alter nevertheless saw distinct change:

> By establishing a sovereign state, Jews have resuscitated the possibility of initiating action rather than merely responding to the action of others, of controlling in some significant degree the conditions that are literally matters of life and death to them. If the painfully limited options open to Israel in foreign policy draw our attention to the naivete of the old Zionist slogan about the Jews being able to 'make their own history' again, it is nevertheless true that the State of Israel represents a radical reorientation of the relationship of Jews to history.[48]

Going on to describe different perspectives on this history as it was being articulated in responses to the current situation, in which the justifications for and the price of the Zionist project were being argued, Alter addressed recent changes. He saw the classical Zionist messianism now most visible in the Greater Israel group, contrasting it to those like Ernst Simon who wrote in the early fifties that the most Jewish quality of Israel would be its resistance to a messianic conception of its own existence. In Alter's view, "The moral and spiritual authority of institutional Judaism has only been compromised by the mode of coexistence with political power that it has assumed in Israel. Having become, in the proper sense of the term, an established religion, official Judaism in Israel has in far too many instances been more narrowly self-interested, more venal, more cynically indifferent to serious social questions and ethical concerns, than it ever was in its decentralized, non-political condition in the Diaspora."[49]

As Israeli Jews were dividing between religious nationalists and others who supported annexation of the conquered territories, as opposed to those who worried about the effect of occupation on the state, Alter was exploring the fate of Zionism as it took physical shape:

Israel came into being as the embodiment of a historical paradox. The Zionist idea could not have been conceived, could have had no motive force, without a deep emotional and imaginative loyalty to the Jewish past, not only the biblical past, but in a more complicated way, even to the Diaspora past where, after all, much of the life and memories of the people to be saved was embodied. On the other hand, Zionism was of course a manifesto through action that the previous two thousand years of Jewish history were all wrong, that the national values implicit in the experience of exile, helping to prolong it, had to be radically transformed. . . . In other words, the doubleness of attitude of Zionist beginnings continues today in the ongoing ambivalence of Israeli society toward the Jewish past.[50]

Citing the universalism of George Steiner in contrast to the particularism of Shlomo Avineri, Alter makes evident the ongoing impact of place on the consideration of Zionism and its moral constitution:

With the translation of the Jewish state from the realm of ideology to history, the strange, submerged life Zionists led has surfaced in Israel, whose citizens are daily confronted in a variety of ways with the palpable consequences of the ideas from which their nation has drawn being and sustenance. It is not an easy confrontation; at times it may seem almost an unbearable one; but at least it makes unillusioned clarity a necessary element of national existence, and as we try to imagine a future we would want, for Jews, for all men, perhaps the last thing we can afford to be is self-deceived.[51]

These writings are merely a small selection of all that was being written and discussed. They make clear both the multiple levels at which discussions took place and the differing frameworks through which Israeli and American Jews saw the aftermath of victory in 1967. With few exceptions, Palestinians remained absent.

As it became clear that there would be no rapid resolution, conditions in the region were changing and having an impact on the assessments of policymakers. The War of Attrition on the Egyptian-Israeli border was finally halted by a ceasefire in the summer of 1970. In the meantime, the efforts of Secretary of State William Rogers, based on Resolution 242, proved fruitless. Soviet resupply of Egypt and provision of technical support did little to encourage the hopes of those who believed that the US and the USSR, working together, could procure an agreement. In the US, Kissinger and Nixon were inclined to give priority to preventing an active or ongoing Soviet role. As a result of these conditions, Israeli and American policies increasingly led to maintaining the status quo of no war, no peace. Support for this absence of active efforts at resolution was only heightened by the development, on the one hand, of PLO activism in the form of terrorist attacks and, on the other, the statement of the Arab League in August 1967 refusing recognition of Israel, negotiations, or peace with Israel. For those already certain that existential vulnerability was Israel's condition while Arabs were the aggressors, these actions only confirmed their point of view. For US government officials, however, Israeli military strength was clear, and by 1969 Nixon accepted Israel's nuclear capacity, conditioned by ambiguous opacity, as well. The choices for American policymakers in any case were largely framed by the Cold War and Soviet intentions, as well as broader interests in ensuring oil supply and preventing revolutionary nationalisms in the Third World.[52]

In September 1970, developments in Jordan helped to further American and Israeli reluctance to alter the status quo. The death of Nasser, following the defeat of the PLO in Jordan and its displacement to Lebanon, introduced new uncertainties. Despite initiatives by President Sadat, neither the Israeli government nor US representatives took these efforts seriously enough to engage in productive negotiations. Although operating from different positions, there was insufficient motivation to engage in efforts to clarify the possibilities for resolution. For Israelis, there was little apparent incentive to withdraw from the territory they held. For Americans, even after Sadat asked that the USSR withdraw its advisors, there was little incentive to put pressure on the Israeli position. In the meantime, Israeli settlements continued, as did political debate about the occupation.[53]

It was not until the next war, in October 1973, that the structures of regional relationships began to settle into new forms.[54] Israeli dependence on US resupply during the war was accompanied by an American policy valuing Israeli military strength, in conjunction with Egyptian separation from the USSR. The PLO, which was experiencing its own internal conflicts, gained greater support from the Soviet Union as well as from much of the Third World, now with a growing presence in the UN. Despite a brief Geneva Conference, which included representatives of the USSR and suggested a new international attempt to negotiate peace, it was the United States, now represented by Secretary of State Henry Kissinger, that sought a gradual process of disengagement rather than final resolutions. This process had the goal of strengthening the American position in Egypt as well as Israel, enhancing perceptions of the US as the power most likely to succeed in managing the Arab-Israeli conflict. It was also a process that continued to rely on state-to-state relations while largely marginalizing Palestinian representation. By 1975, Kissinger solidified this reality when he made a commitment to Israel that the US would not enter into discussion with the PLO until it recognized Israel's right to exist, as well as accept Resolution 242.[55]

The war of 1973 and the oil crisis that followed were ultimately to have profound effects on the ways in which Jews, and American Jews in particular, viewed and discussed the Israeli-Palestinian conflict. The shock of the war itself generated a response in Israel very different from that of six years before: anger and loss, isolation and fear, intelligence and military failure punctured the confidence of 1967. Despite the ultimate victory, it left Israelis shaken.

Before 1967, American and Israeli Jews were, in very different ways, faced with the fruits of their own successes. The Zionist movement had resulted in a Jewish state that absorbed large numbers of Jewish immigrants, reinforcing the mission attributed to the state as a historical necessity. American Jews were finding new political and social voices in the broader landscape of turmoil that characterized the sixties. Anti-Semitism appeared not only lessened but delegitimized. With the Eichmann trial and recognition of the Holocaust as a "war against Jews," Israel was asserting its right to represent victims while simultaneously manifesting the values of Zionism and statehood. Nevertheless, there were new questions: What did Zionism now mean? What kind of state was possible? What was the role of religious law and the authorities representing it? What should be the relationship between Israel and the diaspora? And, in the US, reactions to the civil rights movement contributed to a revival of Jewish ethnic identity and questions about its definition or priority. Fear connected to loss of boundaries accompanied these developments, as they had to some extent in earlier times in Europe. Would integration signal an assimilation that diluted Jewish tradition? Would Arendt's description of a choice between being a Parvenu or a Pariah also apply in the US? American Jews, now increasingly comfortable in American life, had differing ideas about their responsibilities to one another and in the larger world.

The war of 1967 only complicated many of these questions. The fears for Israeli survival that developed in the three weeks before were also reflective of the gap between professional understanding of Israeli military capabilities and popular experiences. Coming as this did shortly after the Eichmann trial, it further strengthened the bonds between American and Israeli Jews. Both groups, in different ways, were just beginning to grapple with the complex factors that had enabled their survival, while most Jews in the Europe they had left behind perished.

In the aftermath of the war, the experience of vulnerability and righteous victory obscured the implications of reuniting the territory of Palestine. The Arab population that was now incorporated in the occupied territories carried what was understood to be not only a competing historical narrative, but one that threatened to undermine precisely the moral legitimacy of Zionist success. The price of Zionism seemed to be taking on a material reality and presence that had been invisible after 1948. As the Palestinian cause assumed the shape of a national movement, institutions, and guerrilla action, it did not pose a military threat to the state, but it did demand a response that would further define the Jewish state. What that should or could be constituted ongoing conversations and debates both in Israel and in the US. These political and intellectual discussions were accompanied by the beginning not only of settlements, but by movements that were to redefine an earlier secular labor Zionism as preparatory to the emerging religious nationalism based on historical Jewish rights.

Two critical challenges were now being decided by daily choices not necessarily based on awareness of consequences. The first challenge was facing or avoiding the return of an earlier history encompassing Palestinian Arabs and Jews who were governed by Great Britain and, after being forced into conflict, emerged to focus on struggles for survival that continued to pit them against one another. By 1967 the power disparities between them were such that facing this history demanded an accounting. The second challenge was defining the physical boundaries of the state and its cultural as well as political constitution. In 1948 armistice agreements had left boundaries that were accepted but in the aftermath of a new war the search for national security entailed questions about how territory did nor did not ensure that goal.

It was not until 1973/74 that the direction of development became clear. With the agreements for troop withdrawals negotiated by Henry Kissinger, the US became directly involved in managing state-to-state agreements that were based on the idea of steps toward defusing conflict, rather than an overall peace process. Integrated into these initiatives was ongoing US military support for Israel along with strategic cooperation. An American policy that sought reliable client states could now move toward combining commitments to Israel, Jordan,and Egypt in addition to the historical ties to Saudi Arabia.

In the US, discussion of Israel was colored by perceptions of its vulnerability in the aftermath of a new war, and by identification with what was viewed as the only democracy in the region, as well as its moral claims, secular and religious. Not many years later, the increasing political voice of evangelical Christians and the increasing strength of religious nationalism in Israel were to undergird these claims. In the aftermath of war, however, there were also prominent Jewish intellectuals and activists who believed that the Israeli future would best be safeguarded by taking initiatives to resolve the specific historical conflict with Palestinians.

In December 1973 a new US-based group announced its goals. Its title, Breira: A Project of Concern in Diaspora-Israel Relations, challenged two competing perspectives. Breira, meaning choice or alternative in Hebrew, contradicted the commonly articulated view that Israelis had *ein breira* (no choice). At the same time, the group was also speaking from a belief in the importance of Israel to the diaspora community and the right of that community to express opinions on Israeli government policy. In its initial statements the group called for Israel to recognize the legitimacy of Palestinian national aspirations, while also making clear its own connection to the ideas of early Zionists with whom they identified. The statement also specifically expressed distress with the pressures in American Jewish life that "make open discussion of these and other vital issues virtually synonymous with heresy."[56]

Ideological differences had already divided Jews both in Israel and in the US after 1967. Following the war in 1973 these became more acute. For those who experienced the war as a further attack on Israel's existence and the PLO simply as terrorists, it was difficult to understand those who saw the war as an effort to change the diplomatic playing field, and who understood the PLO as representing a legitimate national movement that required recognition in the context of efforts to resolve the conflict. Similarly, those who perceived Israel as a powerful state, which reflected the success of Zionism, believed that it should take active measures to resolve conflict with the Palestinians. They were concerned about the ways in which Israel would be transformed by being an occupying power, and had difficulty accepting that there were still genuine reasons to fear for Israel's existence.

Breira, founded in late 1973, sought to offer an alternative to both the American Israel Public Affairs Committee (AIPAC) and to the more militant Zionism of the Jewish Defense League, among others. Critical to understanding Breira's mission was its commitment to maintaining open debate and discussion on topics that were unwelcome by many in the Jewish communal establishment. Those who supported the organization included numerous rabbis who had been active in earlier civil rights and progressive movements, including Rabbi Joachim Prinz. These were by and large individuals with a historical identification as Zionists but who were worried about the ways in which that movement was being redefined. Although gaining broad support in its initial efforts, Breira finally was decimated by attacks from the right and consequent defections from inside. For approximately four years it represented an important effort to bridge the divide between a left that equated Zionism with an Israeli policy of displacing Palestinian Arabs and a right that was intent on preventing criticism of Israel, whose policies (whatever they were) they believed were inherently protective of Jewish rights while under attack.

By 1977, with Breira's demise and new elections in Israel that brought the right-wing Likud Party to power, Zionism as an arena for Jewish politics was closed down. Being Zionist came to be identified with supporting Israeli policy while Jewish criticisms of that policy, as well as alternative views of Palestinian nationalism, were often attacked. Polarization of debate was heightened by the American context in which it took place under new international conditions. Ironically, precisely the fulfillment of earlier hopes for American support to Israel now contributed to new boundaries imposed on political debate. An American foreign policy that favored military strength in its clients, and had begun a "war on terrorism" that saw revolutionary or socialist movements as dangerous, found common ground with an Israel that sought security through military control and action. Questioning these assumptions was now readily ascribed to naïveté as well as betrayal. Under these circumstances the Israel-Palestine conflict inevitably eroded the ground that Breira had sought to protect—that in which there was no contradiction between supporting both Israeli rights to existence and Palestinian rights to recognition.

The Zionism that had started out being precisely a movement that insisted on Jewish choices, as well as the importance of Jewish history, was now lost to a Zionism based on "ein breira" and selective versions of history. A Zionism that worked to create a modern, self-defining Jewish nation that could survive the external forces that, through hostility or absorption, appeared to threaten its existence, now was linked to a state policy based on avoidance of diplomatic initiatives while maintaining its primary focus on physical survival. The perceived need for big power support to maintain the conditions deemed necessary for that survival now also altered the structures of relationships within the international Jewish community. Where the relationship between Israel and the diaspora had taken on varied shapes over the preceding decades, after 1973 there was a decisive shift linking the Israeli and American governments with the American Jewish community, which was expected to act in accordance with the priorities of those states. Neither the Israeli government, nor that of the US, viewed the American Jewish establishment as having a legitimate independent voice to contribute.

Conclusion

In the late 1970s three developments served to harden the lines of US-Israel cooperation, further reinforce a bipolar view of the Palestinian-Israeli conflict, and alter its international context. In 1977 the Likud Party displaced Labor as the governing authority in Israel. With that change came greater commitment to Jewish settlement of the Occupied Territories (now referred to as Judea and Samaria by some on the right) as well as more sympathy for a religious nationalist version of Zionism. When Prime Minister Menachem Begin succeeded in concluding a peace treaty with Egypt, which effectively excluded the Palestinians, regional dynamics shifted to give Israel seemingly greater freedom and security.

Closely following in 1979, the revolution in Iran signaled further regional and international shifts. The overthrow of the shah by a religious nationalist movement mobilized historical resentment of foreign interference, which was now focused on the United States. The resultant rupture only reinforced the role of Israel as an American client state. When Ronald Reagan became president in 1981 the stage was set for renewed Cold War tensions that contributed to decreased US interest in pursuing resolution of the Israel-Palestinian conflict.

In Israel, however, the removal of Egypt as an active threat made it possible to focus on efforts to eliminate the PLO, which was disparaged as a terrorist organization linked to the USSR. In June 1982, with US complicity, Israeli forces invaded Lebanon, gaining the transport of the PLO leadership and Palestinian fighters to Tunis and permitting Christian Lebanese allies to massacre Palestinians in the refugee camps of Sabra and Shatila. This came to be a turning point, not toward security and peace, but toward deeper divisions in an Israel that was now engaged in a war of its own choosing.[1]

In Israel, and in the part of the American Jewish community that was attached to it, the events of 1982 heightened awareness of Israeli power and with it questions as to how that power was being utilized. Attacks on the refugee camps with their civilian populations begged for explanation as well as moral judgments. In Israel, the events led to the Kahan Commission whose findings forced the resignation of Minister of Defence Ariel Sharon. More immediately, public criticism and demonstrations made manifest the divisive effects of this military campaign. Many years later a film, *Waltz with Bashir*, illustrated the impact of the invasion on some who served in the military.[2] In the US, too, the Israeli action, U.S. participation, and the longer-term consequences for both the US and Israel created further division.

By 1987, the First Intifada was instrumental in forcing a direct confrontation that brought home the reality of a Palestinian-Israeli conflict that superseded what had been viewed as an Arab-Israeli contest. Several consequences followed from these developments. It became clear that the hope of eliminating a Palestinian voice through military action and dislocation of the PLO had failed. Israelis watching developments, or acting as part of the military in the Occupied Territories, were now faced with the reality of a Palestinian population reacting directly to Israeli use of force and its limitations. In the US, the implications of an occupation that had already lasted twenty years, and the emergence of a new activist generation among Palestinians living in the Occupied Territories, was coupled with greater attention to the need for a resolution that would protect both Israeli security and American interests in the region.

By 1988 the taboo on negotiating with the PLO was broken when Yasir Arafat spoke the words that had been required by the US. In a speech in Geneva to the UN General Assembly, Arafat renounced the use of terrorism and accepted UN Resolution 242 as the basis for a settlement of the conflict. What followed, however, were twelve years in which the US remained a significant player in what was broadly called a peace process. At times it seemed that there was hope of a two-state outcome and coexistence. That hope, however, was consistently belied by ongoing settlements as well as deep fundamental differences within both Israeli and Palestinian populations. The US acted as a buffer and played a mediating role, but the clear bias toward Israeli positions ultimately weakened its possible effectiveness. That bias, based on strong military and intelligence ties, supported by domestic political interests, was evident following the Madrid Conference of 1991. It took place during the presidency of George

H. W. Bush and for the first time created diplomatic efforts that included Palestinian representatives from the Occupied Territories. Although the Oslo Agreements signed in 1993 appeared to promise a way forward to Palestinian self-government and Israeli security, the years that followed proved critics right, and by 2000 little was left of the original hopes. Central to the ultimate failures of Madrid and then Oslo was the issue of ongoing Israeli settlements in the Occupied Territories as well as challenges by rightwing movements both in Israel and within the occupied Palestinian population.

By 2000, the failure of the Camp David talks attended by Prime Minister Ehud Barak, PLO president Yasir Arafat, and President Bill Clinton, followed by the Second Intifada, erased hopes for resolution and have been followed by developments that have only reinforced the asymmetry of power. At the same time, however, these conditions created room for new conversations about the stakes of an occupation and settlement policy that had lasted for thirty-three years.

Already in 1986 Meron Benvenisti, former deputy mayor of Jerusalem (1973–1978), had warned that developments on the ground in the Occupied Territories would force Israelis to choose between having a Jewish state or having a democratic state.[3] To his surprise, he reported that reactions to his analysis resulted in opposition from his own liberal reference group and support from his adversaries.[4] Benvenisti was speaking from knowing the material changes occurring, which he saw as ultimately driving a transformation in Israeli Jewish options. Already then it became evident that the potential loss of democracy versus the loss of a Jewish state revealed a basic divide in the Israeli Jewish population. American Jews, however, were largely ignorant of this discussion, which challenged the established mantra of Israel as the only democratic state in the Middle East, easily identified with the United States. The underlying, unresolved question of how various groups defined the idea of a Jewish state remained largely hidden for US Jews until more recent years.

The discussions of Zionism traced in earlier chapters of this book took place primarily within Jewish circles. They helped to determine how the state of Israel came into existence, who was included and excluded, as well as which basic assumptions governed policy once statehood was attained. It was only after 1948 and then particularly after 1967 that the elision of Zionism and statehood was accompanied by a growing consensus that linked American and Israeli Jews into a political community. Central to that structure was a shared emphasis on national security that served to decrease discussions about the uses of Israeli and American power.

Within Israel itself political developments continued to be vigorously debated. In the non-Orthodox American Jewish world, however, decreasing tolerance for criticism of Israel gradually alienated those who sought to reconcile their idealized visions of the Zionist project with the increasingly evident Israeli reliance on military strength to control a complex population under its power. As the Arab-Israeli conflict returned to its origins as a Palestinian-Israeli confrontation, the historical attribution of permanent victimhood to Jewish history was less and less accurate or viable as reality belied it. Gradually, the political arena, which had been forged as one inclusive of Israeli and American Jews, broke down.

In the aftermath of the failed Camp David talks of 2000 new conversations and conflicts have become more visible. Central to this process is the emergence of challenges to the political arena that had been constructed by the presumption of an American Jewish and Israeli consensus that gradually become dominant after 1967. At the core of this consensus was a set of relationships assumed to benefit both the US and Israel, with the American Jewish establishment acting to contain critical voices questioning this arrangement or offering alternative interpretations. As this consensus frayed, the way was opened for alternative arenas and political leaderships and thinkers to offer competing ideas about Zionism and Jewish peoplehood. Although these developments were met at times with fears for the unity of Jewish life, this was not the first time that Zionism had to vie with alternative versions of Jewish modernity.

What has seemed at stake in more recent years are competing analyses of the relationship between American and Israeli Jews with regard to political life and action. Although labeled political, these differences inevitably integrate an existing spectrum of views on the desirable relationship between religion and the state. While there are some—particularly the Orthodox Jewish communities with their own leaderships—who continue to maintain traditional communal boundaries, secular Jews—American and Israeli—wrestle with the ongoing challenge of living in a more fluid, pluralistic world while still seeking some forms of Jewish continuity. The challenges inevitably differ for these two broadly conceived groups, but both experience the push and pull of both mutual dependence and separation.

Meron Benvenisti was one of the first to state clearly the expectation that Israelis would have to choose between living in a democracy and maintaining a Jewish state. In 1986 it was still posed as a choice between reversion to the earlier Zionism of Jewish statehood and the transformation of that entity by expansion and domination of a subject population. It was not until after the First Intifada (1987–1991) that the need to recognize Palestinian national claims could no longer be ignored. Over the next years, as increasing settlements accompanied what was known as the peace process, internal contradictions surfaced. They culminated in a Second Intifada (2000–2005), which resulted in consolidation of the separation between Palestinians in the Occupied Territories and Israeli Jews, along with creating a narrative that undercut arguments for coexistence.

Since 2000 a growing set of writings testifies to renewed differences among American and Israeli Jews, but these differences do not necessarily fall along national lines. Rather, polarization in both the US and Israel has gradually been manifest ideologically as well as politically. For Israelis the post-2000 period has been colored by adaptation to a situation characterized, on the one hand, by a narrative claiming that they have "no partner for peace," and on the other, by views that see Israeli and American interests aligned, supporting the expectation of a partner for security.

In place of the largely unquestioned identification of US and Israeli interests, it now became necessary to argue either for this position or against it. As critiques of Israeli policies and support for Palestinian concerns became more visible in the US, responses showed both fear of the consequences and growing alienation from arguments based on zero-sum assumptions. As progressive American Jewish organizations focused on the occupation as responsible for the failure of peace efforts, those who spoke in the name of Zionism attributed responsibility to Palestinian decision-makers.[5] In an earlier chapter, the ways in which the Algerian War entered into responses to the Arab-Israeli conflict were discussed. After 2000 it was the campaign against apartheid in South Africa that provided an alternative framework for the Israeli-Palestinian conflict. On the one hand, the BDS (boycott, divestment, and sanctions) movement sought to mobilize Americans in particular to support nonviolent ways by which governments as well as individuals or institutions could bring pressure to bear on Israel in hopes of ending the occupation. On the other hand, the context of this campaign limited its impact as the post-9/11 focus on terrorism and the wars in the Middle East further strengthened those who saw the interests of the US and Israel aligned. In addition, a context in which Muslims were often seen as suspect added to the plausibility of attributing anti-Semitism to groups that defined themselves as seeking justice for Palestinians. With growing polarization in both Israeli and American political arenas, it became harder to contain recognition of two separate but not equal histories (Jewish and Palestinian), each with its own pain and responsibility.

Recent debates and legal efforts highlight at least one way in which the Israeli-Palestinian conflict contributes to sharpening terminology and, with it, emotions within the American Jewish world. As the conflict has become a focus for Palestinian activism along with growing mobilization by Jewish groups critical of Israeli policies and the occupation, within the United States it has been accompanied by a vigilant Jewish defensive response. The fact that this is occurring at a time when anti-Semitic attacks in Europe and the US mobilize historical fears only complicates the discussions. In response to these developments, efforts to define anti-Semitism and to encode it in law or regulation have sparked an important focus on the ways in which it has become difficult to disentangle anti-Semitism from anti-Zionism. That challenge is rooted in a history that gradually blurred the lines between Judaism and Zionism. Finding a way to separate out these meanings, sought by Jews and Palestinians, has been made much more difficult by the political implications read into the discussions.[6]

Responding to the dilemma of widening gaps within Jewish communities and particularly the struggles of younger secular Jews in the US, a number of writers offered analyses that manifested alternative paths to thinking about the past as well as the future. Daniel Gordis, an American immigrant to Israel, suggested that American and Israeli Jews should complement each other, denying that the occupation was central to their emerging differences.[7] Rabbi Eric Jaffe's review of his book challenged this denial and asserted the centrality of concerns with Israeli policy.[8] Recognizing the effects on American campuses, Kenneth Stern sought to place the conflict into the specific American contexts while Dov Waxman more broadly addressed emerging communal differences.[9] In contrast to earlier questions about the legitimacy of American Jewish criticism of Israeli policies, this literature reflects the growing recognition of alienation. It is in that context that more recent proposals for the future have arisen. Central to them is the emerging discussion about one-state versus two-state solutions to the conflict. Based on the view that time had rendered a two-state outcome unrealistic, Tony Judt and, more recently, Peter Beinart sought to open up conversations that remained connected to earlier Zionist history but recognized the transformative impact of historical developments. They were arguing primarily against the settlement project and occupation as defeating a two-state outcome.

Where Judt's article stimulated a full-throated attack and the publication of Benny Morris's book on the subject, Beinart's work has not aroused comparable responses. Perhaps this too reflects the changing environment of American and Jewish life.[10]

Scanning a select few of the relevant writings published after 2000, it becomes possible to differentiate the historical contexts within which writers place their arguments. What emerges from such an examination are new political arenas that signal the ways in which some Jewish thinkers and writers in the US and Israel are gradually extricating their analyses from the apparent merger of American and Israeli political contests. It is in the questioning of Israeli policies and the rejection of fear-based understandings of Jewish history that new possibilities emerge. Inevitably, these are accompanied by ongoing resistance to arguments based on the need to account for the historical uses of power and its effects both in the US and in Israel.

In a recent book, *The Implicated Subject*, Michael Rothberg provides an argument for considering the role, as well as consciousness, of implicated subjects when thinking about historical conflicts that have been viewed through a bipolar lens of victim and victimizer.[11] This analytical framework is intimately connected to the now globalized realities of transnational populations that span territorial locations and diasporic communities, as well as to the ways in which historical memory has been constructed. As Rothberg notes, this expansion of narratives that have typically been cast in terms of persecutors and victims is particularly pertinent to the complexities of the Israel-Palestinian conflict as well as to the role of American Jews in its evolution.

Another view of current developments is offered by an article in *Ha'aretz* published on May 24, 2020, titled "After Losing Hope for Change, Top Left-Wing Activists and Scholars Leave Israel Behind." The Israeli Jews discussed in this piece have devoted significant efforts over the years to overcoming obstacles to Palestinian and Israeli mutual understanding and coexistence. In different ways, they see themselves as rooted in historical Zionism but are keenly aware of the trajectories that required repairs and transformations that were met with powerful opposition. Eventually, they felt a need to emigrate in order to pursue their work and family lives abroad. Perhaps most telling is the fact that these activists, writers, and scholars did not see a way to educate their children in Israel due to the growing racism, intolerant nationalism, and militarism that they opposed.

At least one of these scholars, Adi Ophir, has found himself replacing "my interest in political Israel with a growing interest in Jewish thought and history. . . . I'm enjoying being a Diaspora Jew."

In his recent book, *The New American Zionism*, Theodore Sasson challenges the idea that American Jews are becoming distanced from Israel.[12] Instead, he argues that "American Jews are increasingly behaving like other contemporary diaspora communities—they are becoming a normal diaspora."[13] Analyzing shifts in the nature of the American Jewish relationship to Israel, Sasson sees a shift from an earlier mobilization model to one of personal direct engagement. Implicit in this transformation is the space for multiple political views toward an Israel increasingly viewed as a "normal" state open to critical assessments as well as support. Also implicit is a relationship that no longer requires Jews to agree in their views because earlier fears no longer govern.

Israel today is the product of the historical European Zionist movement. That movement and its ideologies grew out of an environment that, while unsafe or limiting, or both, for many Jews, was also entirely recognizable in a world transitioning from empires to nation-states. It was a world in which Zionism's aspirations—solving the Jewish Question, transforming Jewish life in its material and cultural aspects, gaining recognition, and becoming modern—could be understood. This context no doubt contributed to the support it was able to garner during and after World War I. Largely shielded by British power under the mandate, Jewish settlement in Palestine provided conditions to build institutions, a governing structure, and contain multiple political forces as well as aspirations.

As fascism and Nazism reinforced the need for Jewish escape, however, it became clear that neither Great Britain nor the US saw their interests aligned with rescue. With the end of World War II, moreover, the recognized annihilation of Europe's Jewish communities coincided with ongoing US and British reluctance to offer safety while American Jews had to wrestle with their own responsibilities. In Palestine, the identification of Jewish statehood with the power for self-defense as well as for separateness from others seen as dangerous, a lack of trust, and a drive to build a larger community all helped shape the ways in which the war of 1947/49 unfolded. Zionism as a field of political thought and action was decisively altered by the establishment of the state of Israel, which now had the tools to craft narratives of Jewish history to be taught in schools and utilized to support the legitimacy of the state, which remained an object of conflict. As a result, Zionism came to be equated with a specific material reality and a state defined as one belonging to the Jewish people wherever they lived. As a state ideology, Zionism ceased to be a productively debated arena for Jewish politics. Coinciding with the decimation of Jewish communities in Europe and the emerging movements for decolonization, the possibilities for a specifically Jewish politics were largely elided, and after 1967 the revival of a politics based on claims of Israeli vulnerability, as well as US support seemingly predicated on the needs of security, further submerged alternatives.

It is therefore useful to consider the more recent emergence of parallel trends in both the US and Israel that signal new arenas in which political conflict has become more visible. In both, debates raise questions about the nature of the state in which competing views of history, as well as values, vie to claim legitimacy. In both, changing demographics and claims to recognition by excluded groups fuel responses to a world in which earlier dominance is at risk. The impact on American Jews is complicated by the possibilities for locating themselves in two very different worlds as they identify with the role of a majority versus a minority. In a related development, how Jews in Israel view their own history—placing themselves in the surrounding world and in relationship to their own minorities—is inevitably governed by the political arena within which they live. In contrast, American Jews have the freedom to choose their own context for both commitment and action. In both cases, however, Zionism as an idea and Israel as a reality have become touchstones for arguing the legitimacy of Jewish actions and views, as well as for assessing the implications of living in a pluralistic world.

The historical Zionist movement succeeded in many ways beyond the dreams of its founders. It did not cure the complex pains and fragilities of adjustments to modernity, nor did it solve the perennial questions attached to Jewish minority existence in the world. If anything, success has uncovered the limitations of achieving military and political power without accounting for the prices paid.

Rather than solving the Jewish Question, it is possible to argue that Zionism strengthened the resources now available for facing all that has been suppressed and ignored. Whether there will be the will to accept historical accountability remains to be seen. In both the US and Israel, the efforts to eliminate alternative political arenas therefore signal an era in which it is likely that newer generations will have to struggle with the difficult choices ahead.

Coda

This book was completed prior to the events of October 7, 2023 and their aftermath. Living still with the repercussions of ongoing violence, now intensified by the results of elections in the US, the future for both Israelis and Americans looks uncertain and precarious as I complete this afterword. As a historian, I can offer insights into the past, but I am also aware that what we see in that past will undoubtedly be revisited as the present and future unfold. It is however already clear that Americans and Israelis are living through a period of radical transformation both in their relationships to one another and internally within each group. For those who have been and remain politically active in the arenas covered in this book—Zionism, Israel, and the US—October 7th and its aftermath has generated added pressure to clarify the choices that will help determine their responses over the longer term. Two books published while I was completing this book represent important interventions in the development of American, Israeli, and diasporic Jewish life. Both contribute to a growing literature of thought about the ongoing challenges for Jews in particular.

In *Tablets Shattered: The End of an American Jewish Century and the Future of Jewish Life*, Joshua Leifer traces the way in which Israel has come to define the positions both of its American supporters and of the American critics of Zionism as Zionism came to be equated with the state of Israel. Leifer's narrative offers a voice of his generation whose consciousness and identity have emerged primarily in the post-9/11 era. As such, his questions as well as commitments offer the reader important insight into the search for a Jewish life, as well as for a politics that is not confined by the earlier boundaries whose construction was detailed in this book. Shaul Magid's *The Necessity of Exile: Essays from a Distance* wrestles with a long Jewish history through essays on exile, Israel, and Zionism. Both of these writers, as well as others now writing in various venues, are documenting the emergence of significant changes in the views, as well as the environment, of American Jews as they struggle with Zionism and its history.

Israel too has changed with the growing role of religious Zionists and militant settlers whose views have been, and are, shaped by the realities of living in a militarized state while defining themselves as Jews in ways often not compatible with historical and secular Zionism. In this book I have not dealt with the transformation of Israeli conversations in parallel with those in the US, but there is little question that political and generational changes are likely to widen the growing gap between American and Israeli Jews. It is increasingly difficult to obscure the fundamental differences of experience between American Jews living as a minority in the US and Israeli Jews, increasingly dominant in demographic terms, and living as a majority controlling a large Palestinian population. Those seeking to understand how the future might unfold for both will need to plumb the depths of those tensions. But to do so will require engaging with, rather than fleeing from, history.

Notes

Introduction

1. Pierre Birnbaum and Ira Katznelson, eds., *Paths of Emancipation: Jews, States, and Citizenship* (Princeton University Press, 1995). While Jews in the Russian Empire participated in a range of political movements, their choices, like that of non-Jewish subjects, were bounded by imperial constraints. See Zvi Gitelman, ed., *The Emergence of Modern Jewish Politics: Bundism and Zionism in Eastern Europe* (University of Pittsburgh Press, 2003).

2. Zionism as an aspiration can be found in the writings of Moses Hess and Leon Pinsker, among others, including Theodor Herzl. Zionism as a political movement can be dated to the first Zionist Congress in Basel, Switzerland, in 1897.

3. Gil Troy, *The Zionist Ideas: Visions for the Jewish Homeland* (Jewish Publication Society, 2018). For a fuller collection, see Jehuda Reinharz and Anita Shapira, eds., *Essential Papers on Zionism* (New York: NYU Press, 1996). These serve primarily as introductions to the subject.

4. Noam Pianko, *Zionism: The Roads Not Taken* (Indiana University Press, 2010), provides an analysis of alternatives in the US. Thomas A. Kolsky, *Jews Against Zionism* (Temple University Press, 1990), is a history of the American Council for Judaism, 1942–1948, which represented American anti–Zionism.

5. See Dmitry Shumsky, *Beyond the Nation-State: The Zionist Political Imagination from Pinsker to Ben-Gurion* (Yale University Press, 2018).

6. Ben-Gurion, Goldmann, and Bloustein played significant roles in Jewish institutional life. Arendt, Magnus, and Jabotinsky each represented or articulated significant critical alternatives to the dominant leaderships. Koestler, Stone, and Uris serve here as writers whose personal experiences (European and American) led to engaged writings on Palestine and Israel.

7. For books that recover the voices of those who are largely unheard in these discussions, see Dov Waxman, *Trouble in the Tribe: The American Jewish Conflict over Israel* (Princeton University Press, 2016); Eric Alterman, *We Are Not One: A History of America's Fight over Israel* (Basic Books, 2022); Daniel Gordis,

We Stand Divided: The Rift Between American Jews and Israel (Harper/Collins, 2019); and Geoffrey Levin, *Our Palestine Question: Israel and American Jewish Dissent, 1948–1978* (Yale University Press, 2023). Yaacov Yadgar, *Sovereign Jews: Israel, Zionism, and Judaism* (State University of New York Press, 2017), and Salim Yaqub, *Imperfect Strangers: Americans, Arabs, and U.S.-Middle East Relations in the 1970s* (Cornell University Press, 2016), provide further context.

8. Two recent valuable contributions to broader discussion are Shaul Magid, *The Necessity of Exile: Essays from a Distance* (Ayin Press, 2023), and Derek Penslar, *Zionism: An Emotional State* (Rutgers University Press, 2023). In *Tablets Shattered: The End of an American Jewish Century and the Future of Jewish Life* (Penguin Random House, 2024), Joshua Leifer addresses "The End of An American Jewish Century."

9. There is a growing literature on Israeli Jews of Middle Eastern origin, on the history of Jewish life in the Middle East, and on the complexities of identities flattened by the pressures of nationalism. See, for example, Yehouda Shenhav, *The Arab Jews: A Postcolonial Reading of Nationalism, Religion, and Ethnicity* (Stanford University Press, 2006); Massoud Hayoun, *When We Were Arabs: A Jewish Family's Forgotten History* (New Press, 2019); and two analyses that challenge boundaries of national separation: Gil Z. Hochberg, *In Spite of Partition: Jews, Arabs, and the Limits of Separatist Imagination* (Princeton University Press, 2007), and Yonatan Mendel and Ronald Ranta, *From the Arab Other to the Israeli Self: Palestinian Culture in the Making of Israeli National Identity* (Ashgate, 2016).

10. The most recent academic considerations of Goldmann's life and work can be found in Mark A. Raider, ed., *Nahum Goldmann: Statesman Without a State* (State University of New York Press, 2009).

Chapter 1

1. Ronald Sanders, *The High Walls of Jerusalem: A History of the Balfour Declaration and the Birth of the British Mandate for Palestine* (Holt, Rinehart and Winston, 1983); Leonard Stein, *The Balfour Declaration* (Simon and Schuster, 1961); and Doreen Ingrams, *Palestine Papers, 1917–1922* (G. Braziller, 1972), 7–18. The text of the Balfour Declaration was brief but it emerged from a longer British colonial history and distinctive negotiations between Zionists and the British government during the war. Its wording allowed for multiple interpretations and its impact on Palestinian Arab elites was immediate.

2. Theodor Herzl, *The Jewish State* (American Zionist Emergency Council, 1946).

3. For a history of early settlement practices, see Derek J. Penslar, *Zionism and Technocracy* (Indiana University Press, 1991).

4. See Amnon Rubinstein, *From Herzl to Rabin* (Holmes and Meier, 2000).

5. Labor Zionism supported the creation of a new Jewish society based on socialist as well as nationalist commitments and sought to recruit those with similar ideological commitments who were prepared to build the new Jewish world. It was not initially meant to rescue Jews from immediate danger and it was expected that the mandate would remain. All this changed with the impact of fascism as well as the growing conflict in Palestine itself.

6. The literature on Ben-Gurion's life and work is extensive. For a short biography, see Anita Shapira, *Ben-Gurion: Father of Modern Israel* (Yale University Press, 2014). For more extensive studies, see Shabtai Teveth, *Ben-Gurion: The Burning Ground, 1886–1948* (Houghton, Mifflin, 1987), and Tom Segev, *A State at Any Cost: The Life of David Ben-Gurion* (Farrar, Straus and Giroux, 2019).

7. For a short biography, see Hillel Halkin, *Jabotinsky: A Life* (Yale University Press, 2014). For an interpretation of Jabotinsky's early years and intellectual development, see Michael Stanislawski, *Zionism and the Fin de Siecle* (University of California Press, 2001). There is also the more complete biography by Joseph Schechtman, *Rebel and Statesman: The Vladimir Jabotinsky Story* (T. Yoseloff, 1956).

8. See *The Autobiography of Nahum Goldmann* (Holt, Rinehart and Winston, 1969), and Raider, *Nahum Goldmann: Statesman Without A State*. For a discussion of the gap between Goldmann's presentation of his activities in his memoirs and his actual activities at times, see Zohar Segev, "Goldmann and the First Two Decades of the WJC," in Raider, *Nahum Goldmann*, 107–24.

9. See Elizabeth Young-Bruehl, *Hannah Arendt: For Love of the World* (Yale University Press, 1982), and Jerome Kohn and Ron Feldman, eds., *Hannah Arendt: The Jewish Writings* (Schocken Books, 2007).

10. See Francine Klagsbrun, *Lioness: Golda Meir and the Nation of Israel* (Schocken Books, 2017). For another perspective, see Pnina Lahav, *The Only Woman in the Room: Golda Meir and Her Path to Power* (Princeton University Press, 2022).

11. See Daniel Kotzin, *Judah L. Magnes: An American Jewish Nonconformist* (Syracuse University Press, 2010).

12. For short discussions of conceptualizations by Ahad HaAm and Theodor Herzl, see Shlomo Avineri, *The Making of Modern Zionism* (Basic Books, 1981). For selections from both their writings, see Arthur Hertzberg, *The Zionist Idea* (Jewish Publication Society, 1997). For biographical information on Ahad HaAm, see Steven Zipperstein, *Elusive Prophet: Ahad Ha'AM and the Origins of Zionism* (University of California Press, 1993). On Herzl's biography, see Amos Elon, *Herzl* (Holt, Rinehart and Winston, 1975), and Ernst Pavel, *The Labyrinth of Exile: A Life of Theodor Herzl* (Farrer, Straus and Giroux, 1989).

13. On the prewar period, see Neville Mandel, *The Arabs and Zionism Before World War I* (University of California Press, 1976). For a broader discussion of the fall of the Ottoman Empire and the post–World War I settlement of the Middle

East, see David Fromkin, *A Peace to End All Peace: Creating the Modern Middle East, 1914–1922* (Avon Books, 1989).

14. By 1920, it had been decided that Great Britain would control Palestine and Iraq as League of Nations mandates while France was recognized as mandatory power for Syria and Lebanon. See Fromkin, *Peace to End All Peace,* 389–420, 493–514. For an understanding of the way in which British economic policy impacted Arabs and Jews in Palestine, see Barbara J. Smith, *The Roots of Separatism in Palestine* (Syracuse University Press, 1993).

15. Henry Feingold, *The Politics of Rescue: The Roosevelt Administration and the Holocaust, 1938–1945* (Rutgers University Press, 1970); David Wyman, *The Abandonment of the Jews: America and the Holocaust, 1941–1945* (Pantheon Books, 1984); Aaron Berman, *Nazism: The Jews and American Zionism* (Wayne State University Press, 1990); Gulie Ne'eman Arad, *America, Its Jews, and the Rise of Nazism* (Indiana University Press, 2000); Richard Breitman, Barbara McDonald Stewart, and Severin Hockberg, eds., *Refugees and Rescue: Diaries and Papers of James G. McDonald, 1935–45* (Indiana University Press, 2004).

16. British Statement of Policy, Cmd 6019 (May 1939), as cited in *The Jew in the Modern World,* ed. Paul Mendes-Flohr and Jehuda Reinharz (Oxford University Press, 1995).

17. See Ylana Miller, *Government and Society in Rural Palestine, 1920–48* (University of Texas Press, 1985).

18. See Avi Shlaim, *The Politics of Partition: King Abdullah, the Zionists, and Palestine, 1921–1951* (Columbia University Press, 1990), 18–38.

19. On an abortive effort at agreement between Ben-Gurion and Jabotinsky, see Segev, *A State at Any Cost,* 247–50.

20. For evidence of more complexity in the relationship between Ben-Gurion and Jabotinsky, as well as an effort to avoid a split in the movement, see "My Dear Enemy . . . ," *Jerusalem Post,* international ed., week ending February 3, 1990.

21. See Kotzin, *Judah L. Magnes,* 169–273; for Magnes's writings, see Arthur A. Goren, ed., *Dissenter in Zion: From the Writings of Judah L. Magnes* (Harvard University Press, 1982); William Brinner and Moses Rischin, eds., *Like All the Nations? The Life and Legacy of Judah L. Magnes* (State University of New York Press, 1987).

22. On the development of Palestinian Arab nationalism under the mandate, see Yehoshua Porath, *The Palestinian Arab National Movement* (Frank Cass, 1977), and Rashid Khalidi, *The Iron Cage: The Story of the Palestinian Struggle for Statehood* (Beacon, 2006).

23. For information on an alternative Jewish plan formulated by the Hebrew Committee of National Liberation, see CAJH Box I–278.

24. See Michael Cohen, *Palestine. Retreat from the Mandate: The Making of British Policy, 1936–1945* (Holmes and Meier, 1978), 66–87.

25. Relevant memoranda, letters, and the summary of a press conference on August 16, 1945, in which Palestine was discussed can be found in the Harry S. Truman papers at the Truman Library, Independence, Missouri.

26. See Susan Hattis, *The Binational Idea in Palestine During Mandatory Times* (Shikmona, 1970). For a more recent and brief discussion, see Benny Morris, *One State, Two States: Resolving the Israel/Palestine Conflict* (Yale University Press, 2009), 44–60.

27. Philip Mattar, *The Mufti of Jerusalem: Al-Hajj Amin Al-Husayni and the Palestinian National Movement* (Columbia University Press, 1988), 99–107. Also Gilbert Achcar, *The Arabs and the Holocaust: The Arab-Israeli War of Narratives* (Saqi, 2010), 140–56.

28. Projects for Arab-Jewish coexistence, such as those for a binational state or a federated one, would have imposed limits on Jewish immigration to Palestine. Such alternatives also foundered on Arab opposition.

29. On Goldmann's role during decision-making about partition, see Raider, *Nahum Goldmann*, 169–203.

Chapter 2

1. Anita Shapira, *Israel: A History* (Brandeis University Press, 2012), 208. See also Tom Segev, *1949: The First Israelis* (Free Press, 1986).

2. Some groups still articulating alternative understandings of the new state have largely been erased from conventional histories. See, for example, "Peter Bergson on the Views of the Hebrew Committee of National Liberation New York Post, December 17, 1947," in the American Jewish Committee Library, CAJH FAD-1, Box 58. In the same box, there is a "Press Survey of Reaction to Creation of State of Israel," June 1948, which reflects the interest of the AJC as it formulated policy. The concerns of the AJC extended to the development of governing institutions. CAJH FAD-1, Box 69, contains a copy of the draft constitution for Israel from 1948 as well as relevant correspondence.

3. For an understanding of Ben-Gurion's views and his communication to an Israeli audience, see the "Address by Mr. David Ben-Gurion to the World Convention of the Ichud [Union of Poale-Zion and Tzeirei-Zion] on August 8, 1951," here translated. Ben-Gurion expresses the view that the state as well as the Yishuv before it were unique and articulates his view of their relationship to Jews outside that territory. CAJH GEN-12, AJC collection, Box 62. This file includes additional material on the Status Law and reflects concerns of the AJC.

4. The Status Law can be found in CAJH GEN-12, AJC collection, Box 62, File 51-2. See files 51–54 for related correspondence.

5. Steps to mitigate the effects of Ben-Gurion's statements on American groups continued to take place in the early 1950s. See Abba Eban to Nahum Goldmann, October 4, 1951, in CZA Z6/466. While the leadership of the AJC operated from commitments to the American Jewish community, Nahum Goldmann was primarily concerned with organizing that community as a way to strengthen its voice vis-à-vis both the Israeli and American governments. In this endeavor, Goldmann sought to be a significant actor between all interested parties. See CZA Z6/659.

6. Melvin Urofsky, *We Are One! American Jewry and Israel* (Doubleday, 1978), 209–34; Henry Feingold, "From Equality to Liberty"; and Mel Scult, "Americanism and Judaism in the Thought of Mordecai Kaplan," in *The Americanization of the Jews*, ed. Robert M. Selzer and Norman J. Cohen (NYU Press, 1995), 97–118 and 339–54. See also Karen Brodkin, *How Jews Became White Folks* (Rutgers University Press, 1998), 138–74.

7. *Autobiography of Nahum Goldmann*, 312–29.

8. Official Israeli concerns are evident in the careful monitoring of American Jewish perceptions and actions with regard to Israel. See as an example the correspondence in ISA, FO 7227/19 and 3379/13. The AJC also closely followed developments. See "Press Survey of Reaction to Creation of State of Israel," 1948, in CAJH FAD-1, Box 58. In the same file, a letter from Richard Rothschild to Louis Bennett, June 15, 1948, discusses the impact of "the Palestine situation on antisemitism in the United States." Included also is a summary on "Peter Bergson on the Views of the Hebrew Committee of National Liberation," *New York Post*, December 17, 1947.

9. Naomi Cohen, *Not Free To Desist: The American Jewish Committee, 1906–1966* (Jewish Publication Society, 1972), 312. This exchange of views is discussed in Ariel Feldestein, *Ben-Gurion, Zionism and American Jewry, 1948–1963* (New York: Routledge, 2006), 33–35, and Charles Liebman, "Diaspora Influence on Israel: the Ben-Gurion–Blaustein 'Exchange' and Its Aftermath," *Jewish Social Studies* 36, nos. 3–4 (July–October 1974), 271–80. A summary signed by both Ben-Gurion and Blaustein in April 1961 can be found in ISA FO3295/6.

10. CAJH, Enclosure dated 11/25/52, Blaustein to John Slawson, October 6, 1954, AJC files, Nationality Law, FAD, Box 71; Abba Eban to Nahum Goldmann, October 4, 1951, enclosing cable, Ben-Gurion to Eban, September 30, 1951, clarifying statement re American Jews, CZA Z6/466.

11. Naomi W. Cohen, *American Jews and the Zionist Idea* (Ktav, 1975), 113–28; Feldestein, *Ben-Gurion, Zionism*. For AJC views on American Jews and Israel from 1953 to 1958, see CJH FAD-1, Box 65.

12. See Moshe Pearlman, *Ben-Gurion Looks Back* (Simon and Schuster, 1965), 238–52. See also Benno Weiser, "Ben-Gurion's Dispute with American Zionists," *Commentary* 18 (1954), 93–101.

13. Nahum Goldmann, Address to Twenty-Third Zionist Congress in Jerusalem, August 1951, in *Community of Fate, Essays, Speeches and Articles* by Nahum Goldmann (Israel Universities Press, 1977), 17–27.

14. See Ronald Zweig, " 'Reparations Made Me': Nahum Goldmann, German Reparations, and the Jewish World," in Raider, *Nahum Goldmann*, 233–54. Also Nana Sagi, *German Reparations: A History of the Negotiations* (St. Martin's, 1986).

15. See Sagi, *German Reparations.*

16. See "Dr. Nahum Goldmann's Views on Israeli Foreign Policy," December 1957, which gives a summary of Goldmann's talk to the Progressive Party in Israel on October 24, 1957, in which he advocated a neutral position for Israel as well as Jews. CAJH FAD-1, Box 69. In the years from 1948 to 1967, Ben-Gurion, Goldmann, and Blaustein continued to articulate differing although often compatible views that reflected their physical and intellectual locations. See, for example, Forum for Jewish Thought. Third Annual Symposium, September 5, 1966, on Jewry and Judaism in the Modern World, in which both Ben-Gurion and Goldmann articulated their views. CZA Z6/2609.

17. For memoranda from Syrian and Lebanese representatives to the US Department of State on the subject of German reparations and the link to the Arab-Israeli conflict as well as to Palestinian refugees, see *Foreign Relations of the United States,* The Near and Middle East, vol. 9, pt. I, no. 408, 410, and 591.

18. See Irwin Wall, *France, The United States, and the Algerian War* (University of California Press, 2001).

19. The Egyptian Revolution of 1952, followed by the ascent of President Gamal Abdel Nasser in 1954, introduced new uncertainties for Israelis. Nasser's aspiration to Pan-Arab leadership was also linked to broader anticolonialism and to support for the FLN struggle in Algeria. By 1956 the convergence of Israeli and French perceptions contributed to the joint action in the Suez/Sinai War. See Gadi Heimann, *Franco-Israeli Relations, 1958–1967* (Routledge, 2017). On the Israeli background, see Avi Shlaim, *The Iron Wall: Israel and the Arab World* (Norton, 2000), chaps. 3 and 4. For a broader analysis, see Michael Laskier, "Israel and Algeria amid French Colonialism and the Arab-Israeli Conflict, 1954–1978," *Israel Studies* 6, no. 2 (Summer 2001): 1–32. On the Algerian Revolution, see Alistair Horne, *A Savage War of Peace: Algeria 1954–1962* (New York Review of Books, 2006).

20. Myron J. Aronoff, "Myths, Symbols and Rituals of the Emerging State," in *New Perspectives On Israeli History*, ed. Laurence J. Silberstein (NYU Press, 1991), 175–92; James McDougall, *History and the Culture of Nationalism in Algeria* (Cambridge University Press, 2006), 225–38.

21. Fanon's depiction of revolutionary violence as necessarily transformative was only part of his contribution to the understanding of colonialism and decolonization as they affected Algerians in particular; *The Wretched of the Earth*

(Grove Press, 2004). For a more recent collection of Fanon's writings, see *Franz Fanon: Alienation and Freedom*, ed. Jean Khalfa and Robert J. C. Young (Bloomsbury Academic, 2018) For information on Fanon's life, see Irene Gendzier, *Frantz Fanon: A Critical Study* (Pantheon, 1973).

22. Michael Rothberg, *Multidirectional Memory: Remembering the Holocaust in the Age of Decolonization* (Stanford University Press, 2009).

23. Jeffrey Isaac, *Arendt, Camus, and Modern Rebellion* (Yale University Press, 1992).

24. Aamir Mufti, *Enlightenment in the Colony: The Jewish Question and the Crisis of Postcolonial Culture* (Princeton University Press, 2007).

25. James McDougall, "Martyrdom and Destiny: The Inscription and Imagination of Algerian History," in *Memory and Violence in the Middle East and North Africa*, ed. Ussama Makdisi and Paul Silverstein (Indiana University Press, 2006), 50–72.

26. See Albert Memmi, *The Colonizer and the Colonized* (Beacon Press, 1967), and *Dependence* (Beacon Press, 1984), to consider the perspective of a Tunisian Jewish intellectual. A broader scope is offered by a recent collection: Sarah Stein and Aomar Boum, *The Holocaust and North Africa* (Stanford University Press, 2018).

27. *Foreign Relations of the United States*, 1950, vol. 5, Ambassador in Israel to the Secretary of State, May 4, 1950; vol. 9, pt. 1, no. 13, Memorandum of Conversation, May 14, 1953, no. 13; Nadav Safran, *From War To War: The Arab-Israeli Confrontation, 1948–1967* (Pegasus, 1969), 100–106; H. W. Brand, *Into the Labyrinth: The United States and the Middle East* (McGraw Hill, 1994), 31–62; Douglas Little, *American Orientalism: The United States and the Middle East* (University of North Carolina Press, 2008), 89–91.

28. Eliezer Don-Yehiya, "Political Religion in a New State: Ben-Gurion's Mamlachtiyut," in *Israel, the First Decade of Independence*, ed. S. Ilan Troen and Noah Lucas (State University of New York Press, 1995), 171–92.

29. David Ben-Gurion, *Rebirth and Destiny of Israel* (Philosophical Library, 1954); Michael Keren, *Ben-Gurion and the Intellectuals: Power, Knowledge, and Charisma* (Northern Illinois University Press, 1983), 100–117.

30. Leora Bilsky, *Transformative Justice* (University of Michigan Press, 2004).

31. Avner Cohen, *Israel and the Bomb* (Columbia University Press, 1998).

Chapter 3

1. See Ylana Miller, "Creating Unity Through History: The Eichmann Trial as Transition," *Journal of Modern Jewish Studies* 1, no. 2 (2002): 131–49. Also, *Hannah Arendt in Jerusalem*, ed. Steven Aschheim (University of California

Press, 2001); Hanna Yablonka, *The State of Israel vs. Adolf Eichmann* (Schocken Books, 2004); and Deborah Lipstadt, *The Eichmann Trial* (Schocken Books, 2011)

2. Peter Novick, *The Holocaust in American Life* (Houghton Mifflin, 1999)

3. To learn about Rabbi Prinz's views and experiences, see the following: Joachim Prinz, *The Dilemma of the Modern Jew* (Little, Brown, 1962), and *Joachim Prinz, Rebellious Rabbi, An Autobiography*, ed. and introduced by Michael A. Meyer (Indiana University Press, 2008). Although they did not always agree, Nahum Goldmann and Joachim Prinz remained friends over the years, corresponding about Jewish institutional developments, sometimes in their native German. For press coverage of a major disagreement between the two, CZA Z6/1894. See CZA Z6/1214 for letters in 1964 and 1965; correspondence dealing with the World Jewish Congress in 1971 can be found in CZA Z6/ 2419. Also J. Prinz to Nahum Goldmann, November 20, 1977, in ISA FO 2389. Both Prinz and Goldmann were active in the Conference of Presidents as well as in American Jewish political activities. See CZA Z6/1216. See, for example, Lucius Battle, Assistant Secretary for the Bureau for Near Eastern and South Asia, FO 3979/8.

4. I. F. Stone, *This Is Israel* (Boni and Gaer, 1948); I. F. Stone, *Underground to Palestine and Reflections Thirty Years Later* (Pantheon, 1978).

5. Stone, *This Is Israel*, 10.

6. Given the existing limitations on immigration and the presence of significant levels of anti-Semitism, the American Jewish leadership could have no expectations that the US would be a refuge. The differences within the community became even more significant during the war when it was known that the camps were exterminating Jews.

7. Stone, *This Is Israel*, 127.

8. I. F. Stone, "Holy War," *New York Review of Books*, August 3, 1967.

9. "Le conflit israelo-arabe," *Les Temps Modernes*, Paris, June 1967.

10. Stone, "Holy War."

11. George Steiner, "How US Jews View the Jewish State," *Life*, August 12, 1957, 106–14.

12. Arthur Koestler, *Darkness at Noon* (Random House, 1941)

13. For the most recent biography, see Michael Scammell, *Koestler: The Literary and Political Odyssey of a Twentieth-Century Skeptic* (Random House, 2009); an earlier study that offers a different perspective is David Cesarani, *Arthur Koestler: The Homeless Mind* (William Heineman, 1998). Koestler himself published two autobiographical works: *The Invisible Writing* (Beacon, 1954) and *Arrow in the Blue* (Macmillan, 1961).

14. Arthur Koestler, *Thieves in the Night* (Macmillan, 1946).

15. Koestler, *Thieves in the Night*, 146.

16. Koestler, *Promise and Fulfillment* (Macmillan, 1949).

17. Koestler, *Promise and Fulfillment*, ix.

18. Koestler, *Promise and Fulfillment*, 41.

19. Koestler, *Promise and Fulfillment*, 279.

20. Koestler, *Promise and Fulfillment*, 289.

21. Koestler, *Promise and Fulfillment*, 335.

22. Leon Uris, *Exodus* (Doubleday, 1958).

23. Ira B. Nadel, *Leon Uris* (University of Texas Press, 2010).

24. Nadel, *Leon Uris*, 109.

25. The review by Uri Avineri is discussed in M. M. Silver, *Our Exodus: Leon Uris and the Americanization of Israel's Founding Story* (Wayne State University Press, 2010), 168.

26. Nadel, *Leon Uris*, 115.

27. Silver, *Our Exodus*, 60.

28. Nadel, *Leon Uris*, 116.

29. On Kollek's suggestion, see Ylana Miller, "Creating Unity Through History."

30. Silver, *Our Exodus*, 124.

31. For a full biography, see Oliver Todd, *Albert Camus: A Life* (Knopf, 1997). For discussion of Camus's work and thought as it developed over time, see Robert Zaretsky, *Albert Camus: Elements of a Life* (Cornell University Press, 2010), and Robert Zaretsky, *Albert Camus: A Life Worth Living* (Belknap Press of Harvard University Press, 2013).

32. Selected writings by Camus on Algeria has been published by Alice Kaplan, editor, in *Albert Camus: Algerian Chronicles* (Belknap Press of Harvard University Press, 2013). See also David Carroll, *Albert Camus, the Algerian* (Columbia University Press, 2007).

33. On the US role and interventions, see Wall, *France, the United States, and the Algerian War*; on the ways in which the Algerian War contributed to altered historical frameworks, see Todd Shepard, *The Invention of Decolonization* (Cornell University Press, 2006), and Robert Malley, *The Call from Algeria: Third Worldism, Revolution, and the Turn to Islam* (University of California Press, 1996).

34. See Paul T. Chamberlin, *The Global Offensive* (Oxford University Press, 2012).

35. For an interesting discussion of the resonances between Arendt and Camus in their political thought, see Jeffrey C. Isaac, *Arendt, Camus, and Modern Rebellion* (Yale University Press, 1992).

36. See Martin Buber, Judah L. Magnes, and Moses Smilansky, *Palestine: A Bi-National State* (Ihud Association of Palestine, August 1946).

37. Jerome Kohn and Ron H. Feldman, *Hannah Arendt: The Jewish Writings* (Schocken Books, 2007).

38. Abba Lerner and Samuel Merlin, *The Palestine Refugee Problem: A New Approach and a Plan for a Solution* (Institute for Mediterranean Affairs, 1958).

39. Raider, *Nahum Goldmann*; Nahum Goldmann, *The Jewish Paradox* (Grosset and Dunlap, 1978).

40. *Autobiography of Nahum Goldmann*, 196. As with any memoir, this one should be understood as offering insight into Goldmann's self-presentation and worldview.

41. *Autobiography of Nahum Goldmann*, 298.

42. *Autobiography of Nahum Goldmann*, 299.

43. *Autobiography of Nahum Goldmann*, 325.

44. *Autobiography of Nahum Goldmann*, 325.

45. Michael A. Meyer, ed., *Joachim Prinz, Rebellious Rabbi: An Autobiography* (Indiana University Press, 2008), 195–200.

46. Meyer, *Joachim Prinz*, 248.

47. Meyer, *Joachim Prinz*, 145.

48. Meyer, *Joachim Prinz*, 147.

49. Meyer, *Joachim Prinz*, 208.

Chapter 4

1. Of the territories governed under League of Nations mandates after World War I, Iraq was the first to gain formal independence in 1932. Syria and Lebanon became independent of French control in 1946. Transjordan, which had been created in 1921, became independent of Great Britain also in 1946. Egypt, occupied by Britain in 1882, underwent a gradual and lengthy process of gaining full sovereignty and independence.

2. For context, see Michael J. Cohen, *Palestine and the Great Powers, 1945–48* (Princeton University Press, 1982), and *Truman and Israel* (University of California Press, 1990). A more recent study of the US role can be found in John B. Judis, *Genesis: Truman, American Jews, and the Origins of the Arab/Israeli Conflict* (Farrar, Straus and Giroux, 2014).

3. Ilan Pappe, *The Making of the Arab-Israeli Conflict* (I.B.Tauris, 1994); Benny Morris, *The Birth of the Palestinian Refugee Problem, 1947–49* (Cambridge University Press, 1987); and Shlaim, *Politics of Partition*, each consider aspects of this period in detail.

4. State of Israel Proclamation of Independence in Walter Z. Laqueur and Barry Rubin, eds., *The Israel-Arab Reader: A Documentary History of the Middle East Conflict* (Penguin, 1995), 81–83.

5. "The Road Not Taken: Constitutional Non-Decision Making in 1948–1950 and Its Impact on Civil Liberties in the Israeli Political Culture," in *Israel: The First Decade of Independence*, ed. Ilan Troen and Noah Lucas (State University of New York Press, 1995), 83–104; Anita Shapira, *Israel: A History* (Brandeis

University Press, 2012). A vocal opponent of the decision to delay a constitution was Hillel Kook. See Joseph Agassi, *Liberal Nationalism for Israel* (Gefen Press, 1999), 32, for his objection.

6. For descriptions of these developments by Israeli writers with a critical perspective, see Amos Elon, *The Israelis: Founders and Sons* (Holt, Rinehart and Winston, 1971), and Tom Segev, *1949, The First Israelis* (Free Press, 1986).

7. On the final negotiations, see Pappe, *Making of the Arab-Israeli Conflict*, chaps. 9 and 10. On the transition for American Jewish leaders, see Zvi Ganin, *An Uneasy Relationship: American Jewish Leadership and Israel, 1948–57* (Syracuse University Press, 2005). On the American Jewish Committee's management of this period, see Marianne Sanua, *Let Us Prove Strong: The American Jewish Committee, 1945–2006* (Brandeis University Press, 2007), 58–66, and Cohen, *Not Free to Desist*, 309–18. For AJC views on American Jews and Israel from 1953 to 1958, see CJH FAD-1, Box 65.

8. For discussions of multiple decisions made in the first years of statehood, see Troen and Lucas, *Israel: The First Decade*, and Silberstein, *New Perspectives*. On political dynamics and relationships, see Joseph Heller, *The Birth of Israel, 1945–1949: Ben-Gurion and His Critics* (University Press of Florida, 2000). For challenges to mainstream assumptions on the relationship between Israeli and Jewish identities, see Boaz Evron, *Jewish State or Israeli Nation?* (Indiana University Press, 1995), and Agassi, *Liberal Nationalism*.

9. On the early history of UN action, see Lex Takkenberg, *The Status of Palestinian Refugees in International Law* (Clarendon, 1998), chap. 1.

10. See Benny Morris, *1948 and After* (Clarendon, 1994), 22–27. For broader perspectives on these years and the presence of alternatives to Ben-Gurion's views, see Heller, *Birth of Israel*.

11. Moshe Sharett served as the first foreign minister (1948–1956) and the second prime minister (1954–1955). For a comprehensive biography, see Gabriel Sheffer, *Moshe Sharett: Biography of a Political Moderate* (Clarendon, 1996). On Golda Meir, see Klagsbrun, *Lioness*, 397–410.

12. For analysis of these developments, see Rashid Khalidi, "Consequences of the Suez Crisis in the Arab World," in *The Modern Middle East*, ed. Albert Hourani (I.B. Tauris, 2004), 535–50. Also Rashid Khalidi, "The Superpowers and the Cold War in the Middle East," in *The Middle East and the United States*, ed. David Lesch and Mark Haas (Westview, 2016), 157–77. For specifics on the arms race before 1967, see Safran, *From War to War*.

13. For a contemporary account of this period in the Arab world, see Malcolm Kerr, *The Arab Cold War, 1958–1967* (Oxford University Press, 1967). For a more recent perspective, see Fadi A. Bardawil, *Revolution and Disenchantment: Arab Marxism and the Binds of Emancipation* (Duke University Press, 2020).

14. For analysis of Palestinian nationalism as it developed historically, see Rashid Khalidi, *Palestinian Identity: The Construction of Modern National Consciousness* (Columbia University Press, 1997).

15. For a detailed history of these years, see Herbert Druks, *John F. Kennedy and Israel* (Praeger Security International, 2005). On the history of Dimona and Israel's development of nuclear weapons as well as the impact on Israeli-US relations, see Avner Cohen, *Israel and the Bomb*. Chapter 6 deals with the period in question.

16. Michael Staub, *Torn at the Roots: The Crisis of Jewish Liberalism in Postwar America* (Columbia University Press, 2002), chaps. 2 and 3.

17. Laura Fermi, *Illustrious Immigrants: The Intellectual Migration from Europe, 1930–1941* (University of Chicago Press, 1968).

18. Goldmann, *Autobiography*, 325–26. For the AJC views that contributed to their remaining outside the Conference of Presidents, see CJH FAD-1, Box 65, and for Minutes of the Conference from 1961 to 1966, see Z6/1880.

19. Goldmann, *Jewish Paradox*, 17.

20. Memorandum to Area Directors and Executive Assistants from Isaiah Terman, July 10, 1957, transmits "The Making of the American Jewish League for Israel and Ben-Gurion's Statement to the Recent Delegation of the American Jewish Committee," July 8, 1957. Nine pages. Center for Jewish History, AJC Collection, GEN-10, Box 315.

21. Alliance Israélite was founded in 1860, centered in Paris. It was particularly active in establishing a network of schools in the Balkans and the Middle East for Jewish education that were intended to improve the social and legal status of Jews. The schools were also intended to disseminate French language and culture. See the *Encyclopedia Judaica*, vol. 2 (Jerusalem, 1973), 647–51.

22. Memorandum to Area Directors and Executive Assistants from Isaiah Terman, July 10, 1957, transmits "The Making of the American Jewish League for Israel and Ben-Gurion's Statement to the Recent Delegation of the American Jewish Committee," July 8, 1957, p. 7. Nine pages. Center for Jewish History, AJC Collection, GEN-10, Box 315.

23. Memorandum to Area Directors and Executive Assistants from Isaiah Terman, July 10, 1957, transmits "The Making of the American Jewish League for Israel and Ben-Gurion's Statement to the Recent Delegation of the American Jewish Committee," July 8, 1957, pp. 8–9. Nine pages. Center for Jewish History, AJC Collection, GEN-10, Box 315.

24. See "Ben-Gurion, Goldmann Exchange Sharp Views on Need of Zionist Movement" and "Dr. Goldmann Reiterates View on International Court for Eichmann Trial," June 6, 1960, available in English at jta.org. For more extensive discussion of the subject with Hebrew references, see Yablonka, *State of Israel vs. Adolf Eichmann*, chap. 3. Press coverage on the tensions between Goldmann and Ben-Gurion can be found at the CZA Z5/8072.

25. See "Ben-Gurion, Goldmann Exchange Sharp Views on Need of Zionist Movement" and "Dr. Goldmann Reiterates View on International Court for Eichmann Trial," June 6, 1960, available in English at jta.org. For more extensive discussion of the subject with Hebrew references, see Yablonka, *State of Israel vs.*

Adolf Eichmann, chap. 3. Press coverage on the tensions between Goldmann and Ben-Gurion can be found at the CZA Z5/8072.

26. See "Ben-Gurion, Goldmann Exchange Sharp Views on Need of Zionist Movement" and "Dr. Goldmann Reiterates View on International Court for Eichmann Trial," June 6, 1960, available in English at jta.org. For more extensive discussion of the subject with Hebrew references, see Yablonka, State of Israel vs. Adolf Eichmann, chap. 3. Press coverage on the tensions between Goldmann and Ben-Gurion can be found at the CZA Z5/8072.

27. The correspondence took place between September 15, 1960 and February 19, 1961. It can be found at ISA, FO 3295/6.

28. The correspondence between Herbert B. Ehrmann, president of the American Jewish Committee, and Ben-Gurion took place between February 28, 1961 and April 23, 1961. Included in the file is also a draft of Ben-Gurion's initial response and suggestions from Ambassador A. Harmon for revisions. See ISA FO 3295/6.

29. Ben-Gurion to Ehrmann, March 15, 1961.

30. Ben-Gurion to Ehrmann, April 23, 1962 Draft.

31. BG to Ehrmann, March 15, 1961.

Chapter 5

1. Yablonka, *State of Israel vs. Adolf Eichmann*, conclusion. More recently, Lipstadt, *Eichmann Trial*, argues that the trial "transformed Jewish life and society," xi.

2. Tom Segev, *The Seventh Million: The Israelis and the Holocaust* (Hill and Wang, 1993).

3. Hannah Arendt, *Eichmann in Jerusalem: A Report on the Banality of Evil* (Viking, 1963). For an Israeli perspective very different from that of Arendt, see Haim Gouri, *Facing the Glass Booth: The Jerusalem Trial of Adolf Eichmann* (Wayne State University Press, 2004).

4. Novick, *America and the Holocaust*.

5. For recent studies that make this connection, see Segev, *Seventh Million*; Novick, *America and the Holocaust*; and Hanna Yablonka, *Medinat Yisrael neged Adolf Eichmann* (Yedioth Ahronot, 2001).

6. Yablonka, *Medinat Yisrael*.

7. For the historical context, see Charles S. Leibman, "Diaspora Influence on Israel," *Jewish Social Studies* 36 (1974): 271–80.

8. B.G. to Herbert Ehrmann, April 23, 1961, letter on the meeting along with a summary of the discussion between Blaustein and Ben-Gurion. In ISA FO 3295/6.

9. Rose Halprin to BG, March 24 1960, CZA Z6/1499 See also Cable, BG to A. Katz, President B'nai Brith, in which BG seeks to reassure Katz that the statement with Blaustein "does not detract in the slightest from the accomplishments and the important role of the Presidents Conference" and states that he deliberately added one reservation that had not been in the 1950 Agreement, "namely that there are differences of opinion on the nature of Judaism within the American Jewish community . . . and particularly between the Jews of Israel and Jews in the Diaspora." ISA FO 3295/6.

10. Goldmann's summary of his meeting and discussion with BG can be found in CZA Z6/1419.

11. Draft response of NG to August 8, 1960 letter from BG. CZA Z6/1499.

12. The questions are included in ISA Prime Minister's Office 6341/1780, letter from Moshe Brilliant to Yitzhak Navon, December 28, 1960. The answers in Hebrew are attached to this letter.

13. American Jewish Committee, *The Eichmann Case in the American Press* (New York: Institute of Human Relations Press, 1961); Yosal Rogat, *The Eichmann Trial and the Rule of Law* (Center for the Study of Democratic Institutions, 1961); Pnina Lahav, "The Eichmann Trial, the Jewish Question, and the American-Jewish Intelligentsia," *Boston University Law Review* 72 (1992): 555–75.

14. ISA, PMO 6384/3657/804/13/1. Teddy Kollek to Alfred Fleishman, June 14, 1960, and Teddy Kollek to Joseph Barnes, June 14, 1960. According to Kollek, Moshe Pearlman had worked in the prime minister's office and was leaving in order to write the book. In an author's note to his first book on the subject (Moshe Pearlman, *The Capture of Adolf Eichmann* [Weidenfeld and Nicolson, 1961]), Pearlman stated that he retired from government service on May 1, 1960, and "at that time I had not thought of Eichmann as the subject of one of my books."

15. ISA PMO 6384/3657/804/13/1, Moshe Pearlman to Teddy Kollek, June 22, 1960. For later discussion of the cooperation between Pearlman and the government, see Teddy Kollek to Isser Harel, November 2, 1960, and Teddy Kollek to Golda Meir, February 15, 1961, in the same file.

16. "Problems of the Eichmann Trial," unpublished memorandum, Anti-Defamation League, "Notes on the Adolf Eichmann Trial," part 1, February 13, 1961, Hoover Library Collection.

17. "Problems of the Eichmann Trial," unpublished memorandum, Anti-Defamation League, "Notes on the Adolf Eichmann Trial," part 1, February 13, 1961, Hoover Library Collection.

18. On the historical significance of the trial, see Yablonka, *State of Israel vs. Adolf Eichmann*, and Segev, *Seventh Million*. Both emphasize the emotional impact of survivor testimony on Israeli society. For discussions of the trial in broader context, see Leora Bilsky, *Transformative Justice: Israeli Identity on Trial* (University of Michigan Press, 2004), and Lawrence Douglas, *The Memory of*

Judgment: Making Law and History in the Trials of the Holocaust (Yale University Press, 2001).

19. Immediately after the trial Ben-Gurion stated: "I believe that trial has achieved its aim. . . . The main thing was to reveal to our youth in this country the tremendous tragedy that befell a dispersed people, at the mercy of strangers, when a brutal regime, devoid of all human conscience, decided to destroy the Jewish people for the sole reason that they were jews [*sic*]. The trial also demonstrated to world public opinion the grave dangers of anti-Semitism and race theory." Answers to Questions Presented to the Prime Minister by Mr. R. Vogel of the Deutsche Zeitung und Wirtschaftszeitung, Cologne, August 13, 1961. ISA PMO 6341/1780. See also Segev, *Seventh Million*, 327–28; Gideon Hausner, *Justice In Jerusalem* (Harper and Row, 1966) 291.

20. On the selection of witnesses, see Hausner, *Justice in Jerusalem*, chaps. 15 and 19. Yablonka, *State of Israel vs. Adolf Eichmann?* chap. 6.

21. For the testimony itself, see State of Israel, Ministry of Justice, *The Trial of Adolf Eichmann* (9 vols.), Jerusalem, 1992.

22. For Ben-Gurion's revision of Hausner's opening argument with regard to the need to emphasize that it was Nazi Germany rather than Germany that was responsible, see ISA PMO 6384/804/13/1, Ben-Gurion to Hausner, March 28, 1961. See also Segev, *Seventh Million*, 346.

23. Hausner, *Justice in Jerusalem*, 345–46; State of Israel, *The Trial of Adolf Eichmann*, vol. 1, 81, 243–44; Yablonka, *State of Israel vs. Adolf Eichmann*, 99–101.

24. See note 14.

25. Hausner, *Justice in Jerusalem*, 295; Yablonka, *State of Israel vs. Adolf Eichmann*, 275; Segev, *Seventh Million*, 341, 348. Also, Yechiam Weitz, "The Holocaust on Trial: The Impact of the Kastner and Eichmann Trials on Israeli Society," *Israel Studies* 1, no. 2 (1996): 1–26.

26. ISA PMO 6384/3657. Paul Jacobs, "Eichmann and Jewish Identity," unpublished manuscript, June 1961.

27. ISA PMO 6384/804/13/1. Theodore Kollek to Mr. Alfred Fleishman, Fleishman-Hillard, Inc., June 14, 1960.

28. Arendt, *Eichmann in Jerusalem*. See also ISA PMO 6384/3657, "Moshe Versus Hannah Arendt in the Eichmann Controversy" [in Hebrew], interview with Moshe Pearlman, where Pearlman's book is explicitly described as an answer to Arendt.

29. The nature of the controversy is reflected both in the collection of Hannah Arendt papers, Library of Congress, and in the correspondence of Teddy Kollek in ISA, PMO, 6384/3657. The impact on Hannah Arendt and her response is evident in her correspondence. See, for example, Hannah Arendt to Karl Jaspers, October 20, 1963, in Hannah Arendt and Karl Jaspers, *Correspondence 1926–1969* (Harcourt, Brace, 1992), 521–25. See also Hannah Arendt and Mary McCarthy, *Between Friends* (Harcourt, Brace, 1995), 145–58. Scholarly discussion of the

controversy has been substantial. See, for example, Elisabeth Young-Bruehl, *Hannah Arendt: For Love of the World* (Yale University Press, 1982), chap. 8; Dagmar Barnouw, *Visible Spaces* (Johns Hopkins University Press, 1990), chap. 6; Richard J. Bernstein, *Hannah Arendt and the Jewish Question* (MIT Press, 1996), chap. 8. For more recent perspectives, see Anthony Grafton, "Arendt and Eichmann at the Dinner Table," *American Scholar* 68, no. 1 (1999): 105–19, and Steven Aschheim, ed., *Hannah Arendt in Jerusalem* (University of California Press, 2001).

30. Hannah Arendt to Vassar College, January 2, 1961, quoted by Young-Bruehl, *Hannah Arendt*, 29. See also Hannah Arendt to Karl Jaspers, December 2, 1960, *Correspondence*, 409–10, in which she says that "I would never be able to forgive myself if I didn't go and look at this walking disaster face to face."

31. On the contact with Shawn, see Arendt and McCarthy, *Between Friends*, 147. The original articles are "A Reporter at Large, Eichmann in Jerusalem," *New Yorker*, February 16, 1963, 40–113; February 23, 1963, 40–111; March 2, 1963, 40–91; March 9, 1963, 48–131; March 16, 1963, 58–134.

32. Hannah Arendt to Karl Jaspers, April 25, 1961, *Correspondence*, 437. Also see Lotte Kohler, ed., *Within Four Walls: The Correspondence Between Hannah Arendt and Heinrich Blucher, 1936–1968* (Harcourt, 2000), 354–65.

33. Hannah Arendt to Mary McCarthy, September 20, 1963, *Between Friends*, 147.

34. Some of these differences became evident in an exchange with an old friend, Gershom Scholem, and H. Arendt, "Exchange of Letters," *Encounter*, January 1964, 51–56. On the differing views of Scholem and Arendt, see Amnon Raz-Krakotzkin, "Binationalism and Jewish Identity," in Aschheim, *Hannah Arendt in Jerusalem*, 165–80. For further discussion, see Ylana Miller, "Fragments of Collective Memory: Jewish Intellectual Exiles as Narrators of History," in *Memory, History and Critique, European Identity at the Millenium, Proceedings of the 6th International ISSEI Conference at the University of Humanist Studies, Utrecht, The Netherlands, August, 1996*, ed. Frank Brinkhuis and Sascha Talmor.

35. See Young-Bruehl, *Hannah Arendt*, 347, and also Bernstein, *Hannah Arendt and the Jewish Question*, 189.

36. *Jerusalem Post*, February 28, 1963, Hannah Arendt Papers, Box 50, Library of Congress, Washington, DC.

37. ISA PMO 6384/3657. Julius Edelstein to Teddy Kollek, March 20, 1963, includes a copy of the ADL memorandum of March 11, 1963.

38. The second memorandum, of March 27, 1963, can be found in the Hannah Arendt Papers, Box 47, Library of Congress.

39. ADL memo of March 27, 1963.

40. ISA PMO 6384/804/13/2, Teddy Kollek to Shlomo Argov, April 17, 1963; and ISA PMO 6384/804/13/3, Shlomo Argov to Teddy Kollek, May 1, 1963.

41. ISA PMO, 6384/804/13/3, Teddy Kollek to Herbert Friedman, October 31, 1963.

42. *American Judaism* (Fall 1963), 20, 60–61, Hannah Arendt Papers, Box 51, Library of Congress.

43. H. Arendt to S. Merlin, June 29, 1964. Hannah Arendt Papers, Box 19, Library of Congress.

44. S. Merlin to H. Arendt, June 12, 1964. Hannah Arendt Papers, Box 19, Library of Congress.

45. Hannah Arendt to Samuel Merlin, June 19, 1964, Hannah Arendt Papers, Box 19, Library of Congress. This letter makes reference to the "Birnblatt trial." A copy of a *Jerusalem Post* article, "Birnblatt Acquittal," May 4, 1964, can be found in Hannah Arendt Papers, Box 50, Library of Congress.

46. The fact that *Eichmann in Jerusalem* was not published in Israel until the year 2000 in itself meant that the discussion was seriously inhibited.

47. On the personal history, see Young-Bruehl, *Hannah Arendt.*

48. The degree to which the Holocaust and Nazism became vehicles for the discussion of the Arab-Israeli conflict and for warnings about the vulnerability of Jews is discussed by Segev, *Seventh Million,* in Novick, *America and the Holocaust,* and is evident in such works as Amos Oz, *The Slopes of Lebanon* (Harcourt, Brace, 1989).

49. Hannah Arendt, *Eichmann in Jerusalem,* 5. On the perspective in Israel, see Segev, *Seventh Million,* chaps. 18 and 29, and Yablonka, *State of Israel vs. Adolf Eichmann.*

50. See Hannah Arendt, *The Jew as Pariah* (Grove Press, 1978).

51. The literature on Arendt's Jewish identity and interests as well as publication of her work in this area is growing. See, in particular, Bernstein, *Hannah Arendt and the Jewish Question,* and Barnouw, *Visible Spaces.* Her unpublished papers also contain significant correspondence and publications reflecting her development.

52. Hannah Arendt to Mary McCarthy, September 20, 1963, *Between Friends,* 148.

53. Arendt, *Eichmann in Jerusalem,* 11.

54. Arthur Hertzberg, "Israel and American Jewry," *Commentary* (August 1967), 69–73.

55. Hertzberg, "Israel and American Jewry."

Chapter 6

1. For a more recent discussion, see Richard I. Cohen, "A Generation's Response to Eichmann in Jerusalem," in *Hannah Arendt in Jerusalem,* ed. S. Aschheim (University of California Press, 2001), 253–77. Even more recent evidence of the ongoing interest in the trial is Rebecca Wittmann, ed., *The Eichmann Trial Reconsidered* (University of Toronto Press, 2021).

2. Hannah Arendt, *The Origins of Totalitarianism* (Harcourt, Brace, 1951).

3. Rothberg, *Multidirectional Memory*.

4. Aamir Mufti, *Enlightenment in the Colony: The Jewish Question and the Crisis of Postcolonial Culture* (Princeton University Press, 2007).

5. For biographical information, see Meyer, *Joachim Prinz*, and Edward K. Kaplan, *Spiritual Radical: Abraham J. Heschel in America* (Yale University Press, 2007). For evidence of the ways in which the AJC office in Israel (established in 1961) continued to work independently, see CJH FAD-1, Box 34.

6. For a detailed history of the US-Israel relationship as it evolved in the early sixties, see Druks, *John F. Kennedy and Israel*; for an interpretive essay, see Melani McAlister, *Epic Encounters: Culture, Media, and U.S. Interests in the Middle East, 1945–2000* (University of California Press, 2005), 43–83.

7. On the visible reemergence of Palestinian identity, see Khalidi, *Palestinian Identity*, 177–209. On the development of the PLO in its international context, see Chamberlin, *Global Offensive*, 14–42.

8. For a longitudinal study of Algerian development, see John Ruedy, *Modern Algeria: The Origins and Development of a Nation* (Indiana University Press, 2005). For work specifically on the development of Algerian nationalism and identity, see James McDougall, *History and the Culture of Nationalism in Algeria* (Cambridge University Press, 2006), and J. N. C. Hill, *Identity in Algerian Politics* (Lynne Rienner, 2009).

9. For a detailed study that includes the historical framework in which Palestinian refugees came to be defined, see Takkenberg, *Status of Palestinian Refugees*, and Michael Fischbach, *Records of Dispossession: Palestinian Refugee Property and the Arab-Israeli Conflict* (Columbia University Press, 2003).

10. On the emergence of Palestinian political activism and efforts to gain statehood, see Yezid Sayigh, *Armed Struggle and the Search for State: The Palestinian National Movement, 1949–1993* (Clarendon, 1997).

11. For the text of the resolution, see Laqueur and Rubin, *Israel-Arab Reader*, 83–86.

12. For a detailed study of the immediate postwar efforts to resolve the conflict, see Pappe, *Making of the Arab-Israeli Conflict*.

13. For an analysis of US policy and impact in the fifties, see Salim Yaqub, *Containing Arab Nationalism: The Eisenhower Doctrine and the Middle East* (University of North Carolina Press, 2004). On regional dynamics, see Roger Owen, *State, Power and Politics in the Making of the Modern Middle East* (Routledge, 1992), 81–107.

14. See Sayigh, *Armed Struggle*, 71–94.

15. The United Arab Republic had united Egypt and Syria in 1958. Its breakdown and the separation of the two states was the outcome of complex political dynamics in both, but it also made clear the distance between aspirations for Arab unity and the reality of diverse state systems. For details, see Kerr, *Arab Cold War*.

16. Gowers and Walker, *Behind the Myth*, 36–39. On the broader dynamics, see Laskier, "Israel and Algeria," 1–32.

17. After President Nasser's nationalization of the Suez Canal Co. in July 1956, Britain and France held consultations that eventually resulted in a plan to have Israel invade Sinai, triggering British and French intervention ostensibly to stop the fighting but with the intention of recovering control over the Suez Canal, with the hope of removing Nasser from power. When the plan was implemented in October 1956, it triggered, instead, American opposition and intervention. By March 1957 Israeli forces had to be withdrawn and Nasser had gained substantial support throughout the Arab world. For an analysis of the longer-term effects, see Rashid Khalidi, "Consequences of the Suez Crisis in the Arab World," in *The Modern Middle East*, ed. Albert Hourani, Philip S. Khoury, and Mary C. Wilson (University of California Press, 1993).

18. For detail on the arms buildups from 1948 to 1967, see Safran, *From War to War*.

19. Little, *American Orientalism*, 157–92.

20. Little, *American Orientalism*, 193–228.

21. Paul W. T. Kingston, "The 'Ambassador for the Arabs': The Locke Mission and the Unmaking of US Development Diplomacy in the Near East, 1952–1953," in *The Middle East and the United States*, ed. David W. Lesch and Mark L. Haas (Westview, 1975), 33–54.

22. Daniel Bell, *The End of Ideology* (Free Press, 1962).

23. On the case of Algeria, see McDougall, *History and the Culture of Nationalism*, 225–38.

24. For discussion of the relationship between writers and the state in its formative period, see Keren, *Ben-Gurion and the Intellectuals*, 118–51, and Keren, *Pen and the Sword*, 33–57.

25. "The Jewish People in the 20th Century," from an address at the World Jewish Congress, July 1966, in *Community of Fate: Essays, Speeches and Articles by Nahum Goldmann* (Israel Universities Press, 1977), 56–65. See also "Forum for Jewish Thought," September 5, 1966, where both Goldmann and Ben-Gurion spoke, CZA Z6/2609.

26. For Goldmann's presentation of his ideas on Israel and the diaspora, see *Autobiography of Nahum Goldmann*, 312–29. For an overview of Goldmann's life and work, see Jehuda Reinharz and Evyatar Friesel, "Nahum Goldmann: Jewish and Zionist Statesman—An Overview," in *Nahum Goldmann: Statesman Without a State*, ed. Mark Raider (State University of New York Press, 2009), 3–59.

27. Goldmann's speeches from this time can be found in the CZA files Z6/2167, Z6/2065, Z6/2758, Z6/2733. His correspondence detailing the work he was doing can also be found in the CZA NG Papers.

28. S. Yizhar, *Khirbet Khizeh* (Ibis Press, 2008). For a review of the book and its postpublication history in Israel, see Jacqueline Rose, "Rereading Khirbet

Khizeh by S. Yizhar," *Guardian*, March 11, 2011. S. Yizhar was the pen name of the Israeli novelist Yizhar Smilansky.

29. David Ohana, *Jacqueline Kahanoff: A Levantine Woman* (Indiana University Press, 2023). For an English translation of work by Kahanoff, see *Mongrels or Marvels: The Levantine Writings of Jacqueline Shohet Kahanoff*, ed. Deborah A. Starr and Sasson Somekh (Stanford University Press, 2011).

30. Ohana, *Jacqueline Kahanoff*, 132.

31. Ohana, Jacqueline Kahanoff, xiii.

32. "Rebel, My Brother," in *Mongrels or Marvels*, 177–192.

33. For the earlier writings, see Kohn and Feldman, *Hannah Arendt: The Jewish Writings*. On Arendt's response in the US, see "Arendt, the Schools, and Civil Rights," in *Arendt and America*, by Richard H. King (University of Chicago Press, 2015), 165–87.

34. The recent debates among Israeli historians were themselves a product of this development. See, for example, "Israeli Historiography Revisited," a special issue of *History and Memory* 7, no. 1 (Spring/Summer 1995).

35. On the one hand, Dina Porat, *The Blue and the Yellow Stars of David* (Harvard University Press, 1990), and Segev, *Seventh Million*; on the other, Morris, *Birth of the Palestinian Refugee*, and Morris, *1948 and After*, as well as Pappe, *Making of the Arab-Israeli Conflict*. See also Smadar Lavie, "Blowups in the Borderzones: Third World Israeli Authors Gropings for Home," in *Displacement, Diaspora and Geographies of Identity*, ed. Smadar Lavie and Ted Swedenburg (Duke University Press, 1996), 55–96. For a more personal example of this process, see Menachem Carmi, "The Psychological Effects of Historical Events: Theoretical Considerations in the Context of the Israeli-Palestinian Conflict," *Mind and Human Interaction* 7, no. 3 (August 1996): 128–38.

36. Segev, *Seventh Million*, 185.

37. Saul Friedlander, *Memory, History, and the Extermination of the Jews of Europe* (Indiana University Press, 1993), 126.

38. The tensions inherent in this position are evident in the interchange between George Steiner and Robert Alter in *Commentary*. See Robert Alter, "Zionism for the '70s," *Commentary* 49, no. 5 (May 1970), 8–14.

39. For a general biography, see Young-Bruehl, *Hannah Arendt*; for Arendt's development and positions on Zionist politics, see a collection of her writings edited by Feldman, *Jew as Pariah*. More recent related studies include Barnouw, *Visible Spaces*, and Richard Bernstein, *Hannah Arendt and the Jewish Question* (MIT Press, 1996).

40. Arendt, *Eichmann in Jerusalem*. Personal papers related to Arendt's responses can be found in the collection of Hannah Arendt personal papers, Library of Congress, Washington, DC. Selected reviews of the work, including those in the German and Hebrew press, can also be found in these files. A letter from Hannah Arendt to Mary McCarthy provides a rare insight into the emotional

drive behind the book: "You were the only reader to understand what otherwise I have never admitted—namely that I wrote this book in a curious state of euphoria. And that ever since I did it, I feel—after twenty years since the war—light-hearted about the whole matter," Hannah Arendt and Mary McCarthy, *Between Friends: The Correspondence of Hannah Arendt and Mary McCarthy, 1949–1975* (Harcourt, Brace, 1995), 168.

41. Reprinted in Feldman, *Jew as Pariah*, 240–51. See also Jasper's comments in his letters to Arendt dated October 2, 1963 and October 25, 1963, *Hannah Arendt and Karl Jaspers*, 525–28. Evidence of the earlier relationship is found in the letters from Gershom Scholem to Hannah Arendt (in German) that are preserved in the Library of Congress Collection of Arendt Papers.

42. Nina Sutton, *Bettelheim: A Life and A Legacy* (Basic Books, 1996), 346.

43. Saul Friedlander, "The Shoah in Present Historical Consciousness," in Friedlander, *Memory, History*, 43.

44. Friedlander, *Memory, History*, 120; Lawrence Langer, *Holocaust Testimonies: The Ruins of Memory* (Yale University Press, 1991), chap. 1.

45. George Steiner, "A Kind of Survivor," in *Language and Silence: Essays on Language, Literature, and the Inhuman* (Atheneum, 1986), 140–54.

46. Arendt, "To Save the Jewish Homeland," 1948, reprinted in *Jew as Pariah*, 179–80.

47. For description of Arendt's personal connections to her "tribe," see Young-Bruehl, *Hannah Arendt*, preface.

48. See, for example, Hannah Arendt, "Zionism Reconsidered," *Menorah Journal*, October 1944, and "About Collaboration," *Jewish Frontier*, October 1948, reprinted in Arendt, *Jew as Pariah*, 147–49 as well as 237.

49. For a short biographical summary and sample of his poems, see *Anthology of Modern Palestinian Literature*, ed. Salma Khadra Jayyusi (Columbia University Press, 1992), 145–59. For an analysis of Darwish's work and that of the Algerian writer Assia Djebar, see Najat Rahman, *Literary Disinheritance: The Writing of Home in the Work of Mahmoud Darwish and Assia Djebar* (Lexington Books, 2008). For an in-depth study of Darwish's work in English, see Anette Mansson, *Passage to a New World: Exile and Restoration in Mahmoud Darwish's Writings, 1960–1995* (Uppsala University Press, 2003).

50. Ghassan Kanafani, *Palestine's Children*, trans. Barbara Harlow and Karen E, Riley (Lynne Rienner, 2000).

51. See, in particular, Fawaz Turki, *The Disinherited: Journal of a Palestinian Exile* (Monthly Review Press, 1972), and *Soul in Exile: Lives of a Palestinian Revolutionary* (Monthly Review Press, 1988).

52. For an overview of developments, see John Ruedy, *Modern Algeria: The Origins and Development of a Nation* (Indiana University Press, 2005), 195–230. For a contemporary commentary on the Algerian War itself by a Berber journalist,

see Mouloud Feraoun, *Journal, 1955–1962: Reflections on the French-Algerian War* (University of Nebraska Press, 2000); for historical studies, see Hill, *Identity in Algerian Politics*, and Ranjanna Khanna, ed., *Algeria Cuts: Women and Representation, 1830 to the Present* (Stanford University Press, 2008).

53. Rothberg, *Multidirectional Memory*.

54. See Bryan Cheyette, *Diasporas of the Mind: Jewish and Postcolonial Writing and the Nightmare of History* (Yale University Press, 2013). On the conversations regarding Jews and colonialism, see *Colonialism and the Jews*, ed. Ethan B. Katz, Lisa Moses Leff, and Maud S. Mandel (Indiana University Press, 2017).

Chapter 7

1. Georges Friedmann, *The End of the Jewish People?* (Doubleday, 1967).

2. Friedmann, *End of the Jewish People*, 228–29.

3. Friedman, *End of the Jewish People*, 270.

4. Friedman, *End of the Jewish People*, 270.

5. Friedman, *End of the Jewish People*, 271.

6. Friedman, *End of the Jewish People*, 283.

7. Tom Segev, *1967: Israel, the War, and the Year That Transformed the Middle East* (Henry Holt, 2007).

8. Segev, *1967*, 33.

9. Segev, *1967*, 42.

10. Segev, *1967*, 62.

11. Historically, there were those who called themselves Hebrews, but it referred to those who lived in Palestine or Israel and whose language/culture was Hebrew.

12. Staub, *Torn at the Roots*.

13. See Karen Bodkin, *How Jews Became White Folks* (Rutgers University Press, 1998), 138–87; Eric L. Goldstein, *The Price of Whiteness: Jews, Race, and American Identity* (Princeton University Press, 2006), 209–39. For analysis of the ways in which US racial politics were linked to the Palestinian-Israeli conflict, see McAlister, *Epic Encounters*, 84–124, and Michael Fischbach, *Black Power and Palestine* (Stanford University Press, 2019).

14. See Staub, "Protect and Keep: Vietnam, Israel and the Politics of Theology," in Staub, *Torn at the Roots*, 112–52. On the evolution of *Commentary* magazine during this period, see Benjamin Balint, *Running Commentary: The Contentious Magazine That Transformed the Jewish Left into the Neoconservative Right* (PublicAffairs, 2010), 97–116. For memos and press followed by the Israeli Foreign Ministry on President Johnson's concerns about Jewish opposition to his Vietnam policies in 1966, see ISA 3979/4.

15. Staub, *Torn at the Roots*, 125–27.

16. Soviet archives as well as those of Egypt, Syria, and Jordan remain largely inaccessible.

17. Cohen, *Israel and the Bomb*, 137–51.

18. See "Memorandum of Conversation," May 26, 1967, Document #77, in Foreign Relations of the United States, 1964–1968, vol. 19, Arab-Israeli Crisis and War, 1967. Included in the conversation is the following statement made by President Johnson to the foreign minister of Israel:

Abba Eban: "The President stressed that all of our intelligence people are unanimous regarding the assessment; that an attack is not imminent; and that if the UAR attacks 'you will whip hell out of them,'" 146.

19. The literature on the crisis in 1967 and the war that followed is voluminous. Broad histories include Segev, *1967*; Michael Oren, *Six Days of War* (Oxford University Press, 2002); and Guy Laron, *The Six Day War: The Breaking of the Middle East* (Yale University Press, 2017). Each brings a slightly different perspective with Laron's work particularly important for its focus on the roles of the US and USSR. In addition, a number of works address specific actors and slices of developments. These include Richard B. Parker, ed., *The Six-Day War: A Retrospective* (University of Florida Press, 1996), the publication of a conference held to mark twenty-five years after the war; Eli Lederhendler, *The Six Day War and World Jewry* (Penn State University Press, 2000); William Roger Louis and Avi Shlaim, eds., *The 1967 Arab-Israeli War* (Cambridge University Press, 2012; Zaki Shalom, *The Role of US Diplomacy in the Lead-Up to the Six Day War: Balancing Moral Commitments and National Interests* (Sussex Academic Press, 2012).

20. Resolution 242 can be found in Laqueur and Rubin, eds., *Israel-Arab Reader*, 116. For a discussion of the US role, see William Quandt, *Peace Process: American Diplomacy and the Arab-Israeli Conflict Since 1967* (Brookings Institution and University of California Press, 2001), 44–47.

21. For a summary of diverging secular views, see Mitch Ginsburg, "In Forgotten Article After Six Day War, Amos Oz Warned of 'Eternal Annexation,'" *Times of Israel*, December 2018. Oz participated in publication of a book that contained interviews with Israeli soldiers immediately after the war: Avraham Shapira, ed., *The Seventh Day: Soldiers Talk About the Six Day War* (Scribners, 1970). In a more recent documentary, *Censored Voices* (2015), filmmaker Mor Loushy corrected the record of those interviews by restoring parts that had not been made public at the time. For more widespread views, see descriptions of the settlement movement that emerged after 1967: Gershon Gorenberg, *The Accidental Empire: Israel and the Birth of the Settlements, 1967–1977* (Henry, Holt, 2006), 99–128, and Akiva Eldar and Idith Zertal, *Lords of the Land: The War for Israel's Settlements in the Occupied Territories, 1967–2007* (Nation Books, 2007), 3–54.

For a more distant, yet engaged, commentary on the deep divisions that had contributed to the war and remained after its end, see I. F. Stone, "Holy War," a review of "Le conflit israelo-arabe," *Les Temps Modernes*, Paris, June 1967, in the *New York Review of Books,* August 3, 1967.

22. For the immediate responses of the US, see Charles D. Smith, "The US and the 1967 War," in Louis and Shlaim, *1967 Arab Israeli War,* 165–92. For an analysis of "Israel and the American Mind: A Study of Press Reactions Since the Six-Day War," by Ruder and Finn in New York, see ISA FO 6557/29. See also memoranda within the Foreign Office and consular officials in the fall of 1967, ISA FO 3979/8. For broader reflection on the effects of Americanization in Israel, see Tom Segev, *Elvis in Jerusalem: Post-Zionism and the Americanization of Israel* (Henry, Holt, 2002). For an interpretation of the post-1967 American views of Israel, see Amy Kaplan, *Our American Israel* (Harvard University Press, 2018), 94–135.

23. Edward Said, *Out of Place: A Memoir* (Vintage Books, 2000), 268.

24. Said, *Out of Place,* 293.

25. For a nuanced and complex view of responses to diplomacy in the Arab states, see Fawaz A. Gerges, "The 1967 Arab-Israeli War," in Lesch and Haas, *Middle East and the United States,* 177–96. On US policy in the immediate aftermath, see Quandt, *Peace Process,* 44–52.

26. For a recent study placing policy toward Palestinians into a longer framework, see Seth Anziska, *Preventing Palestine: A Political History from Camp David to Oslo* (Princeton University Press, 2018).

27. Interview with Golda Meir in the *Sunday Times of London,* June 15, 1969, as quoted in Kathleen M. Christison, "Myths About Palestinians," *Foreign Policy,* no. 66 (Spring 1987): 109.

Chapter 8

1. For a broad introduction to this period in Israel, see Michael Brenner, *In Search of Israel: The History of an Idea* (Princeton University Press, 2018), chap. 5, 166–229. For the view from the US, see Quandt, *Peace Process,* 1–130. For perspective on developments in US policy toward the Arab Middle East, see Salim Yaqub, *Imperfect Strangers: Americans, Arabs, and U.S.-Middle East Relations in the 1970s* (Cornell University Press, 2016), 1–111. On the PLO and its evolution in this period, see Chamberlin, *Global Offensive.* For a detailed history of the war in 1973, largely based on Israeli sources, see Abraham Rabinovich, *The Yom Kippur War* (Schocken, 2004).

2. On the post-1967 debates, see Micah Goodman, *Catch-67: The Left, the Right, and the Legacy of the Six-Day War* (Yale University Press, 2018), and Brenner, *In Search.* In the immediate aftermath of war Israeli representatives in the US paid close attention to concerns and actions in the US. Correspondence

about initiatives by Hillel Kook, memoranda to the Conference of Presidents, letters from the Zionist Organization of America and Philip Bernstein, executive director, as well as the text of an address by Morris Abram of the AJC can be found in ISA FO 3979/9.

3. Dayan quoted in Segev, *1967*, 500.

4. Edward A. Padelford, "The Regional American Press: An Analysis of Its Reporting and Commentary on the Arab-Israel Situation," PhD diss., American University, 1979; Jay S. Levin, "Then and Now: Changing American Periodical Perceptions of the Six-Day War," honor's thesis in history, Duke University, 2008. For an interesting analysis linking responses to the war in Vietnam with the Six-Day War, see McAlister, *Epic Encounters*, chap. 4.

5. Yaqub, *Imperfect Strangers*, 55–66.

6. See Klagsbrun, *Lioness*, 509–13. Also Segev, *1967*, 500–517.

7. Shlomo Ben-Ami, *Scars of War, Wounds of Peace: The Israeli-Arab Tragedy* (Oxford University Press, 2006), 116.

8. Dalia Gavrieli-Nuri, "Saying 'War,' Thinking 'Victory'—the Mythmaking Surrounding Israel's 1967 Victory," *Israel Studies* 15, no. 1 (Spring 2010): 96.

9. Ben-Ami, *Scars of War*, 134–35. Efforts to continue binding the diaspora to Israel after the war are discussed in planning a prime minister's conference on May 15, 1968. See CZA Z6/1241.

10. Quandt, *Peace Process*, 67–70. For a detailed description of diplomacy after UN Resolution 242 was adopted, see Shlaim, *Iron Wall*, 259–318.

11. Already in 1968 Nahum Goldmann was generating significant criticism of his intervention in diplomatic efforts after the war of 1967 resulted in continuing conflict. In April 1968 news of his meeting with Senator William Fulbright became public and gave rise to suspicion that he had asked for the senator to intervene with the US administration. See N.G. to Louis Pincus, Chairman of the Executive, Jewish Agency, April 3, 1968, and J.W. Fulbright to N.G. included in cable to Moshe Rivlin, April 4, 1968, in CZA Z6/1151. In the same file are summaries of very critical Israeli press comments on Goldmann's actions. Partially in response, Goldmann spoke to a press conference in Jerusalem on April 29, 1968. In this six-page declaration he also addressed his views on Israel. See CZA Z6.2733-16-1. Included as well is a letter from Goldmann to Yaacov Herzog in the prime minister's office, August 18, 1968, in which Goldmann enclosed a memorandum on the neutralization of Israel as a solution. He mentions that he has discussed these ideas with Professor Henry Kissinger, Professor Zbigniew Brzezinski, and Raymond Aron, all of whom were impressed.

12. On this episode, see Raider, *Nahum Goldmann*, 297–324, and Klagsbrun, *Lioness*, 526–29. Also, Elinor Burkett, *Golda* (Harper Collins, 2008), 278–81. In the years following the war in 1967, Goldmann spoke regularly about the Israel-diaspora relationship and corresponded with various groups including a representative of the World Union of Jewish Students. See CZA Z6/2390 for 1970

and CZA Z6/2419 for 1971. He also remained diplomatically active, as evidenced in his "Note on Dr. Nahum Goldmann's Conversation with Professor Henry A. Kissinger Washington—April, 1969" in CZA Z6/2720-14.

13. See Nahum Goldmann, "The Future of Israel," *Foreign Affairs* 48, no. 3 (April 1970): 443–59.

14. Nahum Goldmann, "The Future of Israel," *Foreign Affairs* 48, no. 3 (April 1970): 443–59.

15. Goldmann, "Future of Israel," 459.

16. Goldmann, "Future of Israel," 446.

17. Goldmann, "Future of Israel," 449.

18. For contemporary assessments largely sympathetic to the Palestinian national movement, see Russell Stetler, ed., *Palestine: The Arab-Israeli Conflict* (Ramparts, 1972). For a detailed history, see Sayigh, *Armed Struggle*.

19. For a clear exposition of the ways in which the war of 1967 could challenge definitions of Zionism, see Amos Oz, "Meaning of Homeland," *New Outlook*, December 1, 1967. Lyova Eliav, longtime Labor politician, recognized the existence of a Palestinian people. See Gershom Gorenberg, *The Accidental Empire: Israel and the Birth of the Settlements, 1967–1977* (Times Books, 2006), 175–76. On the emergence of the settlement movement and its implications, see Eldar and Zertal, *Lords of the Land*.

20. For an explication of the battle of al-Karama on March 21, 1968, see Khalidi, *Palestinian Identity*, 196. The salient effect and meaning attributed to this battle on Jordanian soil was the attribution of Palestinian capacity to stand and fight Israeli forces despite the inequality of strength.

21. For a contemporary analysis, see Irene Gendzier, "Algeria and Palestine: Warning or Model?," *New Middle East*, no. 25 (October, 1970): 12–14. On the process of attaining recognition, see Augustus Richard Norton and Martin H. Greenberg, *The International Relations of the Palestine Liberation Organization* (Southern Illinois University Press, 1989). Also, Chamberlin, *Global Offensive*, 43–71.

22. While Fatah, led by Yasir Arafat, adhered to a Palestinian nationalism that sought to avoid interference in the affairs of Arab states, the Popular Front for the Liberation of Palestine, led by George Habash, leaned to a Marxist analysis that favored revolution in the Arab world, particularly Jordan. Other, smaller groups contained within the PLO umbrella included the Democratic Popular Front for the Liberation of Palestine and Saiqa.

23. See Kathleen Christison, *Perceptions of Palestine: Their Influence on U.S. Middle East Policy* (University of California Press, 1999), 124–56.

24. For analysis of the impact on Israeli policy, see Shlaim, *Iron Wall*, 258–63. On the American response, see Quandt, *Peace Process*, 46.

25. Quandt, *Peace Process*, 55–78, for a scholarly description. For a subjective view, see Henry Kissinger, *White House Years* (Little, Brown, 1979), 341–79.

26. The September 1970 crisis became known as Black September, resulting in escalating Palestinian-Jordanian conflict as well as international interventions. President Nasser sought to mediate an agreement between the PLO and the Jordanian monarchy, but his death, on September 27, 1970, cut those efforts short. For more details on this period, see Chamberlin, *Global Offensive*, 108–41. For one aspect of the US role, see Kissinger, *White House Years*, 594–631.

27. Yaqub, *Imperfect Strangers*, 44–53. For Golda Meir's perspective on the Sadat initiative, see the most recent biography, Klagsbrun, *Lioness*, 584–609. Burkett, *Golda*, 272–76, offers a less extensive discussion. Golda Meir's memoir, *My Life* (G.P. Putnam's Sons, 1975), 400–402, skirts the subject.

28. For an overview of the context within which Palestinian activism was taking shape in 1968, see Mark Kurlansky, *1968: The Year That Rocked the World* (Ballantine, 2004).

29. On developments leading to the Egypt-Israel peace treaty, see Yaqub, *Imperfect Strangers*, 239–75, and Quandt, *Peace Process*, 177–242. On the Carter administration and the question of Palestinian inclusion, see Christison, *Perceptions of Palestine*, 157–94; for critical appraisals of US policy, see Noam Chomsky, *The Fateful Triangle: The United States, Israel, and the Palestinians* (South End Press, 1983); Rashid Khalidi, *Resurrecting Empire: Western Footprints and America's Perilous Path in the Middle East* (Beacon, 2004); and Naseer Aruri, *Dishonest Broker: The Role of the United States in Palestine* (South End Press, 2003).

30. See, for example, Fischbach, *Black Power and Palestine*.

31. On Arab American organizations, see Yaqub, *Imperfect Strangers*, 55–86. For a historical view of Middle East studies in the US, see Zachary Lockman, *Field Notes: The Making of Middle East Studies in the United States* (Stanford University Press, 2016).

32. For an overview of these years, see Shapira, *Israel: A History*, 307–25. The interviews found in Ben Ezer, *Unease in Zion*, which are contemporary, illuminate the range of discussions in these years.

33. See Reja Shehadeh, *Strangers in the House: Coming of Age in Occupied Palestine* (Steerforth Press, 2002), 48–52.

34. Paul Jacobs, "A Time to Heal," *Ramparts* 6, no. 1 (July 1967), 3–11.

35. Michael Walzer and Martin Peretz, "Israel Is Not Vietnam," *Ramparts* 6, no. 1 (July 1967), 11–14.

36. I. F. Stone, "The Future of Israel," *Ramparts* 6, no. 1 (July 1967), 41–44.

37. *Commentary Magazine* 44, no. 2, August 1967.

38. Arthur Hertzberg, "Israel and American Jewry," *Commentary* 44 (August 1967), 69–73.

39. Hertzberg, "Israel and American Jewry," 72.

40. Theodore Draper, "Israel and World Politics," *Commentary* 44, no. 2 (August 1967) 19–48.

41. Draper, "Israel and World Politics," 19.

42. Amos Elon, "The Israeli Occupation," *Commentary* 45, no. 3 (March 1968), 41–47.

43. Elon, "Israeli Occupation," 46–47.

44. Amos Oz, "Meaning of Homeland," *New Outlook* 10, no. 9, December 1, 1967.

45. Robert Alter, "Zionism for the '70s," *Commentary* (February 1970), 47–57.

46. Alter, "Zionism," 47.

47. The collection was published in English as *Unease in Zion,* edited by Ehud Ben Ezer (Quadrangle Books, 1974).

48. Alter, "Zionism," 50.

49. Alter, "Zionism," 51.

50. Alter, "Zionism," 55.

51. Alter, "Zionism," 57.

52. Cohen, *Israel and the Bomb,* 329–337.

53. Eldar and Zertal, *Lords of the Land,* 3–29. For a more extensive discussion of the settlement movement in the first ten years, see Gorenberg, *Accidental Empire.*

54. The war of 1973 shocked Israelis with the surprise attack launched by Egypt and Syria. In stark contrast to 1967, Israeli forces struggled on both fronts, experiencing serious losses of life. For a detailed history from the Israeli point of view, see Rabinovich, *Yom Kippur War.*

55. Quandt, *Peace Process,* 169, and Anziska, *Preventing Palestine,* 11.

56. Staub, *Torn at the Roots,* 281. For the history of Breira, see Staub, *Torn at the Roots,* 290–308.

Conclusion

1. Elizabeth Stephens, *US Policy Towards Israel* (Sussex Academic Press, 2006), 174–82; Anziska, *Preventing Palestine,* 199–226.

2. *Waltz with Bashir* was an animated film in which the narrator, a participant in the invasion of Lebanon, attempts to process the traumatic experience of witnessing the massacres at Sabra and Shatila. The film was made in 2008.

3. Meron Benvenisti, *Conflicts and Contradictions* (Villard Books, 1986), 175.

4. Benvenisti, *Conflicts,* 180.

5. An instructive view of the very different interpretations that knowledgeable observers offered is in "Camp David: The Tragedy of Errors," *New York Review of Books,* August 9, 2001, followed by responses in issues from September 20, 2001, as well as June 13, 2002. In contrast, see Benny Morris, *One State, Two States: Resolving the Israel/Palestine Conflict* (Yale University Press, 2009), 172–76.

6. Kenneth S. Stern, *The Conflict Over the Conflict: The Israel/Palestine Campus Debate* (New Jewish Press, 2020). This is an ongoing debate. For a contribution that makes reference to the historical context, see Neve Gordon and

Mark LeVine, "Was Einstein an Anti-Semite?," *Inside Higher Ed*, March 26, 2021, accessed April 9, 2021, www.inside.highered.com/views2021/03/26/problems. For an analysis of implications for American politics, see Nathan Thrall, "How the Battle over Israel and Anti-Semitism Is Fracturing American Politics." *New York Times Magazine*, March 28, 2019. For a different view, see David Schraub, "A New Definition of Antisemitism Is Out and the Anti-Semites Love It," *Ha'aretz*, April 7, 2021.

7. Gordis, *We Stand Divided*.

8. Eric H. Yoffie, "This Year's Most Bizarre, Patronizing Misreading of U.S. Jews and Israel," *Ha'aretz*, November 10, 2019.

9. Waxman, *Trouble in the Tribe*.

10. For the articles by Tony Judt, see "The Alternative," *New York Review of Books*, October 23, 2003, and the response, "An Alternative Future: An Exchange," *New York Review of Books*, December 4, 2003. For Peter Beinart's essay, see *Jewish Currents*, July 7, 2020, and a response by Shaul Arieli, "Peter Beinart Doesn't Realize That the Israeli-Palestinian Divide Is Too Wide to Bridge," *Ha'aretz*, July 24, 2020. Benny Morris offers a longer analysis of the subject in his book *One State, Two States*.

11. Michael Rothberg, *The Implicated Subject: Beyond Victims and Perpetrators* (Stanford University Press, 2019).

12. Thoedore Sasson, *The New American Zionism* (NYU Press, 2014).

13. Sasson, *New American Zionism*, 3.

Bibliography

Achcar, Gilbert. *The Arabs and the Holocaust: The Arab-Israeli War of Narratives.* Saqi, 2010.

Agassi, Joseph. *Liberal Nationalism for Israel.* Gefen Press, 1999.

Alter, Robert. "Zionism for the '70s." *Commentary,* February 1970.

Alterman, Eric. *We Are Not One: A History of America's Fight over Israel.* Basic Books, 2022.

American Jewish Committee. *The Eichmann Case in the American Press.* Institute of Human Relations Press, 1961.

Anziska, Seth. *Preventing Palestine: A Political History from Camp David to Oslo.* Princeton University Press, 2018.

Arad, Guli Ne'eman, *America, Its Jews, and The Rise of Nazism.* Indiana University Press, 2000.

Arad, Guli Ne'eman, ed. "Israeli Historiography Revisited." Special issue of *History and Memory* 7, no. 1 (Spring–Summer 1995).

Arendt, Hannah. *Eichmann in Jerusalem: A Report on the Banality of Evil.* Viking, 1963.

Arendt, Hannah. *The Jew as Pariah.* Grove, 1978.

Arendt, Hannah. *The Origins of Totalitarianism.* Harcourt, Brace, 1951.

Arendt, Hannah, and Karl Jaspers. *Correspondence 1926–1969.* Harcourt, Brace, 1992.

Arendt, Hannah, and Mary McCarthy. *Between Friends: The Correspondence of Hannah Arendt and Mary McCarthy, 1949–1975.* Harcourt, Brace, 1995.

Arieli, Shaul. "Peter Beinart Doesn't Realize That the Israeli-Palestinian Divide Is Too Wide to Bridge." *Ha'aretz,* July 24, 2020.

Aruri, Naseer. *Dishonest Broker: The Role of the United States in Palestine.* South End Press, 2003.

Aschheim, Steven. *Hannah Arendt in Jerusalem.* University of California Press, 2001.

Avineri, Shlomo. *The Making of Modern Zionism.* Basic Books, 1981.

Balint, Benjamin. *Running Commentary: The Contentious Magazine That Transformed the Jewish Left into the Neoconservative Right.* Public Affairs, 2010.

Bardawil, Fadi A. *Revolution and Disenchantment: Arab Marxism and the Binds of Disenchantment.* Duke University Press, 2020.

Barnouw, Dagmar. *Visible Spaces: Hannah Arendt and the German-Jewish Experience.* Johns Hopkins University Press, 1990.

Beinart, Peter. *The Crisis of Zionism.* Henry Holt, 2012.

Beinart, Peter. "Yavne: A Jewish Case for Equality in Israel-Palestine." *Jewish Currents,* July 7, 2020.

Bell, Daniel. *The End of Ideology.* Free Press, 1962.

Ben-Ami, Shlomo. *Scars of War, Wounds of Peace: The Israeli-Arab Tragedy.* Oxford University Press, 2006.

Ben-Ezer, Ehud. *Unease in Zion.* Quadrangle Books, 1974.

Ben-Gurion, David. *Rebirth and Destiny of Israel.* Philosophical Library, 1954.

Benvenisti, Meron. *Conflicts and Contradictions.* Villard Books, 1986.

Berman, Aaron. *Nazism, the Jews, and American Zionism.* Wayne State University Press, 1990.

Bernstein, Richard J. *Hannah Arendt and the Jewish Question.* MIT Press, 1996.

Bilsky, Leora. *Transformative Justice: Israeli Identity on Trial.* University of Michigan Press, 2004.

Brand, H. W. *Into the Labyrinth: The United States and the Middle East.* McGraw Hill, 1994.

Breitman, Richard, Barbara McDonald Stewart, and Severin Hockberg, eds. *Refugees and Rescue: Diaries and Papers of James G. McDonald, 1935–1945.* Indiana University Press, 2004.

Brenner, Michael. *In Search of Israel: The History of an Idea.* Princeton University Press, 2018.

Brinner, William, and Moses Rischin, eds. *Like All the Nations? The Life and Legacy of Judah L. Magnes.* State University of New York Press, 1987.

Brodkin, Karen. *How Jews Became White Folks.* Rutgers University Press, 1998.

Buber, Martin, Judah L. Magnes, and Moses Smilansky. *Palestine: A Bi-National State.* Ihud Association of Palestine (New York), August 8, 1946.

Burkett, Eleanor. *Golda.* Harper Collins, 2008.

Camus, Albert. *Algerian Chronicles.* Edited by Alice Kaplan, translated by Arthur Goldhammer. Belknap Press of Harvard University Press, 2013.

Carmi, Menachem. "The Psychological Effects of Historical Events: Theoretical Considerations in the Context of the Israeli-Palestinian Conflict." *Mind and Human Interaction* 7, no. 3 (August 1996): 128–38.

Carroll, David. *Albert Camus the Algerian: Colonialism, Terrorism, Justice.* Columbia University Press, 2007.

Cesarani, David. *Arthur Koestler: The Homeless Mind.* William Heinemann, 1998.

Chamberlin, Paul T. *The Global Offensive: The United States, the Palestine Liberation Organization, and the Making of the Post–Cold War Order.* Oxford University Press, 2012.

Cheyette, Bryan. *Diasporas of the Mind: Jewish and Postcolonial Writing and the Nightmare of History.* Yale University Press, 2013.

Chomsky, Noam. *The Fateful Triangle: The United States, Israel, and the Palestinians.* South End Press, 1983.

Christison, Kathleen M. "Myths About Palestinians." *Foreign Policy,* no. 66 (Spring 1987).

Christison, Kathleen M. *Perceptions of Palestine: Their Influence on U.S. Middle East Policy.* University of California Press, 1999.

Cohen, Avner. *Israel and the Bomb.* Columbia University Press, 1998.

Cohen, Michael J. *Palestine and the Great Powers, 1945–1948.* Princeton University Press, 1982.

Cohen, Michael J. *Palestine: Retreat from the Mandate—the Making of British Policy, 1936–45.* Holmes and Meier, 1978.

Cohen, Michael J. *Truman and Israel.* University of California Press, 1990.

Cohen, Naomi W. *American Jews and the Zionist Idea.* Ktav Press, 1975.

Cohen, Naomi W. *Not Free to Desist: The American Jewish Committee, 1906–1966.* Jewish Publication Society, 1972.

Connelly, Matthew. *A Diplomatic Revolution: Algeria's Fight for Independence and the Origins of the Post–Cold War Era.* Oxford University Press, 2002.

Draper, Theodore. "Israel and World Politics." *Commentary* 44, no. 2 (August 1967).

Druks, Herbert. *John F. Kennedy and Israel.* Praeger Security International, 2005.

Dubnov, Arie, and Itamar Ben-Ami, "Did Zionist Leaders Actually Aspire Toward a Jewish State?" *Ha'aretz,* May 31, 2019.

Eldar, Akiva, and Idith Zertal. *Lords of the Land: The War for Israel's Settlements in the Occupied Territories, 1967–2007.* Nation Books, 2007.

Elon, Amos. *Herzl.* Holt, Rinehart and Winston, 1975.

Elon, Amos. "The Israeli Occupation." *Commentary* 45, no. 3 (March 1968).

Elon, Amos. *The Israelis: Founders and Sons.* Holt, Rinehart and Winston, 1971.

Evron, Boaz. *Jewish State or Israeli Nation?* Indiana University Press, 1995.

Fanon, Frantz. *Alienation and Freedom.* Bloomsbury Academic Press, 2018.

Fanon, Frantz. *The Wretched of the Earth.* Grove, 2004.

Feingold, Henry. *The Politics of Rescue: The Roosevelt Administration and the Holocaust, 1938–1945.* Rutgers University Press, 1970.

Feldestein, Ariel. *Ben-Gurion, Zionism and American Jewry, 1948–1963.* Routledge, 2006.

Feraoun, Mouloud. *Journal, 1955–1962: Reflections on the French-Algerian War.* University of Nebraska Press, 2000.

Fermi, Laura. *Illustrious Immigrants: The Intellectual Migration from Europe, 1930–1941.* University of Chicago Press, 1968.

Fischbach, Michael. *Black Power and Palestine.* Stanford University Press, 2019.

Fischbach, Michael. *Records of Dispossession: Palestinian Refugee Property and the Arab-Israeli Conflict.* Columbia University Press, 2003.

Friedlander, Saul. *Memory, History, and the Extermination of the Jews of Europe.* Indiana University Press, 1993.

Friedmann, Georges. *The End of the Jewish People?* Doubleday, 1967.

Fromkin, David. *A Peace to End All Peace: Creating the Modern Middle East, 1914–1922.* Avon, 1989.

Ganin, Zvi. *An Uneasy Relationship: American Jewish Leadership and Israel, 1948–57.* Syracuse University Press, 2005.

Gavrieli-Nuri, Dalia. "Saying 'War,' Thinking 'Victory'—the Mythmaking Surrounding Israel's 1967 Victory." *Israel Studies* 15, no. 1 (Spring 2010).

Gendzier, Irene. "Algeria and Palestine: Warning or Model?" *New Middle East,* no. 25 (October 1970).

Gendzier, Irene. *Frantz Fanon: A Critical Study.* Pantheon, 1973.

Ginsburg, Mitch. "In Forgotten Article After Six Day War, Amos Oz Warned of 'Eternal Annexation.'" *Times of Israel,* December 2018.

Goldmann, Nahum. *The Autobiography of Nahum Goldmann.* Holt, Rinehart and Winston, 1969.

Goldmann, Nahum. *Community of Fate: Essays, Speeches, and Articles.* Keter Publishing House, 1977.

Goldmann, Nahum. "The Future of Israel." *Foreign Affairs* 48, no. 3 (April 1970).

Goldmann, Nahum. *The Jewish Paradox.* Grosset and Dunlap, 1978.

Goldstein, Eric L. *The Price of Whiteness: Jews, Race, and American Identity.* Princeton University Press, 2006.

Goodman, Micah. *Catch-67: The Left, the Right and the Legacy of the Six-Day War.* Yale University Press, 2018.

Gordis, Daniel. *We Stand Divided: The Rift Between American Jews and Israel.* Harper/Collins, 2019.

Gordon, Neve, and Mark LeVine. "Was Einstein an Anti-Semite?" *Inside Higher Ed,* March 26, 2021.

Goren, Arthur A. *Dissenter in Zion: From the Writings of Judah L. Magnes.* Harvard University Press, 1982.

Gorenberg, Gershon. *The Accidental Empire: Israel and the Birth of the Settlements, 1967–1977.* Henry Holt, 2006.

Gouri, Haim. *Facing the Glass Booth: The Jerusalem Trial of Adolf Eichmann.* Wayne State University Press, 2004.

Gowers, Andrew, and Tony Walker. *Behind the Myth: Arafat and the Palestinian Revolution.* W. H. Allen, 1990.

Grafton, Anthony. "Arendt and Eichmann at the Dinner Table." *American Scholar* 68, no. 1 (1999): 105–19.

Halkin, Hillel. *Jabotinsky: A Life.* Yale University Press, 2014.

Hattis, Susan. *The Bi-national Idea in Palestine During Mandatory Times.* Shikmona Press, 1970.

Heimann, Gadi. *Franco-Israeli Relations, 1958–67.* Routledge, 2017.

Heller, Joseph. *The Birth of Israel, 1945–1949: Ben-Gurion and His Critics.* University of Florida Press, 2000.

Hertzberg, Arthur. "Israel and American Jewry." *Commentary*, August 1967, 69–73.

Hertzberg, Arthur. *The Zionist Idea.* Jewish Publication Society, 1997.

Herzl, Theodore, *The Jewish State.* American Zionist Emergency Council (New York), 1946.

Hill, J. N. C. *Identity in Algerian Politics.* Lynne Rienner, 2009.

Hirschhorn, Sara. *City on a Hilltop: American Jews and the Israeli Settler Movement.* Harvard University Press, 2017.

Horne, Alistair. *A Savage War of Peace: Algeria 1954–1962.* New York Review of Books, 2006.

Hourani, Albert, Philip S. Khoury, and Mary C. Wilson, eds. *The Modern Middle East: A Reader.* I.B. Tauris, 2004.

Ingrams, Doreen. *Palestine Papers, 1917–1922.* G. Braziller, 1972.

Isaac, Jeffrey. *Arendt, Camus, and Modern Rebellion.* Yale University Press, 1992.

Jacobs, Paul. "A Time to Heal." *Ramparts* 6, no. 1 (July 1967).

Jayyusi, Salma. *Anthology of Modern Palestinian Literature.* Columbia University Press, 1992.

Judis, John B. *Genesis: Truman, American Jews, and the Origins of the Arab/Israeli Conflict.* Farrar, Straus and Giroux, 2014.

Judt, Tony. "The Alternative." *New York Review of Books*, October, 23, 2003.

Kanafani, Ghassan. *Palestine's Children: Returning to Haifa and Other Stories.* Lynne Rienner, 2000.

Kaplan, Amy. *Our American Israel: The Story of an Entangled Alliance.* Harvard University Press, 2018.

Kaplan, Edward K. *Spiritual Radical: Abraham J. Heschel in America.* Yale University Press, 2007.

Katz, Ethan B., Lisa M. Leff, and Maud S. Mandel. *Colonialism and the Jews.* Indiana University Press, 2017.

Keren, Michael. *Ben-Gurion and the Intellectuals: Power, Knowledge, and Charisma.* Northern Illinois University Press, 1983.

Keren, Michael. *The Pen and the Sword: Israeli Intellectuals and the Making of the Nation-State.* Westview, 1989.

Kerr, Malcolm. *The Arab Cold War: 1958–1967.* Oxford University Press, 1967.

Khalidi, Rashid. *The Iron Cage: The Story of the Palestinian Struggle for Statehood.* Beacon, 2006.

Khalidi, Rashid. *Palestinian Identity: The Construction of Modern National Consciousness.* Columbia University Press, 1997.

Khalidi, Rashid. *Resurrecting Empire: Western Footprints and America's Perilous Path in the Middle East.* Beacon, 2004.

Khanna, Ranjanna, ed. *Algeria Cuts: Women and Representation, 1830 to the Present*. Stanford University Press, 2008.

King, Richard H. *Arendt and America*. University of Chicago Press, 2015.

Kissinger, Henry. *White House Years*. Little, Brown, 1979.

Klagsbrun, Francine. *Lioness: Golda Meir and the Nation of Israel*. Schocken, 2017.

Koestler, Arthur. *Arrow in the Blue*. Macmillan, 1961.

Koestler, Arthur. *Darkness at Noon*. Random House, 1941.

Koestler, Arthur. *The Invisible Writing*. Beacon, 1954.

Koestler, Arthur. *Promise and Fulfillment*. Macmillan, 1949.

Koestler, Arthur. *Thieves in the Night*. Macmillan, 1946.

Kohler, Lotte, ed. *Within Four Walls: The Correspondence Between Hannah Arendt and Heinrich Blucher, 1936–1968*. Harcourt, 2000.

Kohn, Jerome, and Ron Feldman, eds. *Hannah Arendt: The Jewish Writings*. Schocken, 2007.

Kotzin, Daniel. *Judah L. Magnes*. Syracuse University Press, 2010.

Kurlansky, Mark. *1968: The Year That Rocked the World*. Ballantine Books, 2004.

Lahav, Pnina. "The Eichmann Trial, the Jewish Question, and the American-Jewish Intelligentsia." *Boston University Law Review* 72 (1992): 555–75.

Langer, Lawrence. *Holocaust Testimonies: The Ruins of Memory*. Yale University Press, 1991.

Laqueur, Walter Z., and Barry Rubin, eds. *The Israel-Arab Reader*. Penguin, 1995.

Laron, Guy. *The Six-Day War*. Yale University Press, 2017.

Laskier, Michael. "Israel and Algeria amid French Colonialism and the Arab-Israeli Conflict, 1954–78." *Israel Studies* 6, no. 2 (Summer 2001): 1–32.

Lavie, Smadar, and Ted Swedenborg, eds. *Displacement, Diaspora, and Geographies of Identity*. Duke University Press, 1996.

Lederhendler, Eli. *The Six-Day War and World Jewry*. Penn State University Press, 2000.

Leifer, Joshua. *Tablets Shattered: The End of an American Jewish Century and the Future of Jewish Life*. Penguin Random House, 2024.

Lerner, Abba, and Samuel Merlin. *The Palestine Refugee Problem: A New Approach and a Plan for a Solution*. Institute for Mediterranean Affairs (New Haven), 1958.

Lesch, David, and Mark Haas, eds. *The Middle East and the United States*. Westview, 2016.

Levitt, Laura. "Levitt on Rothberg, 'Multidirectional Memory: Remembering the Holocaust in the Age of Decolonization.'" H-Judaic, June 2010.

Liebman, Charles. "Diaspora Influence on Israel: The Ben-Gurion–Blaustein 'Exchange' and Its Aftermath." *Jewish Social Studies* 36, nos. 3–4 (July–October 1974): 271–80.

Linfield, Susie. *The Lion's Den: Zionism and the Left from Hannah Arendt to Noam Chomsky*. Yale University Press, 2019.

Lipstadt, Deborah. *The Eichmann Trial.* Schocken, 2011.

Little, Douglas. *American Orientalism: The United States and the Middle East.* University of North Carolina Press, 2008.

Lockman, Zachary. *Field Notes: The Making of Middle East Studies in the United States.* Stanford University Press, 2016.

Louis, William Roger, and Avi Shlaim, eds. *The 1967 Arab-Israeli War.* Cambridge University Press, 2012.

Magid, Shaul. *The Necessity of Exile: Essays from a Distance.* Ayin Press, 2023.

Makdisi, Ussama, and Paul Silverstein. *Memory and Violence in the Middle East and North Africa.* Indiana University Press, 2006.

Malley, Robert. *The Call from Algeria: Third Worldism, Revolution, and the Turn to Islam.* University of California Press, 1996.

Mandel, Neville. *The Arabs and Zionism Before World War I.* University of California Press, 1976.

Mansson, Anette. *Passage to a New World: Exile and Restoration in Darwish's Writings, 1960–1995.* Uppsala University Press, 2003.

Mattar, Philip. *The Mufti of Jerusalem: Al-Hajj Amin Al-Husayni and the Palestinian National Movement.* Columbia University Press, 1988.

McAlister, Melani. *Epic Encounters: Culture, Media, and U.S. Interests in the Middle East, 1945–2000.* University of California Press, 2005.

McDougall, James. *History and the Culture of Nationalism in Algeria.* Cambridge University Press, 2006.

Meir, Golda. *My Life.* G. P. Putnam's Sons, 1975.

Memmi, Albert. *The Colonizer and the Colonized.* Beacon, 1967.

Memmi, Albert. *Dependence.* Beacon, 1984.

Mendes-Flohr, Paul, and Jehuda Reinharz. *The Jew in the Modern World.* Oxford University Press, 1995.

Meyer, Michael A., ed. *Joachim Prinz, Rebellious Rabbi: An Autobiography.* Indiana University Press, 2008.

Miller, Ylana. "Creating Unity Through History: The Eichmann Trial as Transition." *Journal of Modern Jewish Studies* 1, no. 2 (2002): 131–49.

Miller, Ylana. *Government and Society in Rural Palestine, 1920–1948.* University of Texas Press, 1985.

Morris, Benny. *1948 and After: Israel and the Palestinians.* Oxford University Press, 1994.

Morris, Benny. *The Birth of the Palestinian Refugee Problem.* Cambridge University Press, 1987.

Morris, Benny. *One State, Two States: Resolving the Israel/Palestine Conflict.* Yale University Press, 2009.

Mufti, Aamir. *Enlightenment in the Colony: The Jewish Question and the Crisis of Postcolonial Culture.* Princeton University Press, 2007.

Nadel, Ira B. *Leon Uris.* University of Texas Press, 2010.

Norton, Augustus Richard, and Martin H. Greenberg. *The International Relations of the Palestine Liberation Organization*. Southern Illinois University Press, 1989.

Novick, Peter. *The Holocaust in American Life*. Houghton Mifflin, 1999.

Oren, Michael. *Six Days of War*. Oxford University Press, 2002.

Owen, Roger. *State, Power and Politics in the Making of the Modern Middle East*. Routledge, 1992.

Oz, Amos. "Meaning of Homeland." *New Outlook* (December 1967).

Oz, Amos. *The Slopes of Lebanon*. Harcourt, Brace and Jovanovich, 1980.

Pappe, Ilan. *The Making of the Arab-Israeli Conflict*. I.B. Tauris, 1994.

Parker, Richard B., ed. *The Six-Day War: A Retrospective*. University of Florida Press, 1996.

Pavel, Ernst. *The Labyrinth of Exile: A Life of Theodor Herzl*. Farrar, Straus and Giroux, 1989.

Pearlman, Moshe. *Ben-Gurion Looks Back*. Simon and Schuster, 1965.

Pearlman, Moshe. *The Capture of Adolf Eichmann*. Weidenfeld and Nicolson, 1961.

Penslar, Derek J. *Zionism and Technocracy*. Indiana University Press, 1991.

Pianko, Noam. *Zionism: The Roads Not Taken*. Indiana University Press, 2010.

Porat, Dina. *The Blue and Yellow Stars of David*. Harvard University Press, 1990.

Porath, Yehoshua. *The Palestinian Arab National Movement*. Frank Cass, 1977.

Prinz, Joachim. *The Dilemma of the Modern Jew*. Little, Brown, 1962.

Quandt, William. *Peace Process: American Diplomacy and the Arab-Israeli Conflict Since 1967*. Brookings Institution and the University of California Press, 2001.

Rabinovich, Abraham. *The Yom Kippur War*. Schocken, 2004.

Rahman, Najat. *Literary Disinheritance: The Writing of Home in the Work of Mahmoud Darwish and Assia Djebar*. Lexington Books, 2008.

Raider, Mark, ed. *Nahum Goldmann: Statesman Without a State*. State University of New York Press, 2009.

Rogat, Yosal. *The Eichmann Trial and the Rule of Law*. Center for the Study of Democratic Institutions, 1961.

Rose, Jacqueline. "Rereading Khirbet Khizeh by S. Yizhar." *Guardian*, March 11, 2011.

Rothberg, Michael. *The Implicated Subject: Beyond Victims and Perpetrators*. Stanford University Press, 2019.

Rothberg, Michael. *Multidirectional Memory: Remembering the Holocaust in the Age of Decolonization*. Stanford University Press, 2009.

Rubinstein, Amnon. *From Herzl to Rabin*. Holmes and Meier, 2000.

Ruedy, John. *Modern Algeria: The Origins and Development of a Nation*. Indiana University Press, 2005.

Safran, Nadav. *From War to War: The Arab-Israeli Confrontation, 1948–1967*. Pegasus, 1969.

Sagi, Nana. *German Reparations: A History of the Negotiations*. St. Martin's, 1986.

Said, Edward. *Out of Place: A Memoir*. Vintage, 2000.

Sanders, Ronald. *The High Walls of Jerusalem: A History of the Balfour Declaration and the Birth of the British Mandate for Palestine*. Holt, Rinehart and Winston, 1983.

Sanua, Marianne. *Let Us Prove Strong: The American Jewish Committee, 1945–2006*. Brandeis University Press, 2007.

Sartre, Jean-Paul, and Claude Lanzmann. "Le conflit israelo-arabe dossier." *Les Temps Modernes*, June 1967.

Sasson, Theodore. *The New American Zionism*. NYU Press, 2014.

Sayigh, Yezid. *Armed Struggle and the Search for State: The Palestinian National Movement, 1949–93*. Clarendon, 1997.

Scammell, Michael. *Koestler: The Literary and Political Odyssey of a Twentieth-Century Skeptic*. Random House, 2009.

Schechtman, Joseph. *Rebel and Statesman: The Vladimir Jabotinsky Story*. T. Yoseloff, 1956.

Schraub, David. "A New Definition of Anti-Semitism Is Out and the Anti-Semites Love It." *Ha'aretz*, April 7, 2021.

Segev, Tom. *1949: The First Israelis*. Free Press, 1986.

Segev, Tom. *1967: Israel, the War, and the Year That Transformed the Middle East*. Henry Holt, 2007.

Segev, Tom. *Elvis in Jerusalem: Post-Zionism and the Americanization of Israel*. Henry Holt, 2002.

Segev, Tom. *The Seventh Million: The Israelis and the Holocaust*. Hill and Wang, 1993.

Segev, Tom. *A State at Any Cost: The Life of David Ben-Gurion*. Farrar, Straus and Giroux, 2019.

Selzer, Robert M., and Norman J. Cohen, eds. *The Americanization of the Jews*. NYU Press, 1995.

Shalom, Zaki. *The Role of US Diplomacy in the Lead-Up to the Six-Day War*. Sussex Academic Press, 2012.

Shapira, Anita. *Ben-Gurion: Father of Modern Israel*. Yale University Press, 2014.

Shapira, Anita. *Israel: A History*. Brandeis University Press, 2012.

Shapira, Avraham. *The Seventh Day: Soldiers Talk About the Six-Day War*. Scribner's, 1970.

Sheffer, Gabriel. *Moshe Sharett: Biography of a Political Moderate*. Clarendon, 1996.

Shehadeh, Reja. *Strangers in the House: Coming of Age in Occupied Palestine*. Steerforth Press, 2002.

Shepard, Todd. *The Invention of Decolonization*. Cornell University Press, 2006.

Shlaim, Avi. *The Iron Wall: Israel and the Arab World*. Norton, 2000.

Shlaim, Avi. *The Politics of Partition: King Abdullah, the Zionists, and Palestine, 1921–1951*. Columbia University Press, 1990.

Shumsky, Dmitry. *Beyond the Nation-State: The Zionist Political Imagination from Pinsker to Ben-Gurion*. Yale University Press, 2018.

Silberstein, Lawrence J. *New Perspectives on Israeli History*. NYU Press, 1991.

Silver, M. M. *Our Exodus: Leon Uris and the Americanization of Israel's Founding Story*. Wayne State University Press, 2010.

Smith, Barbara J. *The Roots of Separatism in Palestine*. Syracuse University Press, 1993.

Sokoloff, Naomi B., and Nancy E. Berg, eds. *What We Talk About When We Talk About Hebrew (and What It Means to Americans)*. University of Washington Press, 2018.

Stanislawski, Michael. *Zionism and the Fin de Siècle*. University of California Press, 2001.

Starr, Deborah A., and Sasson Somekh, eds. *Mongrels or Marvels: The Levantine Writings of Jacqueline Shohet Kahanoff*. Stanford University Press, 2011.

Staub, Michael. *Torn at the Roots: The Crisis of Jewish Liberalism in Postwar America*. Columbia University Press, 2002.

Stein, Leonard. *The Balfour Declaration*. Simon and Schuster, 1961.

Stein, Sarah, and Aomar Boum. *The Holocaust and North Africa*. Stanford University Press, 2018.

Steiner, George. *Errata: An Examined Life*. Weidenfeld and Nicolson, 1997.

Steiner, George. "How U.S. Jews View the Jewish State." *Life*, August 12, 1957.

Steiner, George. *Language and Silence: Essays on Language, Literature, and the Inhuman*. Atheneum, 1998.

Stephens, Elizabeth. *U.S. Policy Towards Israel*. Sussex Academic Press, 2006.

Stern, Kenneth S. *The Conflict over the Conflict: The Israel/Palestine Campus Debate*. New Jewish Press, 2020.

Stetler, Russell. *Palestine: The Arab Israeli Conflict*. Ramparts, 1972.

Stone, I. F. "The Future of Israel." *Ramparts* 6, no. 1 (July 1967).

Stone, I. F. "Holy War." *New York Review of Books*, August 3, 1967.

Stone, I. F. *This Is Israel*. Boni and Gaer, 1948.

Stone, I. F. *Underground to Palestine and Reflections Thirty Years Later*. Pantheon, 1978.

Sutton, Nina. *Bettelheim: A Life and a Legacy*. Basic Books, 1996.

Takkenberg, Lex. *The Status of Palestinian Refugees in International Law*. Clarendon, 1998.

Teveth, Shabtai. *Ben-Gurion: The Burning Ground, 1886–1948*. Houghton Mifflin, 1987.

Thrall, Nathan. "How the Battle over Israel and Anti-Semitism Is Fracturing American Politics." *New York Times Magazine*, March 28, 2019.

Todd, Olivier. *Albert Camus: A Life*. Knopf, 1997.

Traverso, Enzo. *The End of Jewish Modernity*. Pluto, 2016.

Troen, S. Ilan, and Noah Lucas, eds. *Israel: The First Decade of Independence*. State University of New York Press, 1995.

Turki, Fawaz. *The Disinherited: Journal of a Palestinian Exile.* Monthly Review, 1972.

Turki, Fawaz. *Soul in Exile: Lives of a Palestinian Revolutionary.* Monthly Review, 1988.

Uris, Leon. *Exodus.* Doubleday, 1958.

Urofsky, Melvin. *We Are One! American Jewry and Israel.* Doubleday, 1978.

Wall, Irwin. *France, the United States, and the Algerian War.* University of California Press, 2001.

Walzer, Michael, and Martin Peretz. "Israel Is Not Vietnam." *Ramparts* 6, no. 1 (July 1967).

Waxman, Dov. *Trouble in the Tribe: The American Jewish Conflict over Israel.* Princeton University Press, 2016.

Weiser, Benno. "Ben-Gurion's Dispute with American Zionists." *Commentary* 18 (1954): 93–101.

Wittman, Rebecca, ed. *The Eichmann Trial Reconsidered.* University of Toronto Press, 2021.

Wyman, David. *The Abandonment of the Jews: America and the Holocaust, 1941–1945.* Pantheon, 1984.

Yablonka, Hanna. *Medinat Yisrael Neged Adolf Eichmann.* Yedioth Ahronot, 2001.

Yablonka, Hanna. *The State of Israel Versus Adolf Eichmann.* Schocken, 2004.

Yadgar, Yaacov. *Sovereign Jews: Israel, Zionism, and Judaism.* State University of New York Press, 2017.

Yaqub, Salim. *Containing Arab Nationalism: The Eisenhower Doctrine and the Middle East.* University of North Carolina Press, 2004.

Yaqub, Salim. *Imperfect Strangers: Americans, Arabs, and U.S.–Middle East Relations in the 1970s.* Cornell University Press, 2016.

Yizhar, S. *Khirbet Khizeh.* IBIS Press, 2008.

Yoffie, Eric H. "This Year's Most Bizarre Patronizing Misreading of US Jews and Israel." *Ha'aretz*, November 10, 2019.

Young-Bruehl, Elisabeth. *Hannah Arendt: For Love of the World.* Yale University Press, 1982.

Zaretsky, Robert. *Albert Camus: A Life Worth Living.* Belknap Press of Harvard University Press, 2013.

Zaretsky, Robert. *Albert Camus: Elements of a Life.* Cornell University Press, 2010.

Zipperstein, Steven. *Elusive Prophet: Ahad Ha'AM and the Origins of Zionism.* University of California Press, 1993.

Archives

S80: Office of Nahum Goldmann

Z5: Jewish Agency for Palestine/Israel, Central Zionist Archives, Jerusalem

Z6: Nahum Goldmann Papers

American Jewish Committee Papers, YIVO Institute for Jewish Research, New York
Arendt, Hannah. Papers. Library of Congress, Washington, DC.
Center for Jewish History, New York
Central Zionist Archives, Jerusalem
Eichmann Trial Documents
Foreign Ministry of Israel, Jerusalem
Israel State Archives, Jerusalem
Library of Congress, Washington, DC
Office of the Prime Minister of Israel, Jerusalem
Truman Presidential Library, Independence, Missouri
Yad VaShem, Jerusalem

Index